THE FICTION OF VALERIE MARTIN

THE FICTION OF
VALERIE MARTIN

An Introduction

VERONICA MAKOWSKY

LOUISIANA STATE UNIVERSITY PRESS   BATON ROUGE

Published by Louisiana State University Press
Copyright © 2016 by Louisiana State University Press
All rights reserved
Manufactured in the United States of America
First printing

DESIGNER: Michelle A. Neustrom
TYPEFACE: Adobe Garamond Pro
PRINTER AND BINDER: Maple Press

LIBRARY OF CONGRESS CATALOGING-IN-PUBLICATION DATA

Names: Makowsky, Veronica A., author.
Title: The fiction of Valerie Martin : an introduction / Veronica Makowsky.
Description: Baton Rouge : Louisiana State University Press, 2016. | Includes
    bibliographical references and index.
Identifiers: LCCN 2015035236 | ISBN 978-0-8071-6216-3 (cloth : alk. paper) | ISBN
    978-0-8071-6218-7 (pdf) | ISBN 978-0-8071-6217-0 (epub) | ISBN 978-0-8071-6219-4
(mobi)
Subjects: LCSH: Martin, Valerie, 1948– —Criticism and interpretation.
Classification: LCC PS3563.A7295 Z75 2016 | DDC 813/.54—dc23 LC record available
at http://lccn.loc.gov/2015035236

For Lynn Z. Bloom,
Scholar, Writer, Cook, Mentor, and True Friend

Contents

Preface

*I*n this book I hope to introduce readers to the work of a major twentieth- and twenty-first-century writer by pointing out the thematic figure in her artistic carpet, its intricate and intriguing submotifs and allusions, and the techniques that weave them with such skill and complexity. I eschew critical jargon and highly specialized theory in the hope that this appreciative exposition of Valerie Martin's work will help the discerning general reader, as well as academics, find as much pleasure and interest as I do in Martin's thought-provoking, absorbing, expertly crafted fiction. I thank the University of Connecticut for research support. The two anonymous readers for Louisiana State University Press provided substantive criticism and suggestions that were invaluable; I learned a great deal from them, as I hope this book demonstrates. I am especially grateful to Valerie Martin for her generosity in participating in a very helpful and insightful interview ("Transformations"), and, above all, for writing the works that provided me, as I read and pondered them, with a supplementary education as well as much delight.

THE FICTION OF VALERIE MARTIN

Introduction

THE FIGURE IN THE CARPET

*T*he books of Valerie Martin receive significant and largely laudatory reviews, both in the United States and in Great Britain. Martin received the Kafka Prize for her novel *Mary Reilly* (1990), which has been translated into sixteen languages (see Martin's website). For her novel *Property* (2003), she won the United Kingdom's highly prestigious Orange Prize. Martin's body of work is extensive as well as excellent: as of 2015, she had published ten novels, four collections of short stories, and a biography. She addresses important themes, both timely and timeless, with impressively deployed literary techniques.

Yet Martin has little name recognition, and she is not a media presence or celebrity, despite the fact that critics have long predicted her imminent fame. In 1988, John Irwin Fischer, in one of the few and earliest scholarly articles on Martin, saw her on "the verge of being famous" (445). Almost twenty years later, in 2007, novelist Sue Halpern, in a review of Martin's novel *Trespass* (2007), observed, "Valerie Martin's novels and stories, although well-received by critics, have made little dent in the public consciousness." Even the 1996 movie version of her *Mary Reilly*, starring Julia Roberts and John Malkovich, failed to augment and solidify her larger reputation.

The chameleon character of her work, the way that she keeps meeting new challenges in subjects and techniques, probably is the main explanation for her lack of sustained fame. There is no immediately recognizable "product" when a reader picks up one of her books; there is no "Martin novel" in the way one can easily anticipate and identify a novel by Philip Roth or Joyce Carol Oates. Her style tends to be clear and concise, with a transparency that does not call attention to itself, unlike, for one example, John Updike's baroquely elaborate descriptions. Her work does not readily fit into neatly defined literary slots; indeed, when I consulted scholarly books in the three most relevant categories—southern literature, the gothic, and postmodernism—I found her work addressed only once, in a footnote (Massé 110 n5).

In Henry James's story "The Figure in the Carpet," various members of the literary world search for the secret, the treasure, hidden in the work of a well-respected contemporary novelist, his "figure in the carpet." The "figure" in Martin's literary carpet, her distinctive cast of mind, tends to be obscured by the densely woven, allusively rich, and technically expert background of her protean fiction. In James's tale, a maddened and maddening literary critic loses his decency and humanity in a futile quest to find the figure in the novelist's carpet that is rare and mystifying; he thus misses the obvious point that the novelist's greatness, the figure in his carpet, is a quality that is not extraordinary but is available to all: his empathy, his impassioned interest in his fellow human beings, based on his decency and humanity. Martin's work deserves and rewards similarly intense scholarly scrutiny, but, fortunately, in a way that neither needs nor evokes madness. As in the works of two of the most significant influences on Martin—Henry James and his brother, the great psychologist and humanist William James—Martin displays an astute yet compassionate regard for her fellow human beings, combining a spirit of lucid inquiry with an imagination at once playful, intensely serious, and, above all, empathetic. The figure in Martin's carpet is her sympathetic yet discerning exploration of the powers of the human imagination, for good or ill, as exemplified in Martin's own powerful imagination. In order to assist in the appreciation and enjoyment of her carpet's figure, this book attempts to provide an understanding of its background: a consideration of her life and career in the context of southern, gothic, and postmodern literatures,[1] with particular attention to the roles of women. Although women are not always Martin's protagonists, their situations are reliable indicators of Martin's view of a society's health or pathology.

1. In three articles and an interview from 1993 to 1996, R. McClure Smith has pointed out the gothic motifs and postmodern revisions in Martin's early fiction using psychoanalytic theory. In an article on *Property*, Susan V. Donaldson noted Martin's postmodern retellings in that novel of stories about the South, particularly slave narratives and neo-slave narratives.

In 1948, Valerie Martin was born in Sedalia, Missouri, but, she relates, "my family moved to New Orleans, my mother's home town, when I was three, so I think of myself as from New Orleans" (Martin's website). As a child she was drawn to the world of stories, especially those of the supernatural sphere and those of mysterious old New Orleans. In an interview, she recalls spending "a lot of time" at the Robert E. Smith Library in her Lakeview neighborhood, which "had a patio" that was "wonderful, and I'd sit out there with my pile of books" ("Transformations" 26).

> First, I went through fairy tales, which are horrifying, and why they give them to children is a real question; they certainly ruined my life for many years. And then I became really fascinated with New Orleans history because the books that had to do with New Orleans history were right next to the children's section. I started reading those. I particularly loved books by Lyle Saxon [about Louisiana history and legends]. . . . School trips took us around the city . . . we went to Madame John's Legacy, the Cabildo, and other old houses in the French Quarter which brought all the stuff I was reading to life for me. It was just a wonderful childhood. I really felt like New Orleans was an enchanted place that I happened to be living in and I loved this fabulous history of voodoo and pirates and slaves, the rich, and, of course, the poor, the amazing variety of people who came to the city. I think that's what got me writing stories, and I think that I couldn't have had the experience, which so influenced my feelings about what makes a good story, anywhere else. ("Transformations" 26–27)

In Martin's mature fiction, "a good story" usually combines pleasure and fear, with an implicit critique of masochism as in *Love: Short Fiction* (1977), *A Recent Martyr* (1987), and *Mary Reilly*. The allure of the past also matured into the historical research that enriches *Mary Reilly, The Great Divorce* (1994), *Salvation: Scenes from the Life of St. Francis* (2001), *Property*, and *The Ghost of the Mary Celeste* (2014). Although she was not and is not a Catholic, while attending a Catholic girls' high school in New Orleans, she continued what she calls "her romantic education," including "a serious preoccupation with the gothic" (Biguenet Interview 47), which

runs through her works from the early *Alexandra* (1979) to her most recent novel, *The Ghost of the Mary Celeste.*

Martin believes that the romantic influences of her girlhood were
somewhat counteracted when she started college at the University of New
Orleans, where she "was attracted to realist writers like [Albert] Camus
and [Gustave] Flaubert" (Biguenet Interview 47) and was greatly influenced by Professor Kenneth Holditch, renowned for his work on Tennessee Williams and for his profound knowledge of the literary history of
New Orleans. Martin recalls, "He's a great Faulkner scholar and knows all
there is to know about Tennessee Williams, but he also encouraged me to
read writers like Hawthorne and James, whom I totally loved, and so he
formed my taste" ("Transformations" 29). The influence of Hawthorne
and James is particularly evident in Martin's second collection of short
stories, *The Consolation of Nature and Other Stories* (1988), and James's
masterful use of point of view (particularly first-person and third-person
limited omniscient) and of *döppelgangers* is demonstrated throughout
Martin's oeuvre. What she calls "the conflicting attractions" (Biguenet Interview 47) of romanticism and realism are best exemplified in Flaubert's
Madame Bovary (1856), which Martin describes as "a cautionary tale about
a foolish woman whose Romantic education ill fits her for her very ordinary life" (Martin's website). The opposition of romanticism and realism
contributes a central and highly productive tension in her fiction, and in
her life: "I didn't want to wind up like Emma Bovary," Martin wryly observes (Martin's website).

After Martin graduated from the University of New Orleans in 1970,
she declared her career in writing by obtaining her M.F.A. at the University of Massachusetts in 1974. She returned to New Orleans, where she
took a job in a welfare office, began to publish fiction, and took a course
at Loyola University in the fall of 1976 (Tolson 407) with the southern
and Catholic existentialist novelist Walker Percy, greatly acclaimed at the
time for his novel of New Orleans malaise, *The Moviegoer* (1961). She is
careful to point out that Percy did not help her to write her first novel,
Set in Motion (1978) (Biguenet Interview 48). He did, however, give her a
laudatory quotation for publicity purposes (Biguenet Interview 48) after
he read it as an "audition" for entering his class ("Transformations" 30).

Although she did not find him "a gifted teacher" because he was "shy" and "very uncomfortable" ("Transformations" 30), Percy's own character and his fictive protagonists became models for some of Martin's male characters, such as the self-absorbed, ineffectual Claude of *Alexandra;* Percy may have recognized himself on some level when he read "a few chapters" of *Alexandra* since Martin remembers him calling her and saying, "I don't know about this character Claude. Isn't he just kind of a wuss?" ("Transformations" 31).

Percy was a significant influence on Martin in the sense that she recognized in his worldview and works aspects of herself that she wanted to repudiate or at least counteract: romanticism and attractions to powerful cultural narratives like that of the magnolia-infused Old South that is "gone with the wind" and the gothic masochistic attraction of women to powerful but flawed men. In an interview, she acknowledged her kinship with Percy: "Of course, he's a total romantic. Although I told myself I was doing something quite original and new, he spotted me as a kindred soul" (Biguenet Interview 47). Martin also may have sympathized with Percy's need to reject the conventional identity of a southern novelist. In a 1972 interview, Percy comments, "Whatever impetus I had towards writing owes nothing to sitting on a porch listening to anybody tell stories about the South, believe me. I think that the day of regional Southern writing is all gone. I think that people who try to write in that style are usually repeating a phased-out genre or doing Faulkner badly. . . . It's just fifty years later than the time of family stories and sagas and histories and so on" (Carr Interview, 1971, 69). Percy, however, is protesting too much since much of his fiction concerns dysfunctional old southern families and their legacies in the New South while Martin eschews such subject matter, even in her works set in New Orleans.

In contrast to Martin, Percy has often been criticized for his sketchy, flat, and somewhat stereotypical female characters, swept in the wake of the more powerful, though quite confused males, as he himself rationalized in an interview: "I write about women from the exclusive point of view of the hero or anti-hero. As such, the view of women or anyone else may be limited by the narrowness of the vision" (Carr Interview, 1971, 70). Such misogynistic "narrowness" is repeatedly critiqued by Martin in her fiction as she demonstrates its deleterious effects on women such as the title character of *Mary Reilly* or the heroine of *Italian Fever* (1999).

Despite these differences, Martin does share Percy's attention to careful craftsmanship, particularly the precept he imparted to that 1976 seminar, "that the writer should tend to the needs of the reader" (Tolson 408). They differ significantly, however, on what they believe the reader needs. Although Percy is often referred to as a postmodern novelist, this label refers more to his position in time than to his subject matter or technique; he wrote *after* the modernist period of literature in the first half of the twentieth century, exemplified by giants like Faulkner. Percy is not a postmodernist in the sense that Valerie Martin is—one who refuses to present the world according to a single ideology or schema—but, instead, Percy is invested in "telling the reader." "My theory," Percy told an interviewer, "is that the purpose of art is to transmit universal truths of a sort" (Cremeens, "Walker Percy," 23), in his case, Christian (particularly Catholic) existentialism. As Martin's fiction repeatedly demonstrates, such a focused perspective may help organize reality, but limits human freedom, especially as manifested in the creative imagination.

In contrast to the privileged Walker Percy, Martin, in the early years of her career, did not have the financial resources to devote herself to her art, but by becoming a teacher herself, she managed to expand her horizons beyond New Orleans. Her teaching also helped support her writing and her only child, her daughter Adrienne from her marriage to Robert Martin at age twenty-three that ended in an amicable divorce ("Transformations" 28). She taught at institutions ranging from the Southwest to New England, with a focus on the latter: the University of New Mexico at Las Cruces, the University of Alabama at Tuscaloosa, the University of New Orleans, Mount Holyoke College, the University of Massachusetts, Sarah Lawrence, and most recently, at Mount Holyoke again (Martin's website).

While teaching at Tuscaloosa from 1983 to 1984, Martin met the Canadian novelist Margaret Atwood, who was finishing what would become her acclaimed *The Handmaid's Tale* (1985). Their friendship developed because "they lived only a few blocks apart and our daughters were the same age" (Biguenet Interview 50). In fact, Martin states that she was the "first person to read" *The Handmaid's Tale* and told Atwood that she thought the novel would make her wealthy (Biguenet Interview 51). Influence is hard to determine, but it is certain that Atwood and Martin share a gothic theme of female imprisonment in dystopias, as demonstrated in *The Handmaid's Tale* and Martin's *Property,* and that Atwood had a substantial role in promoting Martin's career and ending an eight-year drought between published books.

After the publication of *Alexandra,* her second novel, in 1979, Martin's publications were stalled. She was not suffering from writer's block, but from a new and unfavorable publishing climate: her editor moved from one publishing house to another. When she submitted what would become her third published novel, *A Recent Martyr,* he told her that "there was 'no enthusiasm in the house.' . . . So the book went around to publishers for eight solid years" with only a serious nibble from one publisher who wanted her to change the novel's point of view to a consistent first person, which Martin refused to do (Biguenet Interview 48). During that period, she also wrote a novel that remains unpublished, "The Perfect Waitress," "about a waitress who murders the owner" of the famed New Orleans restaurant Commander's Palace; one other completed and unpublished novel; and three partial novels that were rejected as proposals ("Transformations" 25). Atwood introduced Martin to her own editor, Nan Talese, at Houghton Mifflin, and the doors of the publishing world re-opened for Martin.

In 1990, Martin's first relatively popular success arrived with *Mary Reilly,* her rewriting of Robert Louis Stevenson's *The Strange Case of Dr. Jekyll and Mr. Hyde* (1886) from the maidservant's point of view. Martin calls *Mary Reilly* her "connector" book because it allowed her to expand, make the connection to, another world in time and space: "The point of view was a challenge. I had never tried to leave Louisiana in my novels and here I was penning the diaries of a maid in Victorian Britain," which she found "liberating" and a source of "confidence" ("Transformations" 32). In addition, that novel and its movie sale helped her to pay for her daughter's education at New York University (a "connector" to Adrienne Martin's successful career as professor of philosophy at the University of Pennsylvania) and to spend 1994 and 1997 in Italy with her partner, Robert Cullen, the prize-winning translator, with whom she lives in upstate New

York. *Mary Reilly* was also a "connector" book in that it formed the central panel of a triptych—with *The Consolation of Nature and Other Stories* and *The Great Divorce*—that explores what human beings share with nature, especially their vulnerability to death, and the ways humans use and abuse nature through the stories they tell themselves about nature.

Martin's years in Italy led directly to two books set there, *Italian Fever,* a novel, and her biography of St. Francis of Assisi, *Salvation: Scenes from the Life of St. Francis.* Her Italian sojourn also produced three significant shifts in her themes and one in characterization. "When I look at my books," she told an interviewer," I see them as before Italy or after Italy, and to me there's a real difference" (Biguenet Interview 52). Martin comments on the first thematic shift: "By the time we were back in New York . . . I recognized that my earlier books were obsessed with the problem of power and sexuality, and that I was now more interested in the problem of power and property" (Biguenet Interview 54). This new emphasis, as demonstrated in her next novels, the aptly titled *Property* and *Trespass* (2007), arose from her interest in St. Francis of Assisi: "The more I found out about him, the more he interested me because he was obsessed with something that I was becoming obsessed with, which is how, when you own something, it owns you" (Biguenet Interview 53). Second, she notes that "the Roman's constant preoccupation with art ultimately resulted in my thinking about what artists are, especially painters, and what they do" (Biguenet Interview 52); she explores the relationship between life and art, ethics as well as aesthetics, in *Italian Fever, The Unfinished Novel and Other Stories* (2006), *The Confessions of Edward Day* (2009), and *The Ghost of the Mary Celeste.* Third, by chance in Rome, Martin discovered Anton Chekhov's short stories and "came to see characters as much more volatile and active" ("Transformations" 30), as evinced in *Trespass* and *The Unfinished Novel and Other Stories.* Her predominant themes of nature and art culminate in *Sea Lovers* (2015), which includes five tales from *The Consolation of Nature and Other Stories,* five tales from *The Unfinished Novel and Other Stories,* and two new stories that present these themes with fantasy and a whimsical humor within a section called "Metamorphoses."

Martin's oeuvre is similarly shape-shifting, and intentionally so, as is typical of this writer's writer: "I try to make each one different in order to keep myself engaged" (Kean, "Valerie Martin"), Martin told an interviewer. Her protagonists are multifarious: lower-level government bureaucrats, an administrative assistant, a nun, a veterinarian, the oyster king of Louisiana, a slave owner, a maid, a saint, artists, actors, and writers, seafarers, and spiritualist mediums. The reader who opens a Martin novel could find herself in the early nineteenth century, the present, or the future, and in locales from New Orleans to New York to London to Italy to Croatia to the high seas. To what extent, then, can her chameleon fiction be considered in terms of readily recognized categories, such as southern, postmodern, or gothic literature?

In attempting to classify Martin as a writer, one might argue that since she was raised, educated, and began her career in Louisiana, and since works set in Louisiana comprise roughly half her oeuvre, she must be a southern writer, yet that designation is unsatisfactory in many respects because roughly half of her work is *not* set in the South and because she does not fit comfortably into traditional definitions of southern literature. That mythic yet troubled South, its obsessive subject, no longer exists, as Julius Rowan Raper points out: "Our familiar place of red clay and mules, of piney hills, hamlets, and grandparents soft as the underside of leaves, is vanishing, even in our fiction" (10). Many critics dispute that such a South ever really existed, except as a fascinating story. Jefferson Humphries asserts that "what we mean when we talk about the South, is not a geographical place. . . . The South is instead nothing in the world but an idea in narrative form, a discourse or rhetoric of narrative tropes, a story made out of substories, a lie, a fiction to which we have lent reality by believing in it" (120).

Fred Hobson argues that such southern "fiction" about fiction was defined by the Agrarians of the 1930s, who were representative of a usually male, landed, and educated class, and who valued "an awareness of history, a regard for tradition and hierarchy, an ornamental sense, even in certain respects a sense of place" (22); in other words, writers like William Faulkner. While Valerie Martin certainly has a strong sense of history and place in Louisiana, her style is not baroquely complex and difficult, nor does she identify with male self-styled southern aristocrats, for, as Michael Kreyling has noted, "the interests of southern women writers and the survival of the orthodox canon do not walk hand-in-hand" (xv). In all of her works, and outstandingly in her blistering dissection of the slave system in *Property,* Martin demolishes such a hierarchy.

For similar reasons, Martin does not fit comfortably into the second generation of twentieth-century southern writers, such as Flannery O'Connor, Walker Percy, and William Styron. These canonically southern writers attempt to cope with a South that is rapidly shedding tradition and descending into an absurd or grotesque unknown. Martin, in contrast, would find maintaining such traditions neither comfortable nor desirable. She comments in 2011 about a recent re-reading of Percy's *The Moviegoer*: "As I was reading it, I was not liking it. It's very over-the-top about class and race. It also possesses this reverence for the Old South—the romantic ideal of the Old South—that I find tiresome" (Biguenet Interview 47).

Martin is also unlike Percy and O'Connor in their attempt to eschew an increasingly materialistic world and replace the ostensibly aristocratic values and ritual of southern social hierarchy with the rituals and hierarchy of Roman Catholicism. In *A Recent Martyr,* Martin presents highly critical depictions of priestly authority, female self-sacrifice, and wishful thinking about miracles. Martin recognizes that people want and need illusions, whether societal or religious, but she also shows the destructive nature of such fictions when employed by the powerful against the less empowered, particularly, but not exclusively, women. However, like Percy and O'Connor, Martin abhors the mindless complacency of the materially prosperous, and, like O'Connor, she often uses violence as a means of violating the reader's complacency and drawing attention to the imminence and the eminence of death. As O'Connor acerbically noted, "When you can assume that your audience holds the same beliefs that you do, you can relax a little and use more normal means of talking to it, when you have to assume it does not, then you have to make your vision apparent by shock—to the hard of hearing you shout, and for the almost-blind, you draw large and startling figures" (34). The violent eroticism and sexual power games in many of Martin's early short stories and novels present "large and startling pictures" of a modern life so anesthetizing and meaningless that these benumbed women protagonists will try anything, however dangerous and potentially demeaning, to feel anything at all.

In many ways, the work of Valerie Martin, born in 1948, is more characteristic of what Fred Hobson calls "the third generation of modern southern literature" (8), whose authors' youths or early maturity were in some degree defined by the 1960s. That decade was characterized not only by a nationwide questioning of authority over the Vietnam War, but also by the conflict over civil rights in the South, and that, Hobson states, "in fact, might be seen as pivotal in southern life and letters in much the same way the 1920s was: it was a time of numerous southern crimes against humanity, of notable attention and criticism from without, of great intellectual ferment" (7). Matthew Guinn finds that members of this third generation, comprised of writers like Dorothy Allison, Larry Brown, Richard Ford, and Randall Kenan, "treat the sacrosanct elements of the cultural mythology engendered by southern modernism with disregard or disdain" (xi), a view that Martin certainly shares.[2] Martin does not, though, participate in another trend that Hobson identifies in many third-generation modern southern writers, like Bobbie Ann Mason, who "immerse their characters in a world of popular or mass culture" (10), but instead weaves an allusive web of "high" culture from art, history, and literature.

"Is being southern a category fixed for life? What do you do with the southern writer who leaves the South, both physically *and* in her fiction?" (5), asks John Lowe in his introduction to *The Future of Southern Letters*. One such writer is Richard Ford, who is much discussed in works concerning contemporary southern literature, while Martin's oeuvre is not (see Hobson, Guinn, Bone), although only one of Ford's books, his first, is set in the South, as opposed to about half of Martin's corpus. But like Martin, as Matthew Guinn points out, "his success has hinged on his abdication of the South as subject and setting" (111). In addition, he is comparable to Martin in that, as Hobson states, "Ford's ability to change places is matched only by his ability to change voices and literary modes" (44). Also similar to Martin, he is critical of the aristocratic southern tradition based on male privilege in a hierarchical, place-bound community, as evidenced by his early parody of Percy's *The Moviegoer* in *The Sports-*

2. For further reflections on contemporary southern literature, see Kreyling (*South*) and Romine.

writer (1986; see Bone xi; for another comparison to Percy, see Hobson 56–57). In Ford's recent novel *Canada* (2012), he continues his deflation of the pretensions and pretenses of the traditional southern literature: the narrator's Alabama-raised father, because he cannot come to terms with the realities of modern Western life in Great Falls, Montana (so far away from the South that it's almost Canada), leads his family to a tragically "great fall." Yet despite the paucity of explicit southern references in Ford's work, scholars such as Guinn, Bone, and Hobson can find a place for Ford in southern literature by considering him a postmodern writer, whose fiction, in Guinn's words, "works within a postmodern arena that denies the validity of grand narratives such as Christianity and history that are so vital to his southern predecessors. Frank [Bascombe, protagonist of Ford's trilogy] must achieve self-awareness and redemption using only the materials of individual experience, nothing more" (119), a worldview shared by Valerie Martin.

In some ways, the difficulty of fitting Martin and her works into the largely male and male-determined canons of southern literature echoes that of another Louisiana woman writer, Kate Chopin (1850–1904). Like Chopin, Martin clearly depicts the plight of women in patriarchal societies, in the South and elsewhere, demonstrating her immersion in a wide range of works in both male and female literary traditions. Chopin repurposed the techniques and themes of the great male French writers, particularly the naturalists, of the nineteenth century, for her critique of the plight of women in late nineteenth-century Louisiana. Similarly, Martin allusively subverts the work of many male literary predecessors to provide the woman's version of the tale, as in *Mary Reilly*, which, as mentioned above, tells Robert Louis Stevenson's story of Jekyll and Hyde from the maidservant's point of view.

Martin also shares Chopin's conviction that the ultimate ruling force is nature with its inevitable ending in death; patriarchy is nature's social avatar and the sea is nature's epitome. In Chopin's masterpiece, *The Awakening*, the protagonist Edna Pontellier, unable to imagine a way out of social conventions and the demands of nature as embodied in her children, walks into the sea to her death. As representatives of the literary naturalism that Chopin espoused, her female protagonists remain determined by their bodies and by society and imprisoned in their minds; they, like Edna, are unable to imagine alternatives that would save them. Unlike those of Chopin, Martin's contemporary female protagonists can more readily defy social conventions and endeavor to understand the workings of nature in order to write endings more acceptable to themselves. They do not die for love, but choose to live in order to continue to love themselves, their children, and their chosen companions, as in *A Recent Martyr* and *The Great Divorce*. Many of them walk away from dehumanizing situations, not into the sea like Edna. Even Martin's drowned nineteenth-century protagonist, Sarah Briggs of *The Ghost of the Mary Celeste*, exhibits more autonomy than Chopin's heroines, as well as a socially subversive spirit of inquiry. Sarah freely chooses to accompany her beloved husband on the fatal voyage and, though defeated by nature in the form of the sea, continues to speak to her descendants and to the future as she interrogates the ways of nature and society in her journal. Sarah uses her mind and her imagination to give her life meaning, unlike Edna Pontellier, who had neither the will nor the imagination to pursue her talent for painting.

Happily, though, times also have changed. Martin, at the turn of the twenty-first century, does not share Chopin's blindness to race as a prison. In Martin's *Property*, the slave Sarah justly hates and works with violence and subterfuge against her master and mistress, unlike Chopin's blacks, who are mainly self-destructively and stereotypically devoted to their owners and employers. In contrast, Martin presents white female privileged protagonists who are destroyed by their obsession with people as property: Manon in *Property* and Chloe in *Trespass* lack empathetic imagination and remain cruelly and self-destructively blind to the sufferings of others. Unlike Edna Pontellier, Martin's most successful women characters (as well as some of her men, like Brendan in *Trespass*) are those who can imagine their way out of their own plights and are thus enabled to exercise those powerful and compassionate imaginations for the benefit of others.

As these reflections on southern literature and its critics suggest, there may be little point in trying to place Valerie Martin exclusively into a slot labeled "southern writer" for two reasons. The first is that southern literature no longer exists, if it ever really did, as a homogenous, stable literary genre, and Martin's works contest the hierarchy of power, especially gendered power, upon which the traditional definition of southern literature rests. As Thadious Davis astutely observes, there currently "is no 'master narrative' of the South into which new groups will merely append their stories. Instead, the very discourse of the South is contested" (K718).

The second reason for not attempting to limit Valerie Martin to southern literature is that her work also participates in other major literary trends. As Richard Gray explains, "Writers are, after all, part of an imagined community, itself made up of multiple imagined communities. They talk to many writers outside the South; many writers outside the South, in turn, talk to them. In the process, they turn the intertextual space of southern writing into a border territory" (xi). For example, despite the differences between them, neither Chopin nor Martin can be called a southern writer in a narrow or limiting sense because both ultimately look beyond Louisiana and the South and address broader questions about nature and its embodiment in culture. To the extent that Valerie Martin's work can be considered "southern writing," it can be located on the border with two other "imagined communities," postmodernism and the gothic.

Martin, with one important exception, exhibits a postmodern sensibility more than postmodern technique. The atmosphere of questioning of authority evoked by the civil rights movement and the protests against the Vietnam War and experienced by those, like Martin, coming of age in the South in the 1960s was part of a larger intellectual current in Western culture. As Linda Hutcheon states in *A Poetics of Postmodernism* (1988), "the 1960s were the time of ideological formation for many of the postmodernist thinkers and artists of the 1980s" (8; see also Calinescu 268). Most importantly, postmodernists question what literary critics often call metanarratives, explanatory stories with cultural power, such as Christianity or, as we have seen, the traditional versions of southern history and literature, both rigorously interrogated by Martin.[3] Instead, Martin's approach is closer to what Jean-Francois Lyotard called "incredulity toward metanarratives" (xxv), resulting in a willingness to question and to explore and then to use what circumstances offer on a contingent basis: "There are many different language games—a heterogeneity of elements. They only

3. I base my discussion of postmodernism on Hutcheon, Calinescu, and Nicol.

give rise to institutions in patches—local determinism" (Lyotard xxiv). As Zygmunt Bauman puts it, "All order that can be found is a local, emergent and transitory phenomenon; its nature can be best grasped by a metaphor of a whirlpool appearing in the flow of a river, retaining its shape only for a relatively brief period and only at the expense of incessant metabolism and constant renewal of content" (189). Martin's highly varied oeuvre exemplifies such an "incessant metabolism and constant renewal of content."

Martin's treatment of history in her fiction is similarly postmodern in its contingent nature and its spirit of exploration. Linda Hutcheon identifies a subgenre which she calls "historiographic metafiction" and characterizes its worldview: "The postmodernist ironic thinking of history is definitely not nostalgic. It critically confronts the past with the present, and vice versa. In a direct reaction against the tendency of our times to value only the new and novel, it returns us to a re-thought past to see what, if anything, is of value in that past experience. But the critique of its irony is double-edged: the past and the present are judged in each other's light" (39). Such irony, lack of nostalgia, and dialogic critique of past and present are characteristic of Martin's historical fiction, particularly of *Mary Reilly*, *Property*, the nineteenth-century sections of *The Great Divorce*, the Serbo-Croation war scenes in *Trespass*, the World War II parts of *Italian Fever*, and *The Ghost of the Mary Celeste*.

With her pronounced interest in history and culture, particularly literature, Martin's work can be seen as part of a continuum from modernism to postmodernism, rather than a definitive break from modernism. In *Beginning Postmodernism*, Tim Woods's differentiation between modernism and postmodernism is useful in situating Martin on this continuum. "Postmodernism is a *knowing* modernism, a *self-reflexive* modernism, a modernism that does not agonise about itself. Postmodernism does what modernism does, only in a celebratory rather than repentant way. Thus, instead of lamenting the loss of the past, the fragmentation of existence and the collapse of selfhood, postmodernism embraces these characteristics as a new form of social existence and behavior. The difference between modernism and postmodernism is therefore best seen as a difference in *mood* or *attitude,* rather than a chronological difference, or a different set of aesthetic practices" (8–9). Thus, although Martin participates in a postmodern sensibility, her work is not generally representative of post-modern techniques, though more as a matter of degree than an absolute difference.

Bran Nicol points out three "dominant" techniques of postmodern-ism that provide a useful basis of comparison to Martin's fiction: "(1) a self-reflexive acknowledgement of a text's own status as constructed, aes-thetic artefact[;] (2) an implicit (or sometimes explicit) critique of realist approaches both to narrative and to representing a fictional 'world'[;] (3) a tendency to draw the reader's attention to his or her own process of interpretation as s/he reads the text. The reason why the concept of the dominant is useful is that none of these features are exclusive to postmod-ern fiction" (K159).

On a spectrum from dominant to unobtrusive deployment of these techniques, Martin's work would be located near the unobtrusive end. Martin does not use such techniques blatantly and as ends in themselves, but subtly and supportively, much more as they are used in high mod-ernist fiction, particularly that of Henry James, which is not principally concerned with disruptively breaking into the reader's imaginative immer-sion to point out its artificial nature. For example, Martin uses biased, if not unreliable, narrators in many of her works (Claude in *Alexandra,* the title character of *Mary Reilly,* Manon in *Property*) and inserts documents of various sorts into the narratives. In Martin's works, however, unlike es-sentially postmodern fiction, characterization and themes are much more important than highlighting the fictive nature of the endeavor. What *Mary Reilly* suggests about gender, science, religion, the art of writing, and morality is foregrounded, rather than the fact that Mary is keeping a diary and that the diary has been edited, though the latter facts are also of some significance in interpreting the themes.

Another example of Martin's unobtrusive use of modernist techniques in a postmodern context is her play with the supernatural, which could be considered what Nicol calls "a critique of realist approaches." Does Elisa-beth turn into a vengeful leopard in *The Great Divorce?* Does Dr. Jekyll turn into Mr. Hyde in *Mary Reilly?* Is the title character of *The Confes-sions of Edward Day* pursued by a döppelganger? Do the dead speak to the living and lure them to their doom in *The Ghost of the Mary Celeste?* Do women change into owls, and do mermaids, selkies, and centaurs really exist, as in the tales of metamorphosis in *Sea Lovers*? Does the governess really see two ghosts across the lake in Henry James's *The Turn of the Screw* (1898)? While these examples could be critiques of realism, they also could *simultaneously*, as befits the dialogic nature of postmodernism, indicate the subjective nature of perception, a characteristic preoccupation of modernism, while also supporting the thematic emphases of each work. As Hutcheon explains, such literary movements are not mutually exclusive: "The postmodern clearly also developed out of other modernist strategies: its self-reflexive experimentation, its ironic ambiguities, and its contestations of classic realist representations" (43).

Yet Martin's version of postmodernism—her attachment to history and culture as demonstrated through her extensive deployment of allusion and parody, as opposed to the K-mart realism school of pop culture postmodernism—may be part of the reason for her relative lack of recognition as a novelist. In *Late Postmodernism: American Fiction at the Millennium*, Jeremy Green suggests that the limited audience for fiction such as Martin's (though he does not discuss Martin) reflects a lack of cultural knowledge or memory: "The problem of memory comes to the fore inasmuch as literary activity depends upon and incites acts of remembering. But in the absence of a serious readership, the appeal to memory embodied in texts, particularly texts of the canon, has no resonance" (12). Jean-Francois Lyotard explores the problem of audience in *The Postmodern Condition* through what he characterizes as a limited and limiting focus on a narrow definition of reality. "Those who refuse to reexamine the rules of art pursue successful careers in mass conformism by communicating, by means of the 'correct rules,' the endemic desire for reality with objects and situations capable of gratifying it. . . . As for the artists and writers who question the rules of plastic and narrative arts and possibly share their suspicions by circulating their work, they are destined to have little credibility in the eyes of those concerned with 'reality' and 'identity'; they have no guarantee of an audience" (75). Martin's arguably best-known novel (though hardly a best-seller or airport fiction), *Mary Reilly*, is a parody of a canonical work, Robert Louis Stevenson's *The Strange Case of Dr. Jekyll and Mr. Hyde* (1886), concerning the "unrealistic" transformation of the respectable Dr. Jekyll into the bestial Mr. Hyde. The audience for Martin's brand of postmodernism may be limited by the very allusiveness and imaginative play that contribute to her status as an artist, despite the gothic frissons and suspense of a novel like *Mary Reilly.*

Indeed, as one further explores Martin's "supra" and "super" realities, one might eschew the terms "modernist" and "postmodernist," and consider Martin a double neo-Jamesian who extends the realistic techniques and themes of Henry James's fiction while, as in William James's *The Varieties of Religious Experience* (1902), exploring the realms of the hidden and seemingly inexplicable. Along these lines, one might deploy a more specific subgenre for Martin's use of the supernatural, for example, that which Katherine J. Weese delineates in *Feminist Narrative and the Supernatural.*

> The fiction introduces an event that defies explanation according to scientific, empirical, post-Enlightenment means of understanding the world. The event challenges the way that women's realities have been constructed in a masculinist society and offers alternative feminist understandings of women's experience. The narrative as a whole is constructed in such a way that it includes realistic details of the historical world—indeed may be dominated by such details—but does not conform to the standards of conventional literary realism; it is non-mimetic both in its inclusion of a seemingly impossible event and in its narrative technique, even when the realistic detail dominates the work. The work employs narrative strategies that fracture teleology, defy closure, and highlight ambiguities of meaning. The narrative exhibits a self-consciousness about narratives in general and/or about its own status as a narrative; the fantastic device facilitates this self-consciousness about storytelling practices. The narratives revise conventional literary genres from a feminist perspective. (8)

Although Weese does not discuss *Mary Reilly* (or Martin) in her book, this description fits that novel according to what could be called postmodernist "storytelling practices" and the use of the supernatural to call into question a world dominated by patriarchy supported by the ostensible rationalities of science.

However one might argue the postmodernist nature of most of Martin's techniques in the highly malleable world of literary taxonomy, one of her dominant techniques is clearly postmodernist, her intertextuality as manifested in allusions and parody. One could justly assert that the use of allusions and parody is found in literature throughout the ages, but, again, it is a matter of degree and purpose: important works from Martin's oeuvre deploy these techniques to postmodernist ends as described by Linda Hutcheon. "Parody seems to offer a perspective on the present and the past which allows an artist to speak *to* a discourse from *within* it, but without being totally recuperated by it. Parody appears to have become, for this reason, the mode of what I have called the 'ex-centric,' of those who are marginalized by a dominant ideology" (35). Martin's concerns often lie with women who have been marginalized by many different ideologies, all of which assert patriarchy, from Christianity to science to the arts. For example, *Italian Fever* is a parody of, among other works, Jane Austen's *Northanger Abbey*, which is itself a parody of the popular gothic fiction of Austen's day. Both Austen and Martin recognize their attraction to the genre and speak from "within it, but without being totally recuperated by it."

Hutcheon's further definition of parody is also useful for an understanding of Martin's parodic fiction: "What I mean by 'parody' . . . is *not* the ridiculing imitation of the standard theories and definitions that are rooted in eighteenth-century theories of wit. The collective weight of parodic *practice* suggests a redefinition of parody as repetition with critical distance that allows ironic signaling of difference at the very heart of similarity" (26). In *Italian Fever,* Martin stresses her protagonist's similarities to gothic heroines who fear sinister plots which *do* exist, yet more to Austen's Catherine Moreland, who fears sinister plots that do *not* exist; unlike these late eighteenth- or early nineteenth-century women, Martin's protagonist neither dies nor is married, but marches off independently into the future, having learned much about life and herself from her experiences in Italy.

If parody is Martin's outstanding postmodern technique, the gothic is the object of that parody throughout her career. Michelle Massé's *In the Name of Love: Women, Masochism, and the Gothic* provides a working definition:

The Ur-plot is a terror-inflected variant of the Richardsonian court-ship narrative in which an unprotected young woman in an isolated setting uncovers a sinister secret. After repeated trials and persecutions, one of two possible outcomes usually follows: the master of the house is discovered as the evil source of her tribulations and is vanquished by the poor-but-honest (and inevitably later revealed as noble) young man, who marries the woman; the master of the house, apparently the source of evil, is revealed to be more sinned against than sinning, and he marries the woman. Strangely enough, in both scenarios the narrative is shaped by the mystery the male presents and not by the drama of the supposed protagonist, the Gothic heroine. (10)

Valerie Martin's *Mary Reilly,* the nineteenth-century-Louisiana sections of *The Great Divorce, Property,* and *Italian Fever* fit this definition through the "trials and persecutions" of the heroine, but Martin's "masters" remain sinners (except in the comic *Italian Fever*). In Martin's works, marriage is more often the source of the heroine's problems than it is the solution to them. Martin's heroines do not arrive at happy endings, but ones that are tragic (*The Great Divorce*) or at best ambiguous (*The Ghost of the Mary Celeste*). Most importantly, Martin does shape the narrative according to the drama of the heroine, not that of the men. Ironically, the Martin novel that best fits Massé's definition of the traditional gothic is *Alexandra,* a parody in which Martin assigns the role of the gothic heroine to a middle-aged man.

Although Martin's oeuvre contains works that are explicitly gothic (albeit somewhat parodic), one could argue that most of her fiction is gothic in the largest sense of that term. Her protagonists do not inhabit sinister castles in romantically depicted historical eras, but they are all, in one way or another, isolated and imprisoned by a patriarchal world that limits their choices, whether in modern New Orleans in Martin's first two books or in the Northeast in her most recent books. The true terror, the gothic frisson in Martin's fiction, is evoked not by the evil machinations of men (many too brutal, too obtuse, or both, to scheme well), but by the horrifying ways that the female protagonists internalize patriarchal values.

Masochism, in many forms, is the way that Martin's female protagonists disturbingly internalize patriarchy, as Massé delineates it in gothic fiction: "What characters in these novels represent, whether through repudiation, doubt, or celebration, is the cultural, psychoanalytic, and fictional expectation that they *should* be masochistic if they are 'normal' women" (2). Explicit masochism is most evident in Martin's early fiction, particularly *A Recent Martyr,* but appears in muted forms in later works like *Mary Reilly* through Mary's internal conflict over her own survival versus her continued suffering for the sake of Dr. Hyde. Some of Martin's female protagonists behave masochistically by losing their humanity and becoming like their tormentors, such as Manon in *Property,* who abuses her slave Sarah as she herself has been abused by her husband, or Chloe in *Trespass,* whose possessiveness and power plays lead to the loss of her family and her life. Chloe is not unique in that Martin's women tend to end up dead when they come to believe they are as wicked or worthless as men tell them they are, such as Camille and Elisabeth in *The Great Divorce,* or those who take masochism to the extreme of martyrdom, however ironic, like Claire in *A Recent Martyr.* Martin, however, shows some of her protagonists as struggling with the cultural prescription that good women should happily suffer for the sake of others (*The Ghost of the Mary Celeste*), especially men, and some of these more enlightened or luckier heroines end their novels by literally walking away from masochistic scenarios as in her first novel, *Set in Motion,* and in *Mary Reilly.*

As this discussion suggests, Martin's work can be located at an intersection of postmodern, gothic, and southern literatures. In terms of the postmodern and gothic, as Susanne Becker points out, gothic fiction in the late twentieth century "experienced a revival that is related to the two most powerful political and aesthetic movements of the time: feminism and postmodernism" (1) in that "feminine writing partakes in the more general postmodern challenges to the master narrative of the Subject" (7). Helene Meyers also discusses the intersection of feminism and postmodernism in contemporary gothic literature and stresses how such texts revise traditional gothic scenarios: "Heroine and reader are detectives together as always, however, the narrative structure invites the latter to retain the role beyond the limits of the text. Thus the postmodern features of these texts promote not only female fear but also female agency" (23), as Martin's novels clearly demonstrate.

This concept of "female agency" contesting "female fear" is also part of Martin's redefinition of southern literature through southern gothic. As Teresa Goddu explains, "The gothic, like race, seems to become most visible in a southern locale. Indeed, the South's 'peculiar' identity has not only been defined by its particular racial history, but has also often been depicted in gothic terms: the South is a benighted landscape, heavy with history and haunted with the ghosts of slavery" (147). In *Property*, Martin highlights the gothic imprisonment of slavery, not only through the sufferings of slaves like Sarah and Walter but also by showing how all of southern society resembles a sinister gothic dungeon, in which no one is free, including slave owners like Manon and her husband. Martin, however, emphasizes female agency, for good or ill; the women, slave and free, are not passive pawns waiting for rescue, but must save themselves as Sarah and Manon attempt to do, with a limited success that proffers a tentative hope for future amelioration.

Although Valerie Martin's work has significant commonalities with southern, postmodern, and gothic literature, her work remains uniquely her own. Over four decades, she has, with technical virtuosity, deployed generic conventions to express the figure in her literary carpet, a worldview that remains consistent although its subjects and methods shift in emphasis over time. Martin's great theme, her Jamesian figure in the carpet, is the human imagination and its varied uses for good or ill: to create, to palliate, to deny, to evade, to destroy. In particular, Martin addresses humanity's desperate and futile attempt to evade awareness of death's reality through the anesthetizing banality of materialism and routine or through the illusory, transitory transcendence of romantic love, erotic love, religion, nature, spiritualism, or art: what Robert Frost would call "momentary stays against confusion" ("The Figure a Poem Makes"). Despite the relative bleakness of her perspective, Martin holds out a ray of hope through humanity's ability to use the imagination, in art and in daily life, for a compassionate empathy that leads to a sense of community, however transient and perpetually threatened by life's vicissitudes.

Love and *Set in Motion*

TEDIOUS TRANSPOSITION TO TENTATIVE
TRANSFORMATION

*V*alerie Martin's first collection of short stories, *Love* (1977), and her
first novel, *Set in Motion* (1978), published as she turned thirty, introduce the principal themes of her career, but without the depth of characterization and textured prose of her mature work. They reflect her early
conflict between romanticism and realism in that her protagonists, mired
in boring daily existence, long to find or create meaning, often in self-
destructive ways, much like the title character of Flaubert's *Madame
Bovary* (1857), a novel Martin repeatedly refers to as a major influence. Her
protagonists could also be compared to the questing existential hero of
Camus's *The Stranger* (1942), equally disaffected and rudderless. Martin's
early seekers, based in New Orleans, also bear a significant, and somewhat
parodic, resemblance to those of Martin's teacher, novelist Walker Percy,
but, unlike Percy's, Martin's questers are granted no truly divine revelations, however tentative. And in contrast to Percy's New Orleans, Martin's
city is devoid of a haunted and haunting past, in keeping with her rejection of Old South myths and literary traditions like those of Faulkner.

Although these two early works disavow the past-obsessed South,
Christian existentialism, and romanticism as limiting perspectives, they
maintain a constant postmodern dialogue with them, particularly the literary plot that Martin will continue to revise throughout her career, that
of the woman imprisoned in a gothic dystopia. In *Love* and *Set in Motion*,
her protagonists are prisoners of a boring and benumbing quotidian existence and demeaning relationships; consequently, they desperately seek
authentic feelings and meanings, often through masochism. As Michelle
Massé has aptly observed, "we must consider 'normal' feminine development as a form of culturally induced trauma and the gothic novel its

repetition. That repetition is not generated by masochistic pleasure but instead, like the response to other forms of trauma, is an attempt at mastery and a revised reality principle" (7). Martin acknowledged such repetitively thwarted mastery when she told an interviewer, "My subject isn't love, especially in the collection of stories called *Love*. They're all stories about power relationships" (Biguenet Interview 47).

Martin herself attempts mastery as she repeats and revises the work of a contemporary of the original gothic novelists, Romantic poet and critic Samuel Taylor Coleridge. In *Love* she depicts her female protagonists' attempts to escape their prisons through their minds or what Coleridge would call the imagination. Their methods range from mechanical physical and mental transpositions to imaginative creative transformations. The key to, and measure of, their success is the degree to which they can use their conjectures to conceive, literally or metaphorically, a real bond with another human being, "love," without compromising their freedom as represented by "motion." Is it possible for a woman to love without losing autonomy, the power over herself that allows her to move as an agent, not to be moved by men as a powerless pawn? Can such a love be imagined?

In a sense, the "Love" of Martin's title is her empathetic version of Coleridge's imagination as he describes it in chapter 13 of his *Biographia Literaria*, because, for Martin, the most powerful imaginative speculation is compellingly directed toward other people. Coleridge considers the imagination the highest power, and he divides it into primary and secondary forms. "The primary Imagination I hold to be the living power and prime agent of all human perception, and a repetition in the finite mind of the eternal act of creation in the infinite I Am." With the possible exception of the angels in the short story "Messengers" as manifestations of the "infinite I Am," Martin does not deal with the primary imagination. Instead, she deploys the two powers that Coleridge terms "Fancy" and the "secondary" imagination, as befits one who does not believe in a god but is highly invested in the ways, destructive or constructive, that human beings use or abuse their own abilities.

Coleridge defines "Fancy" as having "no other counters to play with, but fixities and definite. The Fancy is indeed no other than a Mode of Memory emancipated from the order of space and time; while it is blended with, and modified by that empirical phenomenon of the will, which we express by the word CHOICE. But equally with the ordinary memory the Fancy must receive all its materials from the law of association." Fancy is not truly creative; it is merely a means of rearranging the mental furniture in the hope of evoking a new sensation. In Martin's short stories "Love," "Transposing," "Surface Calm," and "The Mechanics of It," the characters are confined to the world of Fancy. In "Contraction" and "The Creator Has a Master Plan," the women find some potential for liberation by employing what Coleridge calls the "secondary" imagination, which "dissolves, diffuses, dissipates, in order to recreate. . . . It is essentially vital even as all objects (as objects) are essentially fixed and dead." These women are poised on the verge of creation, as artists and mothers, but the reader does not know if they actually will be "set in motion," as Helene, the narrator of the novel *Set in Motion*, will be, however tentatively.

The seeming outlier in Martin's short story collection *Love* is "Messengers" with its atypical male protagonist and with angelic intervention, not human creativity, catapulting him out of his rut. The divine messengers, however, are *deus ex machina*, since no transformation comes from Jacob's imagination. This story can also be regarded as Martin's ironic homage to Walker Percy. Like Percy's hubristic heroes, Martin's Jacob Abel thinks that, like the biblical Jacob, he can wrestle with angels and, like Adam and Eve's son Abel, can make a perfect sacrifice for God. Also like Percy's protagonists, Jacob is so mired in the quotidian that even normally undesirable ways of escape seem desirable. When the angels tell him that he is about to have the worst day of his life, Jacob believes that he is hallucinating, but he does not find the prospect of madness repellent since it would at least be different, what Walker Percy would call a "rotation," the quest for novelty: Jacob "would have to go to a psychiatrist; he would probably have to go into debt, tell his wife, maybe even lose his job. The prospect had some vague attraction for him" (26).

Jacob, as is typical of Martin's male protagonists, uses women's pain for his own ends. When his wife, Christina, is hurt in an accident, anesthetics do not dull her pain, which cannot be alleviated, according to the angels, until Jacob burns down his house and its contents, as does the mad title character of Percy's *Lancelot* (1977). *Christ*ina, like Christ, suffers to bring salvation to man and to turn his mind from the material to the spiritual. When Jacob obeys the angels, "Christina's presence flooded through him like a flash of light, leaving a sweet taste in his mouth [like the body of Christ, the host during communion], a warm lassitude in his limbs and an unfathomable serenity in his chest" (32), and so, at the end of the story, he heads for "Christina's door" (33). Jacob may be saved, but Christina is dead; as the doctor indicates, "There's no hope now" (32). Jacob's presumably temporary release from the quotidian is paid for by her death. For Martin, who does not believe in Christ as God, this female sacrifice is for naught: Jacob is alone now, in contrast to Percy's protagonists who continue their struggle with living female helpmeets. Also unlike Percy, Martin does not allow Jacob what she would consider the easy out of a divine plan, the crucifixion, which would forgive and reward his profiting from others' pain. The reader is left to wonder what new "rotation" or "Fancy" will be needed to alleviate Jacob's next bout of boredom and who will be sacrificed for him.

The title story "Love" presents the point of view of the potential female sacrifice who is as deadened by the quotidian as Jacob and fantasizes her pain as a release. The unnamed narrator works in a government bureaucracy in New Orleans, in this case a welfare office, as do many of the protagonists of Martin's early works and as did Martin herself. As is typical of the confines of female masochism, she is allowed some agency in performing a role in which she is ostensibly sacrificing herself for others, but she subverts this role by refusing to give emotionally and by hoarding her feelings in fantasies that she controls. The narrator creates this scenario about the client across the table from her: "He could grab me by my hair and pull me forward easily, turning my body away as he pulled me by the hair so that I would be stretched backward across the table and he could bring the blade down along my throat" (1). The hair pulling and the exposed, menaced, or damaged throat are key elements in the masochistic fantasies of many of Martin's female characters; a slit throat would silence the woman by ending her voice and agency. The narrator of "Love" fantasizes that after her throat were cut, the blood would form a mask "over my chin, my face, into my nostrils and over my eyes. Since it is my eyes that he particularly despises" (1). In Martin's early work, the eyes are the still-living part behind the death mask that women wear to conform to society's expectations and are the only remaining challenge to men.

The narrator's fantasies are merely mechanical Coleridgean "Fancy" and cannot change her life, yet she rejects any real possibility of Love, the story's ironic title, in either the sense of *agape* in caring for her clients or *eros*, both loves that could transform her existence. The client, of course, does not enact the narrator's fantasy. Instead, when the narrator of "Love" is seeing him out and she "misses a step" (5) on the stairs, he grabs her elbow and saves her with an expression of "concern" (5) and "tenderness" (5); he sees, reciprocally, in her "eyes a rush of gratitude and confidence" (6). They both shy away from the reality of this encounter, "forgetting all about the rent receipt, so eager are we both to be free of the sight of one another" (6). She turns back to the welfare office for presumably another rotation of boredom and fantasy since she realistically fears the entanglements and loss of autonomy of a "love" relationship under patriarchal terms. In other words, this latter-day gothic heroine is not paranoid; masked forces do threaten her agency, as the other stories indicate.

Like the narrator of "Love," the also-unnamed narrator of "Transposing" realizes the futility of her attempts at alleviating the boredom of her everyday existence, her "usual numbness" (60), with husband, children, dog, cat, houseguests, students; she is even arriving at a similar realization about the futility of a lover. Her death-in-life is signaled, as it often is in Martin's work, by feeling cold and seeking warmth, in this case through the mechanical artifice of a heat lamp (60–61). As is also typical of Martin's early female protagonists, the narrator wears a mask of conventional expressions and gestures while experiencing quite different feelings beneath the surface. In the story's last scene, with her husband watching her as she awaits a call from her lover, she washes the dishes like "a ceremony, an incantation" (63). Although she wears the mask of the model wife, she is actually manipulating her husband, who senses something that he cannot identify and "this unnerves him" (62). Her power, however small or futile, and achieved through seeming docility or acquiescence, is also characteristic of Martin's early female protagonists. Michelle Massé considers such a strategy typical of a gothic heroine: "She more often exaggerates ever so slightly the behavior the dominator claims to want, verging on parody in her fidelity to stereotype" (251).

Rearranging the prison's furniture, not true freedom, is the source of relief sought by the female protagonists of *Love*. "Transposing" can mean a change in form as a synonym for transformation, but its other meanings involve mechanical changes like moving a term from one side of an equation to another, changing a musical key of a composition, changing a sequence, or moving from one place to another; these are ineffectual strategies much like that of the gothic heroine's exaggerated acquiescence. The narrator of "Transposing" realizes the futility of her hopes for transformation, as she, while answering questions from her psychiatrist, fantasizes about making this statement to her lover: "This is as good a time as we get. There's nothing to transcend here. . . . It works pretty well to pretend you're not in your real life. I'm doing it myself. But I am in your real life and so are you" (58). She sees their lives as endless transpositions or rotations with no transformation or transcendence: "I see him. Time passes, then I see him again" (58).

In contrast, in "Surface Calm," in order to feel something and gain some control, Martin's female protagonist, Ellen, inflicts pain upon herself, but, in this story, a patriarchal order replaces the divine plan of "Messengers" as the punitive metanarrative. John Irwin Fischer, in the first scholarly article on Valerie Martin, noted in 1988 that although "Martin writes about women who are masochists" (445), "one must expand one's notion of masochism well beyond *reductive* clinical etiologies" (447) and consider, among other elements, "a society that regards [Ellen's] vacant life as normal" (447). Ellen uses knives, chains, and wire to cut and prick herself in order to act and to feel in a life that otherwise lacks agency and purpose. She has no job beyond housewifery; no children beyond herself, "a childish woman"; and seemingly no history of independence before and beyond the time when she was "running to meet him [husband Neil] at the door of her mother's house, years ago" (11). When her husband leaves for a week on a business trip, she is forced to recognize the death-like chill of her life: she believes her house is "always cold, no matter what the temperature" (20); she visits a hardware store "as dark and musty as a cellar"

(13), and after a phone call from her husband "she felt as if her face had frozen" (12).

As in the case of other female protagonists in *Love,* Ellen's "frozen" face is a death mask surrounding the still-living eyes. When she looks in the mirror, she prophesies that, "in a few years . . . she would be like all those other middle aged women who look at their reflections only under extreme provocation, at which time they ignore the eyes and examine the makeup instead of the face" (14). Her masochism is her means of dealing with what she now cannot avoid seeing: "The marks of her ritual, which multiplied daily, became her only source of consolation for the hours in which her eyes were open" (15) and not covered by her anesthetizing mask. Her "ritual" is mechanical Coleridgean Fancy since she merely re-arranges the source of her pain, moving it from her life under a patriarchy to the metal cutting implements that she believes give her some control. When Ellen's husband Neil returns from his trip, he expresses horror at the sight of her wounded body but does not look deeper, past her mask, into her eyes, and "though he was convinced that she was mad he still wished to make love to her" (19), exploiting a woman's pain, like Jacob in "Messengers."

Martin believes that most women have very limited power in our culture as she told an interviewer in 1992: "There may be some strong women doing well out there, but they're certainly a minority, and most of them are doing as poorly as they were ever doing" ("Interview," Smith 13). After her husband's trip, Ellen stops hurting herself by fantasizing that she is "someone else, someone she had read about. The cuts were healing and she saw herself as one just coming to life, slowly, but with great promise, from the inside out" (21). This is a mere fantasy because Ellen is not really healing herself; she is still dependent on her husband, though she now uses her cutting as a way of gaining some power over him by linking her "healing" (21) to his coming home from work for lunch every day and "convincing herself again and again, by recalling a nod, a smile, a half-conscious caress, that he loved her to the exclusion of all else and that he thought her the perfect wife" (21). She keeps her mask, the parodically exaggerated acquiescence of her "Surface Calm," in place until the day that he cannot join her for lunch: "she felt chilled" and yet goes into the tomb-like shed, where she "was enveloped in a sudden rush of cold and dusty air" (22). Even "the sun was not warm enough to please her" (22), so she strips the thorns from the roses and pricks herself with them to break through her icy mask and experience emotion, "laughing and crying in alternate bursts of fear and pleasure, anger and relief" (22). Another round of "rotation," "Fancy," or transposition begins, and there is no promise of transformation in Ellen's life.

"The Mechanics of It," as the title indicates, also concerns "Fancy," this time with an emphasis on memory that demonstrates Martin's repudiation of the southern literary obsession with the past. As Coleridge states, "The Fancy is indeed no other than a mode of memory emancipated from the order of space and time; while it is blended with, and modified by that empirical phenomenon of the will, which we express by the word CHOICE." The unnamed narrator seeks relief from the daily life of husband and child by compulsively and repetitively returning to a memory— "Twenty times a day, forty, God knows how many" (35)—from five years earlier when she bit her lover Jerome on the thigh and he responded by pulling her head back by her hair and slapping her face, exposing her mouth and throat in the typical posture of a silently masochistic Martin female protagonist. Her repeated fantasy is only a transposition of memory, a Fancy, and so the Mechanics of It don't change anything: she keeps hoping for a letter from Jerome that will change everything. She has learned nothing from the repetition as the last line of the story indicates: "I can't think of any explanation for this" (38).

As John Irwin Fischer notes, in Martin's early works "mothers divide their time between a compellingly erotic heterosexual relationship and the company of their only daughters" (446). In "The Mechanics of It," what is more chilling than this woman's futility is the fact that she models such behavior for her daughter. She sees her daughter's desire to go outside to her friends as similar to her own desire to contact Jerome (37), using masochism as a response to lack of power. "If I were to tell her she could not go out to the other children she would become so angry at me she wouldn't be able to control herself. I have seen her like this, in a rage at me, biting her own knuckles and pulling at her hair because she is afraid to do what she would like to do, kick at me and leave, laugh at me. She is like me" (36). Even in her one possible creation, her daughter, she does not see herself transformed, but only a repetition, a copy, the Mechanics of It. Even the future seemingly holds no hope for the gothic heroine's liberation.

Reproduction, in the senses of copying and parturition, is also probed in "Contraction." Marta, the central consciousness, has two possible ways out of her quotidian impasse: creating fiction and creating a child, but she regards these transformative possibilities as either/or, not both/and, so she seems likely to end up with neither. Marta is obsessed with a short story collection by a writer who seems to resemble Joyce Carol Oates: "slightly protruding eyes" (43), a professor who has "no children" (41) and writes prolifically with "a lot of violence, curtly presented, neatly dispensed with" (40). Marta rejects her as a role model, using the excuse that the author "was so willing to give up her life for a bunch of fiction, for a bunch of stories" (42), as if a mother could not write. Her real reason, though, is fear of confronting her own demons since she finds the author's stories too much like the "content of her dreams" (40) and so are "too close to home" (40). Yet Marta cannot stop reading her work and begins to read a short story called "Contraction" in the bathtub, putting off the attentions of a lover to do so.

While the "Contraction" of the stories could be birth pangs, Marta uses them to reduce or contract her possibilities: she is too fearful of what her inner self would produce, either as writing or as a child, so she remains like a fetus herself, contracted in the amniotic fluid of the bathtub, unable to transform herself or create. After trying unsuccessfully to get pregnant by her husband, Marta is now attempting to conceive by her lover, interestingly enough a writer himself of "dull" (45) fiction, whom she hopes will do better as a biological progenitor. Before getting in the tub, she notices a spot of blood and is terrified that she is losing a pregnancy. She remembers a pregnant woman whom she had seen earlier on the streetcar and fantasizes that the woman is afraid that the child will look like her lover and not like her husband; Martin's story "Contraction" ends with the remembered woman merging with Marta and frantically wondering "whose child is this? Whose child is this?" (50). "Mart"a could also be a "contraction" of "Mart" in herself, a successful mother and author, who uses döppelgangers in her later fiction to show unattractive alternative selves in the manner of Henry James's "The Jolly Corner" or the many döppelgangers who haunt gothic fiction.

The narrator of "The Creator Has a Master Plan" is a creator of both fiction and a child, but the story is unpublished, the baby is unborn, and the first line is unpropitious: "The last time you rejected me" (64). Despite these parlous circumstances, this narrator, unlike the masochistic protagonists of the other stories in *Love,* is angry about being controlled by patriarchy. She has revenge fantasies against the unknown editor who has rejected another one of her stories. She pictures him discovering that his mistress keeps a hunting knife in her lingerie drawer, a threat that parallels her own purchase of an antique rifle at a shop on Royal Street. The narrator, a clerk at a New Orleans welfare office, also fears for her biological progeny since she is six hundred dollars short of what she will need for the pregnancy and birth. The rifle cost one hundred and fifty dollars that she can ill spare, but it makes her feel capable, "like a pioneer stalking through the wilderness" (75). In addition to the rifle, she consoles herself by dancing naked and imagines that her dance would ignite a fire that would burn up desk, papers, and editor.

Since her own creativity, as author and mother, is threatened, the narrator uses the rifle as a phallic symbol, and she plans to learn how to shoot it, perhaps part of her "Master Plan," though it would be destructive rather than creative. She would, though, give herself the same powers as the men, the "masters," who try to thwart or destroy her creativity: the editors who reject her work and the lover who expected her to have an abortion. The story ends with her "rubbing and polishing this useless weapon until it gleams" (79). The weapon may be as "useless" as her dance, but both serve to make her believe herself powerful enough to survive until a story is accepted and her child is born. "The Creator Has a Master Plan" is the last story in *Love* and indicates that Martin the creator has a master plan for her collection, showing the range of possibilities from "Fancy" to imagination, from transposition to creativity, as she revises patriarchal cultural narratives from religion, literature, and romance.

Martin's first novel, *Set in Motion* (1978), continues to probe women's responses to patriarchal structures, a spectrum from the parodically excessive acquiescence of masochism to writing her own story through a revision of the Coleridgean Romantic imagination. The novel, through its narrator, gives "a local habitation and a name" (Shakespeare, *A Midsummer Night's Dream*, 5.1.17) to many of the nameless female protagonists of *Love*. Like them, Helene Thatcher, age twenty-seven, works in a welfare office in New Orleans and seems to be leading a rather aimless existence after quitting work on her PhD. The narrative and Helene are "set in motion" when Helene receives a phone call from her former dissertation director, Clarissa Pendleton, summoning her for a visit to Baton Rouge on a Friday evening. *Set in Motion* explores the ways in which this phone call and other aspects of Helene's life—a gothic imagination, her clients at the welfare office, her women friends, and actual or potential male lovers—could "set" Helene "in motion" to use her imagination to change or transform her life, rather than just transposing its pieces with her Fancy.

Martin explicitly invokes Coleridge on the imagination through Helene's recognition that she has a "diseasedly retentive imagination" (48). In a letter to Robert Southey on August 14, 1808, Coleridge gives what he calls "a clue to the whole mystery of frightful Dreams, & Hypochondriachal Delusions": "an *aggregation* of slight feelings by the force of a diseasedly retentive imagination" (974). As Daphne Merkin notes, like Walker Percy's *The Moviegoer*, Martin's novel exhibits "a common concern with a state of irredeemable enervation" (15). Helene tries to relieve her ennui by masochistically terrifying herself with the gothic legend of a former client of the welfare office who was denied benefits, murdered an elderly black woman and, unapprehended, is repeatedly spotted in New Orleans holding up her decapitated head by its white hair (51–52). With her friend Maggie, another case worker, Helene speculates on the deterioration of the head as time passes and fears that the man will appear on her doorstep with the grisly prize (52–53). Through this Coleridgean "'aggregation of slight feelings,'" Helene may have hoped for a boredom-alleviating, almost enjoyable *frisson,* but, like a gothic heroine, she instead realizes that she has become "trapped by my own imaginings" (55) to the point that she feels that she cannot stay alone in her apartment and takes refuge with her friend and quondam lover Reed, a bartender and drug addict. Like a typical gothic heroine, Helene flees a male villain to the arms of a male savior who is not up to the job (see Meyers 23).

Martin parodies both religious and romantic "saviors" in Helene's liaison with Richard, the husband of her best friend, Maggie. In her next novel, *Alexandra* (1979), Martin alludes to Matthew Lewis's wildly popular *The Monk* (1796), in which an ostensibly saintly monk uses his cloister, prestige, and power for sensual gratification, including rape. In *Set in Motion,* with the drunken and troubled Richard, Helene uses St. Louis Cathedral for some potentially erotic games with Richard by playing at confession in the deserted sacred precincts in the middle of the night. She mock-confesses to lying, disobedience, and being "incapable of true contrition" (60). Richard, as "priest," responds, "I'm going to beat it out of you" (61), a reference to Helene's masochistic pleasures and to another influential novel for Martin, *Dangerous Liaisons* (1782), by Pierre Choderlos de Laclos.

As in Lewis's and Laclos's novels, religious mockery turns to terror for Helene: "Gradually I became aware of the silence that stood trembling at the edge of our laughter, and then I was laughing only to avoid that silence, full and hysterical, which stood around in the corners of the place, like pools of shadow ready to rush up the walls" (61). Like her fear of the decapitated head, Helene's trepidation at the silence indicates her fear of death at the hands of men, not only actual death, but the death-in-life which characterizes her aimless boredom. The decapitation by a former client and Richard's mock-threat to beat her show that Helene sees pain at the hands of a man as a feasible way out of ennui, indicative of a "contracted" or "diseasedly retentive" imagination as symbolized by a missing head now controlled by a man.

Helene's masochism is her response to her sense of powerlessness, which is reinforced by her job at the welfare office. Although she claims to have "cultivated . . . a studied indifference to the problems of my clients" (36), she realizes that "I hated myself and my work, because I was helpless and preferred to be helpless" (47). Helene has resisted the draining trap of female self-sacrificial caring only to retreat behind the equally dispiriting mask of the insensate bureaucrat. Neither attempt is entirely successful because some of her clients manage to touch her humanity. After watching the disabled Mr. Williams slowly and painfully struggle to maintain his dignity by signing his own name, Helene recognizes "his determination, and his pride which would not be shaken" (44), but she retreats from this insight by calling it "an animal's patience" (44). When she suggests another round of visits and paperwork to another client, Mr. Bodely, who has lost his toe, he places his shriveled, amputated toe on the desk before her and tells her, referring to much more than his toe, "There ain't no way to repair this kind of damage to a man" (99). When she remains obdurate, despite the evidence before her, he declares, "Miss, you don't understand nothin' about nothin' and that's a fact" (100).

A possible female role model piques Helene's interest at this critical juncture when she begins to realize her dilemma: she will kill her humanity if she resists the female role of caring, and she will kill her humanity through emotional exhaustion if she accepts it. Helene's ninety-two-year-old client Mrs. Hudson, like Mr. Bodely, tries to make Helene "understand" through her example; she enjoys her life despite her infirmities, and cares for others, especially her old dog and her grandson. She tells Helene, "Every person you meet be someone . . . and every li'l thing you see is something to see" (115). When the visit ends, "Mrs. Hudson put her hand out to me and I took it in my own gratefully. I felt that her touch filled me with strength, with her pleasure in life. I wanted to go out the door with her. She released my hand and turned from me, leaving me excited. By the time I got to my desk, I felt impatient and alone, convinced that I would not be like her and ashamed of myself for pretending, even for a moment, that I might" (117–18).

Mrs. Hudson almost "set" Helene "in motion," but though she did not succeed, she at least motivates Helene to attempt to empathize with her friend and fellow caseworker Maggie. Helene tells Maggie, "When I was in high school, the nuns used to say that the soul was like a container of grace, everybody could fill their container, but some people, like saints, had great big containers and others had little ones. I think mine's a thimble" (118). Even though she does not follow Mrs. Hudson's saintly example of putting others first, Helene's thimbleful of grace does move her to the charitable gesture of trying to probe Maggie's barely contained fatigue and hysteria, though she gives up fast, "determined not to push her to an untimely confession" (119), an incomplete gesture toward female mutual assistance or community. Helene cannot move definitively in either direction: she is stuck, damned if she follows the female script of caring and damned to resemble the vampire-like men if she does not.

Standing by your man, following the heterosexual romance plot, is an equally distasteful and self-destructive modus vivendi for women. As in her relations with her welfare clients, Helene maintains her reserve; she keeps male secrets even from the ostensibly close female friends who are affected. When she is summoned by her former dissertation director, Clarissa Pendleton, to Baton Rouge, Helene finds the house empty and so she looks for Clarissa at her department at the university. There she meets another professor, Michael Pitt, and goes to his place where they engage in some rough sex. He does not tell Helene that he is Clarissa's fiancé, nor does Helene tell Clarissa about her encounter with Michael when she later learns of the engagement from Clarissa. Even more remarkably, Clarissa does not call off her wedding when Michael tells her of what, by then, had become a series of sexual encounters with Helene. Like the eponymous title character of Samuel Richardson's novel, whose name she shares, Clarissa passively continues her commitment to a cruel man.

Helene's friend Maggie is equally blind to any alternatives to the conventional female script of standing by your man as masochistic renunciation of self: Maggie's husband, Richard, treats her with contempt. In a scenario resembling the Clarissa-Michael-Helene triangle, Richard attempts, though unsuccessfully, to have an affair with Helene, and Helene does not tell Maggie about Richard's advances, their conversations, or their games in St. Louis Cathedral. As Richard becomes increasingly strange and troubled and Maggie more careworn, Helene does at least warn Maggie, "You've got to do something" because Richard is "taking you with him" (94). Maggie cannot act because she is simultaneously in denial and in thrall to the masochism of danger; she tells Helene, "I can't believe he'd really hurt me" (92) and "I want to see what's going to happen" (92). Both Clarissa and Maggie have been set in motion, but in the sense of inertia: they continue to move in a straight line unless and until they are moved by another force.

Helene rejects another alternative to female masochism, female defiance, as too dangerous. She is initially intrigued by the story of a New Orleans woman who lived and succeeded, the Baroness Pontalba (1795–1874), who survived her father-in-law's attempt to kill her but literally incorporated his real motive, to weaken her sense of agency and control: "The shot was never removed, and as an old woman she lost control of her hands, so that they jerked about uncontrollably" (105). The caretaker of the Pontalba Museum tells her that the father-in-law "wanted her to sign her money over to him and she wouldn't. She was strong-willed. She did as she pleased." Helene responds, not by considering the Baroness's accomplishments such as erecting the Pontalba buildings on Jackson Square, but by focusing on the damage done by her defiance, "And got shot for it" (147) (for more on the Baroness Pontalba, see Vella). Helene is more interested in maintaining control over her own body, so that, repulsed by the Baroness's jerking hands, she cannot perceive wider realms of potential action and success. Significantly, Helene has this conversation after evading her secret lover Michael Pitt by leaving him at her apartment without telling him she was going and then wandering around the French Quarter; unlike the Baroness Pontalba, she does not confront, but instead continues to evade, solving nothing.

Through two strategies, Helene does attempt to maintain some degree of power in her relationships with men, albeit negative and reactive: the mask of withholding and the motion of flight. This is easiest with Michael Pitt, Clarissa's fiancé, since he is so blinded by his convictions about his own power and the stupidity and passivity of women. Fittingly, as an academic, he studies Theodore Dreiser and social determinism and counts himself among the strongest who will survive. Helene enjoys the sexual power play but refuses to participate in his mental power games. When he starts to prod her about women's liberation, to his annoyance, she picks apart the terms of his questions and tells herself "I don't care" (123). When he taunts her about "self-respect," she muses, "What would he do when he realized—he would have to sooner or later—that the word meant nothing to me, that the loss of that commodity was as insignificant to me as paring a fingernail?" (137). Like Camus's Meursault in *The Stranger*, a novel that greatly influenced Martin, Helene tries to maintain her emotional numbness by refusing to acknowledge society's hierarchy and conventions; also like Meursault, she protests too much and is only partially successful; meanwhile neither Pitt nor society is altered.

In the character of Richard, Maggie's husband, Helene sees an aspect of herself, her emotional twin or male döppelganger. Unlike the oblivious Pitt, Richard, a painter, is excessively affected by society and other people. He drinks, he wanders the city, he stalks Helene, and he writes obsessively in his journal. Like Helene, he feels the faceless oppression of mass society; one of his paintings depicts "a bunch of figures falling past a city down a plastic chute" (90). Helene recognizes their affinity when she reads his journal. "I was queasily conscious of how the writing had struck me. It wasn't alien at all. I had felt from start to finish a persistent lucidity, so that even as one part of me responded, This is madness, this is confusion, another followed the sentences with a sense of righteous satisfaction; yes, this came first, this was the obvious conclusion of that" (198–99). Like Jacob in Martin's "The Messengers" and like the title character of Walker Percy's *Lancelot,* Richard burns down his home, but in this case in the hope of relieving his own pain, not that of his wife Maggie, whom he has already psychologically incinerated: "Maggie has no electricity. She is burned out. I burned her out, but it is her own fault, because that's what she wanted" (188). Helene rejects the masculine alternative of alleviating her own pain through another's suffering.

Mutual wound licking is the unsavory alternative presented by the third man, Reed, an uneducated bartender and drug addict, with whom Helene must come to terms as she attempts to find her modus vivendi. Reed and Helene's relationship resembles that of Binx and Kate in Walker Percy's *The Moviegoer* (1961) in that they seem to have complementary weaknesses and act as mutual caretakers. Helene tries to get Reed to consume food, not just drugs, and she brings him to the hospital when he overdoses; he watches over her as she sleeps nightly at his apartment until the decapitator is caught. Helene tells Maggie that loving Reed would be "pointless" (94) because their relationship will not develop or create. Helene and Richard are like the carrier pigeons that Helene keeps at her apartment. When Maggie asks Helene if they laid eggs, Helene observes that "the birds were nestled close together, the male shielding the female's head against his chest," and she replies to Maggie, "They seem to like each other, but nothing comes of it" (165).

In *Set in Motion,* Martin presents a contemporary gothic dystopia in which women's possibilities seem confined to versions of female suffering. Yet, in contrast to the static and passive heroines of gothic fiction, Helene chooses motion over confrontation as a response to male demands and as a means to power, however limited: "What I liked best was to be in transit . . . to go from a lover to a lover, to a room, across a room, to close one door, moving to open another door, being in motion" (97). She muses, "I knew, had always known, that I could have power over a certain kind of man if I wanted it. The power of weakness, the possibility that indecision hides a variety of strength" (97). She compares herself to "a slave who knows his master can't understand the language of slaves and has no power in that language" (103) and so she believes "I had a certain indestructible freedom" (103). This passage is key to understanding the female "masochism" in Martin's early works. In a world in which women have limited power, they choose evasion, flight, masks of "weakness" and "indecision," and incomprehensibility to gain some control over their situations. In that sense, the "masochism" is not a passive love of pain inflicted by others; it is a state of awareness and a choice among limited options. It may be better than unthinking docility, but these women are further limiting their options by believing that slaves cannot escape; they can just wander in surroundings circumscribed by their masters. In a patriarchal society, Helene and her women friends attempt to figure out how much freedom they really can have and if they are already too damaged to enjoy it, dilemmas faced by women in the Old South in Martin's later novels *The Great Divorce* (1994) and *Property* (2003) since the slave system is the ultimate gothic dystopia for black and white women.

By the second half of the novel, through Helene's further interactions with other similarly entrapped women, Martin suggests that an active, mutually helpful female community could help revise or at least partially subvert the alternative of female masochism. Helene becomes less convinced of the efficacy of her emotionless mask and of the desirability of motion that only leads to pain, madness, and death, a lie where "nothing comes of it" (165). When Clarissa comes to Helene's apartment, apparently to have a confrontation about Helene's affair with Michael, the two women instead have an amicable discussion based on their understanding of Michael's lies and inflated ego. Michael told Clarissa the falsehood that Helene knew that he was engaged to Clarissa when they had their first sexual encounter the night Clarissa was out of town. He also claimed that Helene was in love with him, but Clarissa knows Helene's emotional reserve too well: "The idea of you being in love with anybody didn't strike me as very plausible" (140). Helene points out Michael's psychological crudity in that men like him use "honesty" (141) to "whip their victims into submission" (140), but "I don't think he's consciously cruel. If he were, he'd be more subtle" (141). Helene and Clarissa part, "surprised and ill at ease at how easily we had settled this matter between us, how clearly we saw one another's position" (142). They are ill at ease because they are like slaves, conniving to deceive a cruel and egotistical master "who can't understand the language of slaves and has no power in that language" (103). This time, however, Helene heads for freedom and escapes Michael, by leaving him in her apartment without telling him she is going.

An additional sign of renewed agency appears through another female döppelganger when Helene starts to work on the welfare case of a young, pregnant African American woman, Mae Ella Cunningham. Helene feels stirrings of disgust at her own emotional detachment from her work with needy people: "I felt as a prostitute must feel who discovers that she despises a regular and financially generous client—I could close my mind, turn off every spontaneous response, and do it" (150). Helene gradually realizes that "Miss Cunningham" is "Ella," the woman whom she had picked up and given a ride on the way to visit the missing Clarissa in Baton Rouge. On that journey, which is the opening scene of the novel, Ella disappeared at a rest stop after Helene snapped at her when she noticed a tear on Ella's cheek: "For Christ's sake. . . . Please don't cry" (9). Helene feared any feeling that might evoke a commitment that would end her own numbness and motion: "Now we were going to have an emotional explosion. I would have to stop the car. I would wind up looking after this poor creature for the rest of my life" (9). Weeks later, in the welfare office, Helene reacts very differently and runs after Ella, calling her name, but she has once again disappeared. Helene is now "unable to quell an insidious suspicion that she knew something about me no one else knew. How useless I was. To myself" (152).[1]

Through Helene's next encounter with a female double, Martin suggests that evasion is not the most desirable strategy in the face of patriarchal demands. Helene now "regretted running from [Michael]. I regretted running. Am I changing? I thought. Is something changing me?" (158). Some confirmation comes when Helene does not push away the next desperate woman she encounters as she repelled Ella. When Maggie is homeless because Richard has burnt down their home, Helene invites Maggie to live at her apartment and realizes "I want to be involved in it. That's so unusual for me" (166). She talks, eats, smokes, and shares her clothes with Maggie. She even asks herself, "Is it a man I need? I just don't think so" (167).

Martin shows how easily female bonds can be broken at the behest of men, especially when a man's stature seems to be threatened by a newly empowered woman, and when women identify, not with the empowered woman, but with what society would regard as the inconceivable situation of a newly powerless man. Helene's tentative sense of community with Maggie is jeopardized when Maggie discovers Richard's obsession with Helene by reading his journals. After reading the journals, Helene tries to convince Maggie of her innocence, while identifying with Richard, whom she now perceives as powerless because "[Maggie] was in the center of it all now; she had complete control over his fate, and this pleased her. In fact, now that she had this power over him, I could see that she could no longer remember not having it. So she thought Richard chose me because of her. I didn't try to dissuade her from this reasoning, there was no point in that. I would let her think what was most useful to her to think, and in the morning, I decided, I would go to the asylum and try to see Richard" (199). This is Martin's version of Henry James's trope of the "sacred fount" in which every couple has a finite amount of élan vital; when one partner flourishes, the other dwindles (*The Sacred Fount*, 1901). When Maggie is burnt out, Richard is empowered; now that Maggie is feeling livelier and healthier, Richard seems "small" and "frail" (204) when Helene visits him

1. Helene's relationship with the enigmatic Ella presages Manon's equally vexed relationship with her willfully, silently subversive slave Sarah in *Property* (2003).

in the hospital and starts to have sex with him until the attendants pull them apart.

Anatole Broyard, in an early review of the novel, sees Helene as trying to be Richard's savior: "Helene visits him and tries to give him what he wants, not because she loves him, but because she believes in saving people. Though she has never allowed Richard to touch her before, they embrace passionately in the doctor's office until the attendants rush in and separate them. It is a beautiful scene and I felt that Helene might actually have succeeded in bringing him back into the world." It seems just as likely that Helene is trying to suck up Richard's remaining life force and be the empowered partner herself and that neither Richard nor Helene may regard his return to the banality of existence as desirable. Indeed, Helene rejects the role of savior as she thinks of Richard on her way back from the hospital: "I knew that what made him mad was his willingness to give himself up to strangers. I blessed my own sanity, seeing for the first time what was at the core of it, my determination never to give up my freedom. I would never, never give up the option to walk away" (206).

The novel ends with Helene walking away, this time from Reed after arriving at his apartment in tears from her charged encounter with Richard in the hospital. At first they seem to enact their mutual caretaking with Reed agreeing to stop trying to kill himself and Helene consenting to get up off the floor (209), an initial step up from female abjection. He falls asleep with his head in her lap until "I eased myself out from under Reed's weight" (210). In the last line of the novel, Helene is "anxious to leave the dark, dreamy gloom of Reed's apartment behind me and go out into the bright sunlight on the street" (210). The novel's ending is ambiguous: although Helene engages more with others in the second half of the novel, her last gesture is walking away as if any relationship is a "weight" that will slow down her motion.

In *Set in Motion*, Martin depicts a world of power struggles between the weak and the strong in the context of the female gothic dilemma and presents only one unsatisfactory, temporary, and endlessly repetitive solution: however the balance of power in any heterosexual relationship may shift, the only way a woman can maintain her integrity is by walking away. The problem is that the female self in motion, while remaining unconquered, is also inert, and loses its capacity for feeling, the good as well as the bad. Although Helene is "set in motion" at the beginning of the novel by Clarissa's summons, and, as in a classic bildungsroman, she appears to develop more meaningful relationships with others over the course of the novel, she is actually "set in motion" in the sense of being set in her ways. She believes that she has evaded the "weight" of relationships, but her motion may just be another form of inertia in which it is impossible to halt unless stopped by a greater force. In *Set in Motion,* Martin presents the truly terrifying gothic spectacle of a female heroine in a contemporary patriarchal dystopia who can only move from one entrapment to the next, with only the most provisional suggestion of the "greater force" of female bonding as a utopian hope, utopian in its ideal nature and utopian in its impossibility of achievement. However, without this hopeful Coleridgean exercise of the creative imagination, all that would remain is the "diseasedly retentive imagination" that compulsively repeats the gothic plot against women.

2

Alexandra

GOTHIC PARODY, PERPETUAL QUANDARY

*I*n her review of Valerie Martin's second novel, *Alexandra* (1979), for the *New York Times Book Review,* Francine du Plessix Gray expresses an exasperation arising from the frustration of admiration mingled with confusion. Gray praises Martin's "skill in creating psychological atmosphere through a detailed depiction of place" (Sec.7, 10), and she recognizes Martin's intent to create a "neo-Gothic" (Sec. 7, 10). Her puzzlement arises from Martin's "trouble making her narrator's voice credible. It becomes extremely difficult for the reader to know whether the frequent silliness of the novel's prose style is parodic or not" (Sec. 7, 10), but she is sure that Martin's "male narrator remains a caricature" (Sec. 7, 15).

Gray's perplexity is understandable because *Alexandra* is postmodern parody seemingly gone wild. Martin is not only writing what she calls "reverse gothic" ("Transformations" 31);[1] she is also transposing gender roles, mocking southern plantation fiction and belles, rewriting Henry James's "The Beast in the Jungle," parodying Walker Percy's fiction, and mingling Christian and pagan mythologies: all this related by a biased first-person narrator who is recollecting his past despite the fact that he believes that memory is unreliable. The key to all of these clamorous and entangling narratives, the Jamesian figure in this novel's intricate carpet, is actually right under the reader's nose, hidden in plain sight. The title of the book is *Alexandra,* and if we reverse the carpet and look at it with the title character, not the male narrator, as its dominant motif, we recognize that this novel is another version of Martin's earlier works in which a female protagonist tries to relieve the tedium of the quotidian with masochistic

---

1. Martin is aware of her audience's confusion about what she calls the "reverse gothic": "I thought that was funny, but nobody else did" (McCay and Wiltz 7).

pleasures and uses a withholding mask and the evasion of motion to preserve some degree of freedom. By placing a male of advanced middle age
in the role of the imperiled gothic heroine, Martin scathingly displays the
absurdity of woman's plight in a man's world. She also compels her readers
to realize that due to our cultural biases we tend to look toward the man's
story as the real or important one, despite obvious indications, like this
novel's title, that the woman's tale is at least equally significant.

Martin describes the basic gothic plot that she is parodying in *Alexandra*: "It's always a woman taken away to the house where strange things
are going on, so I wanted to have a man taken away to a house where
women were doing strange things; that was pretty much the rationale of
that novel and why I call it a reverse gothic" ("Transformations" 31). If we
readers fail to notice the "reverse gothic," Martin gives us a broad hint by
placing a copy of the Ur-gothic, Matthew Lewis's *The Monk* (1796), in the
library of Beaufort, "the house where strange things are going on." If one
reverses the genders in the following plot summary, one can perceive the
major characteristics of a classic gothic narrative: female imprisonment in
a mysteriously labyrinthine male dystopia where the heroine's female predecessors were abused and/or destroyed, and with abounding male and female döppelgangers presaging the life-altering experiences of the heroine.

Claude Ledet, the narrator, agrees to give up his job and home in New
Orleans to accompany an enigmatic and compelling woman whom he has
recently met, Alexandra, to an estate, Beaufort, deep in the bayous, which
is ruled by the goddess-like Diana with the help of two other women,
Alexandra and Collie. The mystery in the women's past is the fate of a man,
John, whom Claude strongly resembles and whom Alexandra and Diana
either killed or did not, with Collie's collusion. Diana warns Claude not to
talk to Beaufort's caretaker, Banjo, who lives in isolation near the labyrinth
that he has created. When Claude does visit Banjo and hears his account
of John's demise, Claude is afflicted with a mysterious illness. In his delirium, Claude believes that Alexandra and Diana are considering killing
him. When Claude recovers, Alexandra abandons him, leaving him de-
spairing; he believes he is spoiled for other women and that his life is over.

Although the similarities are evident, the differences between Martin's
novel and a generic gothic are significant, most importantly in the rever-

sal of gender roles. In the initial phase of his relationship with Alexandra, Claude enacts the traditionally female role of his and earlier eras. He refers to Alexandra with the male nickname of "Alex." He waits for her to make the first moves ("Suppose she didn't call?" [28]) and remains passive ("I sat next to my phone" [29]). She tucks into a steak and he daintily eats a salad (20). The sugar he puts in his coffee meets with her scorn (46). Her sport or hobby is knife throwing. He worries about how she rates him in bed: "She was delighted with my performance" (27). He wants to be a part of her life, but knows he must do so without threatening her independence: "Already I could see that she was willing to let me stay or go, whatever I wanted, as long as I didn't leave my things about and try to make her change her solitary ways" (24). If these obsequious strategies to please appear silly in a man, why not in a woman?

Through Claude, Martin also parodies some of the classic neo-gothic belles of the Southern Renaissance. Like the hyperfeminine Blanche Du-Bois in Tennessee Williams's *A Streetcar Named Desire* (1947), expelled from her beautiful dream of the plantation home, Belle Reve, Claude likes hot baths on hot days, and he tells Alexandra, as Blanche similarly tells the hypermasculine Stanley Kowalski, "It refreshes me" (105). Blanche is frequently compared to a moth who will burn in Stanley's flame; Claude sees himself as a moth who "has no choice" (46) about his flame, Alexandra. Another infamous southern belle, Faulkner's Temple Drake, the foolish virgin of *Sanctuary* (1931), is abandoned in her own neo-gothic labyrinth of horrors at Frenchman's Bend and rightly fears that "something is going to happen to me." Claude also anticipates that "something will happen to me" (81). For Blanche with her impoverished ladyhood, Temple with her debutante's destiny, and Claude with his government clerkship—as for sheltered and bored gothic heroines—this is a partially pleasurable terror and a fate as much desired as dreaded because it apparently provides a means of egress from the mundane and predictable. Claude observes, "Mine had always been the heartless struggle of an animal who has the intelligence to comprehend the efficient calculation of the trap into which he has stumbled," and he sees Alexandra and Beaufort as freedom: "Somehow, in spite of my hopelessness, I had escaped it" (97). And in accordance with the gothic plot, Claude will find what he believes to be horrors, like those of Frenchman's Bend, under the Belle Reve of "Beaufort," a name that suggests handsome and strong men as a refuge, a reversal of the feminine Belle Reve and the fact that Beaufort is controlled by women.

Claude, however, is not a young innocent thrust against his will into thralldom in a gothic enclosure. He is forty-nine years old, if we are to believe what he tells Alexandra (46), and he has been engaged in a long-running sexual relationship with Mona, a prosperous widow. In a gothic tale, the heroine often has a persistent suitor from whom she is fleeing, but runs away into a new trap, the gothic prison. In New Orleans, importunate suitor Mona had tried every wile to get Claude to live with her. When she later goes to Beaufort to "rescue" him, Claude learns that he has not received Mona's letters because Alexandra has been reading and keeping them (163), the act of a gothic abductor. Claude, however, feels contempt for Mona, "a big fat insect I wanted to slap" (10), but "for a long time I enjoyed Mona's affections and bank account" (4); no virginal ingénue, he has been exploiting her. Consequently, he does not want to be rescued from Beaufort, where he is living in luxury on Diana's bounty. In this reverse gothic, the prospect of property, possessions, and power, not love, are what truly lure Claude to Beaufort, foreshadowing the themes of Martin's later great novels *Property* and *Trespass*.

Gothic imprisonment turns to "door-slamming" farce because Claude is far too old and experienced to be eligible for gothic Stockholm Syndrome; unlike gothic heroines or modern kidnap victims, he chose his fate. Alexandra "saves" Claude from Mona by wounding her with one of her throwing knives. Maddened by Mona's accurate parting prophecy that his "young girl" (164) will not desire him much longer, Claude states that "never had I felt such a desire to hurt a woman" (164), but instead he "left the room, slamming the door behind me" (164), exhibiting the ineffectual rage of the traditional woman scorned. Like the similarly aging Dr. Faust, Claude muses, "If some phantom had risen up and offered me an infernal contract in exchange for stopping time dead for a few years, I would have signed eagerly" (44). In contrast to gothic heroines in masochistic thrall to love, Claude, under the guise of love for Alexandra, lusts for power as much as Dr. Faust and makes his own diabolic bargain.

In another twist of the reverse gothic, Martin shows the male version of the sheltered gothic heroine's longing for the dangerous excitements of love as she parodies Henry James's "The Beast in the Jungle" (1903). Claude is so eager to make his Faustian pact because he wants to avoid a fate similar to that of James's protagonist John Marcher. Like Claude, John Marcher is a bureaucrat with "his little office under Government" (K31002). He also shares Claude's belief that "something will happen to me" (81), in Marcher's case, as described by his confidante, May Bartram, "the sense of being kept for something rare and strange, possibly prodigious and terrible, that was sooner or later to happen to you, that you had in your bones the foreboding and the conviction of, and that would perhaps overwhelm you" (K30848). Marcher thinks of this "conviction" as "the crouching Beast in the Jungle" (K30969) whose pounce would result in "possibly destroying all further consciousness, possibly annihilating me; possibly, on the other hand, only altering everything, striking at the root of all my world and leaving me to the consequences, however they shape themselves" (K30862). Marcher spends his life waiting for the Beast to strike and so becomes "the man, to whom nothing on earth was to have happened" (K31591). While she is dying, May Bartram attempts to alert Marcher to her love for him, that passion which could have "alter[ed] everything" (K30862) for him. He failed to see "the Beast" in May's proffered love until it was too late, after her death and at the end of his wasted life.

Through parody, Martin brilliantly points out that one could read "The Beast in the Jungle" as James's male, modern version of the female gothic, a longing for dangerous passion that liberates one from the bureaucratic quotidian and allows one to evade, rather than deal with, things as they are, one shared by Martin's contemporary heroines in places like the welfare office in New Orleans in *Love* and *Set in Motion*. In the scene where Claude prepares to escape his office and leave for Beaufort, he is assisted in his packing by his unappreciated May Bartram, Miss Babar. She offers him, at the conclusion of their labors, half of her "fragrant tangerine" (63), as if wishing him well in his new life since tangerines are tokens of luck in Chinese New Year celebrations. She also points out the imminence of death in any life when she notes that while his "termination is rather sudden" (63), "who among us has not [contemplated termination]?" (63). Like May Bartram, Miss Babar is aware that death awaits her, and also like May, she wants to consume life to its dregs while she can, so she "ate two more slices, delicately sucking her fingertips after each" (64). As May recognizes Marcher's obdurate obtuseness in their final conversation, so Miss Babar realizes Claude's when she confirms that he is "running away with a young woman" (64) and observes, "You are the sort of man who must do that sort of thing, I suppose" (64), while Claude cluelessly "wondered why we had never shared a tangerine before" (64). Babar means "lion" in Hindi, and Miss Babar is the unrecognized beast in Claude's office jungle, but he instead leaves for the jungle-like foliage of Beaufort with Alexandra. Despite Claude's attempt to avoid John Marcher's fate as "the man, to whom nothing on earth was ever to have happened" and Claude's belief at the end of the novel that he has been "altered, entirely altered" (176), he remains as self-centered, possessive, jealous, and unobservant as ever.

Along with romantic and gothic love as seemingly salvific traps for women, Martin also rejects religion as she parodies the basic plot of Walker Percy's novels. Martin was drafting *Alexandra* while she was taking a writing course with Percy at the University of New Orleans, and she has acknowledged that "Walker Percy was a model for Claude" ("Transformations" 31). Ironically, after reading the novel, the unwitting Percy called Claude "kind of a wuss," and Martin agreed ("Transformations" 31). The irony here receives a turn of the screw in that Percy, in a self-mocking self-interview, described himself to himself as "rather negative in your attitude, cold-blooded, aloof, derisive, self-indulgent, more fond of the beautiful things of this world than of God" (*Conversations* 176), an apt characterization of Martin's Claude.

Percy's typical protagonist is a man mired in the banality of the quotidian. Regarding himself as a seeker, he embarks on a quest for life's meaning during which he meets many representative figures, some of whom tempt him to the grave sins of despair and suicide. At novel's end, Percy's seeker has rejected his hubristic goal of solving or curing the enigma of human existence and settled down with a complementary woman to find God's love in other human beings. Percy's novels are comedies in the traditional literary sense of ending in a marriage, in the Christian sense of finding salvation through faith in God, and in the sense of humor that Percy manifests during the risible adventures that puncture his protagonist's pride.

The characters in *Alexandra* would in many ways feel quite at home in a Percy novel. Claude, the bored seeker of the bureaucratic quotidian, begins the novel "glum, poverty-stricken, dull and thin" (4) in an equally dull job of making the "latest projection for the future cost of Social Security" (36). Mona is like the heartily practical, fleshy, and bossy women who try to mother the Percy protagonist, for example, Kitty in Percy's *The Second Coming* (1980). Alexandra, functionally illiterate and psychologically damaged, resembles Percy's hurt heroines, such as Kate in *The Moviegoer* (1961) and Allison in *The Second Coming* (1980), who find their complement in the seeker. There are good and bad African Americans as in Percy's novels: Banjo serving as the "bad nigger" in contrast to the faithful Collie, loyal like the breed of dogs. Diana could be one of Percy's representatives of southern stoicism who believe, like Aunt Emily in *The Moviegoer* and father figures in other Percy novels, that since the world is in decline, they can only uncomplainingly maintain their high standards. Diana tells Claude why she will keep her soon-to-be-born child away from the world: "The future is for madmen. There's a great future in the world for madness and anarchy and hate. It gets worse every year. . . . It can't be changed and it doesn't even matter whose fault it is. The end of it is despair" (143).

Claude, in contrast to Walker Percy's protagonists, remains uninterested in large social and religious systems; indeed, he may well be one of Diana's "madmen" since he remains obsessed with possessing and controlling Alexandra and has no religious epiphany at the end of the novel that would give him any fellow feeling or empathy. For Percy, Claude would be a castaway (from God) on an island who does not recognize that he is a castaway and believes that he could be happy on the island, in Claude's case, if he could possess Alexandra; Percy characterizes such delusory, impossible happiness away from God as "despair" (144). While it is hardly surprising that the selfish Claude does not experience a religious conversion, he attributes his despair at the novel's end to unrequited love. Religious issues seem equally irrelevant to the other characters and to Martin's plot. Martin is interested in the power dynamics that fracture human relationships, not in man's fractured relationship with divinity.

Martin also includes other parodic references to Christianity as it is practiced by the hypocritical and used by the strong to hurt the weak, the opposite of Christ's message. John, Claude's putatively murdered precursor among the women of Beaufort, is a pornographer, unlike the ascetic John the Baptist, and he appropriately prefigures the selfishly sadistic sexuality of Claude, not the compassion of a self-sacrificing Jesus. (The parody is further complicated if one considers the John/Claude pairing an early instance of Martin's use of the döppelganger.) The role of Christ is multivalent, however, since Diana takes that role when she offers to wash Claude's feet "just like in the Bible" (105). A later coming of the Messiah is also suggested by the name of Diana's baby son, Christopher, meaning "Christ-bearer," a reference to the patron saint of travelers. Claude is temporarily brought closer to the meaning of Christianity through baby Christopher, for whom he acted as midwife during Diana's labor and whom he enjoys holding and tending. Love for Christopher, though, is not enough for Claude, who ends the novel by leaving Christopher and heaven to court drink, despair, and death as means of spiting Alexandra for leaving him. Like the sexual sinners in the windy second circle of Dante's *Inferno,* Claude can make Christian allusions and perceive them around him, but he cannot learn from them. Of a sexual encounter with Alexandra, he comments, "I felt as if we were being lifted in the air and turned upright, so that we whirled in a column together, our heads above the atmosphere" (134).

Parodic references to classical literature and myth abound as well, more cultural scripts whose implications Claude cannot recognize. Diana is tall, pregnant, and wears white as a latter-day Artemis, the Greek version of the Latin goddess Diana, patroness of the hunt and fertility. She is not only accompanied by dogs, but she also turns her followers into dogs. Collie, her faithful retainer, is named after a breed, and Collie compares Alexandra to a dog following Diana (87). Claude, after Christopher's birth, also exhibits a dog-like devotion to Diana. Banjo has rejected the role of Fido and has built a maze at Beaufort, making himself a rival monarch to Diana by emulating King Minos at Crete, who built the labyrinth inhabited by his creature, the Minotaur. Martin's Alexandra tells Claude that she is leaving him to avoid a future in which she would be "wandering around after you like some dog, whimpering for you, any time, anywhere" (174), but Claude dismisses her Cassandra-like prophecy as "lies" (180).[2] The *Alexandra* is a poem by Lycophron (c 285 BC), where Alexandra is another name for Cassandra, whose particular torment was to have her accurate prophecies constantly disregarded.

The novel *Alexandra*'s multitudinous and complex web of allusions, also reminiscent of Lycophron's *Alexandra,* is further complicated by the use of an unreliable narrator, Claude, who, as we have seen, seems oblivious to these many relevant and instructive references. Henry James, whom Martin greatly admires, sometimes uses unreliable male narrators to convey a woman's story of exploitation and misinterpretation through implication, much as Alexandra's story must be discerned by the reader through the erroneous and self-serving narration of Claude. Similarly, the story of the title character of James's *Daisy Miller* (1878) is related through the central consciousness of Winterbourne, who fails to understand and truly love Daisy, a failing shared by Claude toward his title character in *Alexandra.* Martin is also parodying the southern version of this paradigm, Faulkner's *The Sound and the Fury* (1929), in which three brothers essentially blame their sister Caddy for their unhappiness in three separate monologues; Caddy does not have her own monologue and the reader must try to piece together her story and her feelings through the male narration, as in *Alexandra.* Martin is satirizing the male tendency to silence women in favor of their self-serving tales as she emphasizes the necessity for women to voice their own version of events.

Probably the most important narrative model for Martin in *Alexandra,* however, was *Naomi* (1924), by the renowned Japanese novelist Junichiro Tanizaki, whom Martin has repeatedly cited as an influence on her work. In *Naomi,* Joji believes himself to be a selfless Pygmalion as he adopts the lower-class teenager Naomi, who eventually becomes his mistress and

---

2. Martin could also be alluding to Rasputin's evil influence over the Russian tsarina Alexandra (1872–1918).

then his wife. Although he believes he is molding her, Naomi is actually in control, as suggested by the title of the novel, and she uses him to support her pleasures, her dalliances with other men, and her independence from control. By the end of the novel, Joji is reduced to a masochistic subservience in order to keep Naomi with him. Since we do not receive an account from Naomi, the reader must deduce Naomi's strength and Joji's blindness by examining what happens in the novel, not by accepting Joji's self-justifying narration.

Like Joji, Claude wants to force Alexandra to follow his Pygmalion fantasy: "She could not have been (couldn't be) more to my taste had I molded the curves of her superior clay with my own hands" (10). Dissatisfied with perfection, like Pygmalion, Claude wants a response from Alexandra, especially to his sexual performance, not a statue's stasis: "The dull expression on her face made me want to shake her" (80); he starts "biting her, tearing at her, dragging her about so viciously I thought I must pull her apart" (80), yet Alexandra "remains uncomplaining" (80). He realizes: "I had never reached her, never touched her, she was unmoved and unmarked by me" (99), so he devises a way to manipulate her. "I thought that if I could force Alex's body to acknowledge me, then her mind must follow, or vice versa. I chose to attempt a sensual possession, as I would not have known (and still do not know) where to begin to engage her thinking" (100). What he believes to be love is actually a desire to possess and use as property. His inability to understand her proves his undoing since she eventually learns to "engage [his] thinking" and leaves him when she believes his scheme is becoming too effective. Like Helene in *Set in Motion*, she walks away.

In *Alexandra*, Martin challenges the reader to find the female title character's true story behind a male's self-serving narration, a tale further complicated and obscured by the novel's dense and sometimes distracting labyrinth of allusions. However, if the reader looks at *Alexandra* as Alexandra's story, not Claude's, Alexandra can be seen as a parodically empowered sister of Martin's earlier female protagonists, particularly Helene of *Set in Motion*, and of Tanizaki's Naomi in that they wear masks of passivity and compliance and use "motion" to get away from men in order to keep their independence.

Under Claude's obscuringly egotistical verbiage is Alexandra's story, a Victorian female bildungsroman with gothic overlays and some significant twists. According to faithful retainer Collie, Alexandra is the illegitimate daughter of the sister of Diana's mother's secretary and is taken in by Diana's mother as a child (86). Like many Victorian orphans in tales like Charlotte Brontë's *Jane Eyre* (1847) or Jane Austen's *Mansfield Park* (1814, the source of *Alexandra*'s epigraph), Alex is different from conventional children, neglected by her rich benefactor, comforted by the servants, and forced to develop strengths of her own. Diana's mother leaves her to Collie's mother, the cook, whom Alexandra calls "Mama" (86). Alex is practically illiterate, and can read only with great difficulty, but she seems to compensate by developing conventionally male skills: she is a whiz at math and memorization. According to Collie, she "rides a horse better than Diana"; can "fix cars" and "sing Italian songs" (88); and can throw knives with accuracy and finesse. Like Jane Eyre, or Fanny in *Mansfield Park,* she is scorned by the beautiful and pampered child of the house, Diana, who, Collie relates, "amused herself by treating Alex like an idiot because she couldn't read very well" (86).

Alex, like a gothic heroine, is lured from a bad situation to a worse one by an enticing villain, but she is not saved by a male hero; instead, she saves another woman from that villain. When the girls become adolescents, Diana begins to see Alex as a project for her benevolence, "something rare and exotic" (88). Unfortunately, as in the case of the title character of Jane Austen's *Emma* (1815), who tries to benefit the illegitimate Harriet but ends by hurting her, Diana's patronage leads to trouble for both Alex and Diana. Alex meets handsome John (Claude's precursor, look-alike, and döppelganger) at a bar, and she becomes embroiled with Diana in a rivalry for him, although Collie considered him "worthless" (88), an uneducated braggart and swaggerer. Since, Collie asserts, John was following the money, he leaves the house one night with Diana, not Alex, in an apparent elopement. According to Diana, John had bound her to a bed in a motel room in order to make pornographic films of her. Alex, not a male hero, finds Diana, frees her, and goes home with her, but it is not clear whether Diana, Alex, both of them, or neither of them killed John (123–24). This mysterious death from the past, a staple of the gothic, is what obsesses Claude, who misses the essential point: who deserves individual credit (or perhaps blame for murder in Claude's view) for annihilating the villain is far less important than women forming an alliance against him since, Collie relates, after these events Diana and Alex seemed "real pleased with each other" (90).

Claude hears this tale of his precursor, John, as gothic heroines hear the tales of their deceased predecessors, as warnings about his own peril, rather than as information that explains Alex's strategies for self-defense. When Alex first meets him at the bar she is tending and picks him up, she is evidently attracted to him because of his resemblance to John, but she initially insists on maintaining her independence and pointedly tells Claude that she ejected "a leech" and "had the locks changed the day before" (21). At the bar where she works, Claude sees her fell an importunate drunk with a heavy glass; she tells Claude, "If Pete [her co-worker] hadn't come in when he did, I would have killed him" (43). He reinterprets the defenses she has developed as a result of her experiences with John as a murderous aggression that could be directed toward him. When Claude is later delirious with fever at Beaufort, he believes he hears Diana and Alex considering whether to leave him to die in the labyrinth (130). But much like the obliviously self-endangering heroines of gothic novels, he disregards this possible warning, again like gothic heroines in the name of love, but in reality due to a desire to regain possession of, and authority over, Alex.

Alex, in contrast to a gothic heroine, does not wait for a male to rescue her, but takes action to free herself. She takes responsibility for her initial failure to see Claude as another alluring entrapment like John. When Claude asks her if she "killed the man who looked like me," Alexandra responds from her new recognition that self-knowledge is power and only replies, "I never could see the resemblance" (175). Although Claude is the one who sees a snake when he enters the paradisiacal Beaufort (74), he is actually the Serpent in Alexandra's Garden because he threatens her independence. She tells Claude that when she was a girl, "I used to imagine that I would be a saint" (170, as did the double protagonists of Martin's next novel, *A Recent Martyr*). Alexandra's sexual addiction to him and her jealousy of his new bonds with Diana and baby Christopher make her realize how far she remains from her goal of independence from the bondage of earthly desires. To redeem herself, she decides to exile herself from this paradise and return to a life of labor in the fallen world of

New Orleans without Claude. In Martin's parody of Genesis and Milton's *Paradise Lost* (1667), the Garden's luxury, like the female gothic enclosure, loses its seductive charms when the heroine realizes it keeps her under the control of various patriarchs; independent toil outside the silken prison is preferable and paradise lost is really paradise gained. Although Jane Eyre takes a similar path when she initially leaves Rochester's supposed loving manipulations for the world of independent work, she returns to tend the maimed Rochester, in what may be another trap concealed by a more equal balance of power and by the masochism of self-sacrificial love; in contrast, Martin's Alexandra keeps moving away, despite Claude's pleas of pain, since, for Martin, enclosures that ostensibly exist for women's protection and comfort are smothering prisons, even when the women seemingly have the upper hand as the titular wardens.

One such initially enticing prison is female masochism, in this case during sex with Claude. Alexandra, however, is conscious of its deceptive allure, unlike Martin's earlier female protagonists who use pain as a means to feel anything at all in their outwardly comfortable female prisons where they are actually powerless inferiors at work and at home. As Alexandra tells Claude that she is leaving Beaufort and him, she provides frightening details of the psychological prison that our culture would identify as romantic love; her identity and spirit are abducted to a horrifically gothic enclosure.

> It goes like this. I wake up and feel awful and ashamed. Then I go over whatever we did in bed the last time, and I go over it again and again until I feel sort of dreamy and warm. And then I get up and start prowling around here, waiting for you. . . . I have one thought, will he make love to me soon. . . . I can't think. . . . I can't concentrate. . . . There's nothing left of me that I can recognize. I don't have any sense, my judgment is shot, my sense of humor is perverse. When I listen to what I'm thinking it makes me sick. When you talk to Diana, when you go off with Christopher, I feel such rage I can hardly catch my breath. I'm lost to myself. (173–74)

Either obliviously or mendaciously, Claude, who had plotted her sexual thralldom, replies to her anguish, "I never meant to make you unhappy" (174), to which Alex astutely retorts, "Are you kidding? . . . Do you think

I don't know what you want? This is exactly what you want. Nothing could suit you more than to have me wandering around after you like a dog, whimpering for you, any time, anywhere. I may have lost my senses, but I know you've done this to me and done it with a vengeance" (174). Alexandra can see through the patriarchal romance plot as a lie that was designed to "make [her] unhappy" and keep her powerless. Unlike James's *Daisy Miller* or Faulkner's Caddy, Alexandra speaks and gives her own version of events.

If *Alexandra* ended here, Martin's novel would be an optimistic feminist novel about a woman's empowerment through the self-knowledge that sets her in motion, away from a self-destructive prison called love. The novel, however, continues for several pages with Claude's response to his experiences with and abandonment by Alexandra. Claude states, "It has been my experience that the last version of a story is the one that vibrates in the imagination with the ring of truth" (145), returning us full circle to *Alexandra*'s epigraph from *Mansfield Park* that reminds us that "our powers of recollecting and of forgetting do seem peculiarly past finding out." Martin leaves us with Claude's version because she is demonstrating that even if a woman asserts and uses a voice and mobility, she remains endangered, because, although she has changed, men have not: they still think and feel the same way. As he watches Alexandra sleep after their confrontation, Claude bitterly reflects:

> I watch this sleep and think it must be the sleep of a dictator. Or a murderer. With this innocence, this unshakeable certainty about the road to survival, no matter how cruel and senseless, no matter what the cost, with this conviction, she closes her eyes upon the outside without regret.
>
> Is there much sleep like this in the world right now? More than before? Is the mechanism of self-defense this operative in many of us today? Are we really coming out of the darkness of self-sacrifice and guilt and duty into the light of what? Self-knowledge? Is this what it will look like? (176–77)

Claude, the epitome of selfishness, wants Alexandra and all women to practice the traditional female virtues of "self-sacrifice and guilt and duty" so that he can complacently have what he wants. In the last lines of the novel, Claude wants to push Alexandra right back into dutiful self-sacrifice by trying to make her feel guilty; he imagines telling her that, after drinking himself to sleep, he wants only the arms of death, a possible suicide threat to make her conform: "And that is the only other embrace I care to contemplate, if you are interested Alex, if you should ever care to know. At this point, nothing less will do" (180). As Kate Ferguson Ellis asserts in *The Contested Castle: Gothic Novels and the Subversion of Ideology,* "the Gothic villain wants to return to a shame culture where conscience—embodied in the woman as mother and helpmeet—cannot follow. In his castle, his monastery, or his lab, he attempts to establish a base from which he can attack his home, where guilt is produced under the rule of women" (xiv). Despite the "reverse gothic," Claude is revealed as the villain, not the victim he claims to be, but one who can wield a woman's ostensible weapon, guilt, against her.

Martin depicts a world where female empowerment is temporary and perpetually menaced if men do not also change. "Reader, I married him" (in life or death), the nineteenth-century female writer's ending, is just a temporary palliative. Their heroines are succeeded by the oblivious male narrators of James, Faulkner, and Tanizaki, and given a turn of the screw through Claude's prototypically female, neo-gothic experience, but the result remains the same. Not only is there no change or improvement in gender relations, but the reader can easily be bewildered or seduced by the dominant voice of the male narrator. Martin seems to be challenging her readers, male and female: if you can discern truth through this bewildering net of allusions to traditional patriarchal narratives as described by a selfishly conventional male narrator, there is some hope for you; however, since most people accept these conventions and respond to them as the rightful imperatives of the dominant male voice, women will continue to confront the perpetual quandary of male power's selfish brutality hidden beneath alluring gothic enticements.

3

A Recent Martyr

RENOUNCING MARTYRDOM, CHOOSING LIFE

*I*n *A Recent Martyr* (1987), Valerie Martin consolidates the ideas and
narrative techniques of her early fiction in a powerfully compelling
novel that is complex yet accessibly attractive. The novel marks a significant transition for Martin, both in themes and techniques. Although the
narrator, Emma Miller, resembles Martin's earlier bored and directionless
female protagonists in *Set in Motion* and *Alexandra,* Emma moves beyond
Helene's and Alexandra's inchoate need for independence represented by
directionless movement to a sense of community based on humanity's
common plight of mortality. Emma may learn and develop more than
Helene and Alexandra because she has a more formidable array of forces
with which to contend: in addition to the usual sadistic lover, she must
deal with a postulant nun as döppelganger, a vulnerable child, and a New
Orleans under quarantine for plague. Emma learns to reject female masochism as a viable plot for her life, whether in the religious form of martyrdom or the secular form of heterosexual "romance." Emma's understanding of her inner and outer life deepens as she meets these challenges
because, unlike Martin's earlier heroines who walk away, she makes not
only renunciations but also positive and intentional choices.

Like Martin's earlier works, *A Recent Martyr* is a postmodern parody of
many works, most prominently Gustave Flaubert's *Madame Bovary* (1856)
and Albert Camus's *The Plague* (1947). Here, though, Martin suggests a
way for women to employ the human need for stories to their advantage,
rather than struggle to live according to male scripts. As a revision of canonical cultural narratives, Emma writes her own story, and it is the story
that she needs in order to survive and mature. She is a thoughtful and
articulate narrator who grapples with what Martin considers the tragedy
of the human condition. Emma muses, "We long for a life we never had

but of which we seem to have a clear memory; a life in which there is no longing" (97). As Martin has stated, such "loss" is "what romantic poetry is all about" (McCay 10). Emma is an artist in that she uses her imagination and the act of writing her journal to create stories that make her life meaningful to herself while assisting those entrapped with her in the human existential plight, a theme that will become increasingly prominent in Martin's work in first-person novels such as *Mary Reilly* and *Property*. For Martin, the stories these women create are not dominating cultural narratives, like religion or romance; instead, they are Jean-François Lyotard's "local determinism" (xxiv) or, like Robert Frost's definition of poetry, "momentary stay[s] against confusion." These stories sacrifice none of their aesthetic quality for their ethical and practical utility.

Emma in some ways reprises Martin's own development as a thinker and writer. Martin is a romantic at heart who sees the world realistically and "set out on my quest to de-romanticize the world in my fiction" (Martin's website). Her guiding light in many ways is Flaubert, of whom Martin has said that there is "no writer more important to me" ("Interview," Smith 10), particularly his *Madame Bovary* (1856), "a cautionary tale about a foolish woman whose Romantic education ill fits her for her very ordinary life" (Martin's website). Like Flaubert, Martin "felt a strong attraction to realism, both as a method and a world view," and she wryly asserts, "I didn't want to wind up like Emma Bovary" (Martin's website).

A Recent Martyr can be considered Martin's tribute to Flaubert as well as her resistant rewriting of *Madame Bovary* in that both novels realistically depict a bored wife and mother trying to break free of the quotidian; a transient desire for sainthood; an imagination inflamed by sensational literature; an adulterous and consuming sexual relationship full of power games; a good but limited husband; a young and vulnerable daughter; and the equation of sexual passion with religious fervor. Martin's Emma, however, does not commit suicide as does Emma Bovary, whose orphaned daughter consequently becomes a downtrodden child laborer in a cotton factory; Emma Miller chooses to live with and for her daughter.

Emma's conscious choice to love and nurture another person arises from the fact that *A Recent Martyr* is also a homage to another of Martin's favorite novels, Camus's *The Plague*. Martin's early novels follow the same progression that she describes as characteristic of Camus's works: "As I have grown older, I have come to see that the romantic notion of the outsider in love with death doesn't solve a thing. It only makes life worse. We have to find ways to create communities. This is exactly the progression Camus makes. In *The Stranger*, the hero is the outsider, the murderer, but in *The Plague*, there is a sincere argument for the necessity of community. There is no God, but there is a need to hold on to what is good" (McCay and Wiltz 19).

In this declaration about community, Martin also reflects a postmodern view of community, as both necessary and tentative, here expressed by Zygmunt Bauman:

> It is for this reason that postmodernity, having privatized modern fears and the worry of coping with them, had to become an age of *imagined communities*. For the philosophers and the ordinary folk alike, community is now expected to bring the succour previously sought in the pronouncements of universal reason and their earthly translations: the legislative acts of the national state. But such a community, like its predecessor, universal reason, does not grow in the wilderness: it is a greenhouse plant, that needs sowing, feeding, trimming and protection from weeds and parasites. Even then it leads but a precarious existence and can wither away overnight once the supply of loving care runs out. It is precisely because of its vulnerability that community provides the focus of postmodern concerns, that it attracts so much intellectual and practical attention, that it figures so prominently in the philosophical models and popular ideologies of postmodernity. (xviii–xix)

Because Emma narrates her story, the reader can closely participate in her struggle to act and think morally and responsibly as she moves, however tentatively, away from solipsism and toward imagining the community that she must nurture in order to survive herself.

Although first-person narration contributes to the reader's engagement with and understanding of Emma, it raises other issues in terms of reliability. Emma does not appear to be a consciously deceptive narrator (or

a self-deceiver like Claude in *Alexandra*), but the reader still needs to account for her biases and for what she simply cannot know. Emma is telling her story after the quarantine for the plague has been lifted and she
has recommitted to her relationship with her daughter. Her account is
based on "a journal" (171), which she describes as a "treatise on my affair"
(171). She also relies on what others have told her, marked with phrases
such as "I later learned" (37) and "But I didn't know any of this then"
(94). She speculates about motive: "I didn't think it entirely an accident
that we met" (91) and uses what she believes to be superior hindsight:
"Though I have entered her thoughts freely in this narrative, I confess to
not having seen entirely into them at that moment" (127). Emma's version
of events is pieced together from her memories, her journal, hindsight,
hearsay, and speculation. She creates the story that she needs to make
sense of her life and to make conscious and committed choices.

Emma is fairly reliable in her unreliability, however, because she tries
to recognize her prejudices and lacunae; in this sense, her narrative could
be considered a confession, though it lacks that genre's self-lacerating yet
self-congratulatory tone.[1] For example, she retrospectively acknowledges
the distortions caused by her self-serving attitude toward Claire, the Car-
melite postulant who aspires to sainthood: "I wondered if perhaps her
greatest accomplishment in this time hadn't been to separate me from Pascal [Emma's dangerous lover]. . . . So I imagined myself superior to her,
more complicated, hence more interesting" (183–84). Emma also doesn't
know, though she would very much like to, what happened in Claire's
final interview with Pascal. She can only note that Claire became "unac-
countably cheerful" (178) afterward, as if there might be a cause-and-effect
relationship.

Emma begins her moral development at what seems to be the nadir
of ennui typical of many of Martin's early protagonists. Emma recalls,
"I saw for myself a future of unrewarding jobs, days that stretched out

---

1. R. McClure Smith, in his article on *A Recent Martyr*, regards Emma's narrative as
part of her masochism in that "confession is masochistic desire in perfect action" (402) as
he explores the masochistic patterns in psychoanalytic terms in Martin's early works. He
also identifies Thérèse of Lisieux, *Madame Bovary*, *The Plague*, and the *Pensées* as important
allusions within the context of masochism.

meaninglessly. I had no wish to destroy myself nor to endure, so what was there, I thought, to do?" (20–21). She believes herself unable to set her own course, admitting "my own unwillingness to make decisions" (21), but ironically she actually does decide to surrender her volition: "I truly wished someone would show me where to go, what to do, tell me what to say" (25). Emma is presented with two such directors representing the masochistic cultural narratives of heterosexual love and patriarchal religion: Pascal with his path of physical ecstasy and Claire with her path of spiritual ecstasy. Ultimately, though, it is the communal extremity of the plague, not the dichotomies of individuals, which helps Emma to find her own middle way of moderation and fellowship, based on what she has learned is important to her.

Her initial "director," Pascal Toussaint, becomes Emma's partner in increasingly perilous games of sadomasochism. These encounters follow the patterns of Martin's earlier works in which the man holds the woman by her hair and cuts off her voice by applying pressure, in Emma's case augmented by intensifying knife play. Pascal is something of a hypocrite because, although he finds Catholicism despicable and wants his mother to be freed from a religion that he believes has enslaved her (7), he himself wants to sexually dominate women, including Claire (10), whom he first meets as a postulant and a guest in his parents' home. His surname is ironic in that Toussaint ("all saints") Louverture ("the opening") freed Haiti's blacks from slavery while perverse Pascal wants to enslave women other than his mother, though he may simply object to the fact that his mother is enslaved to his father, not to him.

His Christian name, Pascal, is also ironic. The philosopher Blaise Pascal (1623–62) was, among many other things, a devout Catholic who tried to improve the Church, while Pascal Toussaint uses his intellectual powers to undermine the faith of others. He is intelligent, proud, and rebellious like Satan in John Milton's *Paradise Lost* (1667), and, like Satan, because he is unhappy in his loss of innocence, he wishes to ruin the happiness of others through undermining their beliefs with mockery. When Emma tries to formulate her ideas about religion, he accuses her of making "a fool of yourself . . . when you talk about religion" (86), which she considers the "cruelest thing he had ever said to me" (86–87). Father

Paine, Claire's confessor, is quite clear about the diabolical threat that Pascal poses to Claire's faith and happiness when he tells Emma, "But I do believe in evil. . . . I think there are forces, sometimes embodied in people, that operate for ill, for the universal ill" (154). Pascal attempts to shake Claire's faith and aspirations for sainthood by contaminating them through sexual associations, first by flirting with her and then by telling her that "religious ecstasy" (63) to him is "like masturbation" (63).

In this novel in which a child, Emma's daughter *Christ*ine, is, in a sense, her savior, Pascal's callous indifference toward children reinforces his role as a satanic tempter, as Emma realizes retrospectively:

> His theories about child rearing ran the narrow gamut from disinterest to insensitivity. He didn't appear to remember his own childhood, and nothing, save speculation about the nature of good and evil, irritated him more than talking about children. The subject, he often observed, bored him. Growing up, it seemed, was simply a matter of learning stoicism. It took me a while to understand what he meant by this but finally I concluded that this stoicism was simply a blatant refusal to put any emotional conviction he might experience before his pride. (86)

Like Satan, his pride has led to a self-destructive envy. Pascal can accept neither innocence nor attempts to move beyond ignorance because individuals in either state would be outside his control and have an opportunity of happiness he has denied himself.

As a revision of Milton's Satan, Pascal is, however, a less compellingly tragic figure and not as successful as a Tempter because, unlike Eve, two women, at least, can see through his alluring tale of power through knowledge and recognize it as a self-serving lie. Emma ultimately does not exile herself from happiness; instead, she rejects Pascal's sexual allurements when she realizes that their sadomasochistic games will lead to her death. Claire is firm in her resolve to return to her convent, despite whatever blandishments or mockery, unknown to Emma and the reader, Pascal may have proffered during his final interview with Claire.

As in *Alexandra,* the women turn the tables, reverse the paradigm of patriarchal authority, by influencing and then abandoning the man who believes he can manipulate them. Pascal is actually much more controlled by than in control of the women in his life. He lives at home and his relationships with the rest of his family and his attitudes toward women stem from his devotion to his mother. When he watches Claire as she listens to Mendelssohn during a concert,[2] he lowers his eyes as she does, and, according to Emma, is "unconscious of the fact (nor did he ever know it) that he had imitated her" (8). Emma sees him not as her guide, but as a similarly lost wayfarer: "Pascal was, in fact, in the same condition, but with less to fall back on than I had. . . . He was not, I thought, enjoying any of it very much at all. He just didn't know what else to do" (21, 26).

Emma's second "director," the spiritual Claire, is another of Martin's döppelgangers, borrowed but significantly revised from gothic fiction. Claire superficially appears to have little in common with the carnal and skeptical Pascal, but Pascal and Claire share a pride in themselves that they believe permits them to disregard the feelings and welfare of others as they pursue their own ends, the roles they see themselves playing in their chosen fictions. While Pascal sees himself as a glamorous Satan or as Satan's successor as in the Byronic heroes of romanticism and the gothic, Claire wants to be a saint because, like Pascal, she "had never expected to be ordinary" (82); "There was some part of her that longed for glory, that wished to rise through the ranks of God's beloved to a position of importance" (84).

Also like Pascal, Claire is quite selfish and incapable of Christian charity. She does not regard other people as a means to God through seeing Christ within them and treating them with empathy and respect. Instead, she regards others as obstacles on her path to sainthood. After ten years at the convent at Lacombe, she wishes to make her vows, but the convent's superior wants her to spend time in the world as a test. Claire does not strive to engage with others when living outside the convent, but tries to act as if she were still within the convent by maintaining her rituals of prayer and self-flagellation. When Pascal's family invites her to dinner, she accepts although she is in the middle of a fast; she refuses to eat at the dinner, putting her own goals before the feelings of others who want to enjoy

2. Claire's religious name is Sister Claire D'Anjou (145), and that name, with her love of music, may allude to a contemporary French singer, Claire Danjou, who "se consacre aujourd'hui entièrement à la musique" ("Claire Danjou").

the occasion, not watch a penance. As she blurts out to Pascal, "Human love . . . is hell. I want nothing to do with it" (151).

Ironically, when Claire declares her rejection of human love, she is standing next to a statue of St. Thérèse of Lisieux (1873–97). According to Emma, Claire is well aware of Thérèse and her example: during a meditation, Claire is "thinking of St. Thérèse's poor health and of her own state of constant blossoming" (37). Claire does share certain superficial similarities with Thérèse. Like Claire, Thérèse was thwarted temporarily in taking her religious vows, died young, and had miracles attributed to her. As Thérèse nursed her fellow nuns during an influenza outbreak, so does Claire assist the citizens of New Orleans during the plague. As Thérèse relates in her autobiography, *The Story of a Soul* (1898), she, also like Claire, suffered from scruples, an overly tender consciousness of sin which leads to preoccupation with self rather than to saintly self-abnegation.

Despite these similarities, Claire will never be a true saint because she is proud and selfish and cannot empathize with others in a community. Thérèse is known as "The Little Flower of Jesus" because she believed that the way to God was through humility, recognizing one's smallness in the face of God's greatness and surrendering to his will. Thérèse dreamed of missionary work and martyrdom, but she overcame her pride to find God in a relatively humdrum existence in a provincial convent and learned to embrace the tedium of the quotidian, which Emma and Claire both find a source of enervation and ennui. Unlike Claire, who rejects human love as hell, Thérèse purposely put herself in the way of those sisters who would irritate her in order to show them sympathy and kindness. In contrast to the fastidiously fasting Claire, Thérèse ate what she did not like or want as an offering to God. Thérèse's popularity as a saint comes from the accessibility of her "Little Way" to an ordinary person faced with the trials and tribulations of everyday life, many of which involve a choice between selfishness and selflessness on a mundane basis, not on the dramatic scale of martyrdom. Claire's rejection of the "ordinary" (82) is inextricably linked with her view of other people as barriers to, not occasions for, saintliness. It is also Martin's tribute to Walker Percy's protagonists, who seek God in daily life with their families and fellows, in many ways a greater ordeal than martyrdom.

Martin uses motherhood as a paradigm for a mutually nurturing community; Emma's maternal love for her aptly named daughter, Christine, will help save Emma as well as Christine. Claire's relation to maternity, in contrast, is a degraded version of not only Emma's but that of Thérèse of Lisieux. During a serious illness, before she entered the convent, Thérèse had a vision in which the statue of the Virgin Mary in her sickroom smiled at her with great compassion. Thérèse had been depressed and repressed following the death of her mother, to whom she had been devoted, and she saw in Mary's smile her acceptance as a beloved child. Claire still has her mother, to whom she is also devoted, and who supports her in her desire to become a nun and a saint, so she finds no need for a divine mother or to become spiritually a little child like Thérèse. Claire's visions are also less benign, and one seems to prefigure the plague that is about to overwhelm New Orleans. When on a streetcar with her mother, Claire perceives the air as "something fetid, teeming with life, but not with life as we like to think of it; rather, full with insect and worm and vermin life, such as overtakes our own lives" (39), and she sees a small child-like woman with a blood-red eye who spouts steam and calls Claire's name (40). Rather than being filled with Christian compassion, Claire is repelled by this vision of suffering humanity in the form of a "child." Indeed, this "child" presages Claire's violent death as the "vermin life" foreshadows her grave.

Through the rumors of miracles and martyrdom that swirl around Claire after her death and the subsidence of the plague, Martin indicates the way that human beings tend to choose the most expedient cultural narrative, a tired default, rather than examine the facts and create a new paradigm that might lead to further revisions and development. With Martin's characteristic postmodern irony, after her death Claire is credited with miracles that save children.[3] Pascal's family believes that Claire

3. Claire's putative saving of New Orleans is an ironic revision of the story of the saint for whom she is named, Clare of Assisi (1194–1253), who renounced the world and its pleasures (and to whom Martin will return in her *Salvation: Scenes from the Life of St. Francis*). St. Clare was greatly influenced by St. Francis of Assisi and founded the ascetic order of the Poor Clares. The citizens of Assisi "credited Clare with twice saving the city from destruction" and "with other miracles in life and after death" ("Saint Claire of Assisi").

performed a miracle when she supposedly saved Pascal's nephew, a tod-dler, by a remarkably skillful throw of a stone at an ostensibly menacing king snake (65–66, 201). The miracle, though, is problematic since king snakes are not venomous. Later, during the plague, Mrs. Leary, who also believes in Claire's miracles, begs her to heal her stricken child because "you saved Lottie Pratt's girl. . . . You prayed over her and she didn't die" (145). Claire replies that "I pray for all the children here. . . . Some die, some don't" (145), and Mrs. Leary's daughter dies. After Claire's death, the mother-general of her convent shows Emma a stack of letters attest-ing to Claire's miracles (199–201), though both women agree that Claire never performed miracles (201). Despite this lack of evidence, the plague-stricken, panicked community defaults to the story that it needs to take heart, survive, and recover.

Emma also revises the story of Claire's "martyrdom" for her own needs. Because of the gasoline shortage, Claire was walking back to her convent from New Orleans through a deserted countryside where she was raped and stabbed to death by two unknown assailants. Claire's violent death was regarded by the New Orleans faithful as a kind of martyrdom due to her zeal to rejoin the saintly life of her order; thus Claire's martyr-dom resulted in the putative miracles in which they need to believe. Al-though Emma rejects the populace's unrealistic view of Claire as a miracle worker, she describes Claire's rape and murder in terms of Emma's own experiences with Pascal: held by her hair, her breath and voice cut off, and menaced by a large knife. Emma sees Claire as courting danger, walking alone to the convent despite warnings, in order to be united with her di-vine lover, much as Emma had played with death in her increasingly dan-gerous sadomasochistic games with Pascal. By the time of Claire's death, Emma has split with Pascal and she projects the fate that she has rejected onto Claire as if to reinforce the moral that a woman dies when she gives up her volition and acts like a submissive dog,[4] an inglorious *recent* martyr in a long succession throughout history, both secular and sacred.

4. According to Emma, Claire had compared herself to a favored "hound" (47) of God. Allowing oneself to be treated like a dog is a bad sign in Martin's work. Alexandra, the title character of Martin's second novel, leaves Claude because she believes he has made her be-have like a slavish dog (174).

Emma constructs her version of Claire's life from positive and negative examples since Emma needs both in her attempt to find her own middle ground. Claire's unwillingness to engage with reality is a negative sign in the context of Martin's strong convictions about the necessity for realism: "Claire hated being realistic. She believed it meant embracing personal failure, and failure was what she could not bring herself ever to embrace" (125). Although Claire rejects external reality, she is highly attuned to an inner reality that Valerie Martin finds necessary but lacking in contemporary life. According to Emma, Claire muses: "To fear an inner life . . . was the greatest foolishness. It was like fearing a breath of air. Why did people find it harder to admit to a universe within than without? Why trust, for a moment, one's own absurd measurement of either?" (136). In *Salvation: Scenes from the Life of St. Francis* (2001), Martin provides an explanation for her fascination with Francis of Assisi that also helps illuminate her characterization of Claire in *A Recent Martyr:* "I do believe, as he did, that the relationship between material prosperity and spiritual progress is nil, and I know that for those who are convinced that the most salient fact of our existence is the certainty that we must leave it, spirituality, by which I mean the apprehension of another (not necessarily an after-) life, offers egress from a prison" (13). Martin published this argument for the necessity of spirituality more than a decade after the publication of *A Recent Martyr,* but Claire's beneficial effect on Emma indicates the emerging importance of this theme in Martin's early work, for example, in this passage where Emma and Pascal encounter Claire near the cathedral: "Pascal stood clutching the iron bars of the fence like an imprisoned man. I sat down again in the gutter beside him. I was thoroughly disgusted with him and considered the evening to have been misspent" (35). Emma is subconsciously beginning to respond to the example of Claire's spirituality, her inner reality, while Pascal persists in "clutching" his carnal imprisonment.

As this scene by the cathedral and Emma's imaginative recreation of Claire's death indicate, although Emma's encounters with Claire are far fewer than her meetings with Pascal, Claire becomes the stronger influence upon Emma because Emma believes that they have a great deal in common. Through her narration of events, Emma creates the döppelganger that she needs. Emma recalls that "when a girl I too had nurtured a great love of God" (76). Unlike Claire, however, Emma believed herself unworthy of God because of the "genuine disorder" (77) of her soul and her "dark spiritual landscape" (77), much as Helene of *Set in Motion* believes her soul is only big enough for a "thimble" of grace (118). As is characteristic of the adult Emma (and of Martin), the girl Emma does not expect her prayers to be answered.

> I remembered once throwing myself on the cold tile floor in the chapel where I prayed, alone and at the close of day. I had watched the sunlight failing to illuminate the stained glass windows (how each figure faded from the heart outward), and it seemed to me that I was next in the great withdrawal of light. Struck by this, I threw myself over the last rays on the floor, but no sooner had I touched the spot where they fell then they were gone.
>
> Nor was I ever enlightened. (77)

One may consider Emma as praiseworthily realistic, but she is also manipulating a situation into giving her the answer that she wants and that will free her from attempting to live according to God's will, not her own.

Emma believes she has freed herself from subjugation to a patriarchal God, yet she remains, like Claire, a woman who strives to reach her potential in a world dominated by men. Claire does not have a husband or male employer as Emma does, but she does have spiritual directors, first the obtuse patriarch Father James, who "attributes her visions to nervous exhaustion or the proximity of her menstrual period" (41). Like Emma with Pascal, Claire makes the decision to surrender herself to a powerful male, God. Emma, who has been reading Matthew Lewis's violent and erotic gothic novel about decidedly carnal priests and nuns, *The Monk* (1796), imagines Claire sensuously looking at the crucifix in the home of Pascal's parents while "her mouth opened slightly as she looked at it, and then her tongue came out and moistened first the upper and then the lower lip" (12). As Emma realizes her fatal attraction for Pascal, she sardonically observes of Claire, "There is something to be said for a lover with whom one can be united *only* in death" (138).

Emma wants to be the winner in the competition with Claire that she created in her own mind, initially in response to Pascal's attraction to Claire, a rivalry to which Claire is oblivious. Ironically, however, it is through her unrealistic characterization of Claire as döppelganger and competitor that Emma is spurred to win both her life and a tentative degree of happiness. Claire's saving of Emma is foreshadowed when Emma watches two girls, one barefoot and one with shoes, pause before crossing a road so hot "that it appeared to be a sheet of gleaming metal. . . . The barefoot girl climbed onto the back of her more fortunate friend and was carried to the safety of another patch of grass" (101). Claire's "shoes," her antipathy toward "human love" (151), protects her from Pascal's sexual heat, so that she may deliver Emma to a new chapter in her life. This scene also suggests St. Christopher carrying the Christ child across a river, much as Emma will save herself by carrying her daughter *Christ*ine through the plague.[5] As Emma pursues her civic service during the plague, she notes that "Chris walked with me or I carried her on my back" (143).

Like Helene and Maggie in *Set in Motion* and Alexandra and Diana in *Alexandra,* Emma and Claire have an uneasy and tentative sisterhood, inconsistently empathetic and trusting, but rising to meet an urgent need. After Emma is almost killed by Pascal as he throttles her in one of their sadomasochistic sex games, she regains consciousness and she recalls, "I thought of Claire. I didn't have a vision of her, but I thought of her. I knew all at once, as if the information came to me through the floor, what I had done and what I would do" (167). Emma defensively tells us that she did not experience a miracle, "a vision," but that she believes she has learned from Claire's example: "What Claire said she wanted, I had: a lover who would consume me entirely" (167). Emma frames her renunciation of her secular Satan and his temptations in religious language associated with Claire: "I have read that repentance is the act by which we put the past behind us, and if that is true, at that moment I repented of ever having loved, touched, wanted Pascal. I repented of it all" (167–68).

5. The scene of one girl carrying another across a hot street may also be a tribute to Margaret Atwood, presumably the "M.A." to whom *A Recent Martyr* is dedicated, since she helped Martin end a decade without a published book when she sent Martin's manuscripts, including *A Recent Martyr,* to her own editor, Nan Talese.

Emma's resolve to amend her life is catalyzed by her relationship with Claire, which gives her a way of perceiving and analyzing the patriarchal imperatives that control them both. Her newfound resolve is reinforced by the plague that strikes New Orleans. The disease resembles Emma's infatuation with Pascal, which she initially fears is "an illness from which I couldn't be cured" (53–54): the citizens of New Orleans, like Emma, are initially willfully blind to its portents and refuse to take responsibility for their failure to contain a potentially fatal contagion. When Emma meets Pascal for the first time, a rat brushes her ankle, but, although she feels "revulsion" (27), she does not regard it as a warning about the prospects for her relationship with Pascal, the welfare of the city—or even her own health. She reports: "I came down with a mysterious illness that lasted four days. I ran a high fever and was so weak at times I found it difficult to walk" (70). Father James's pants are inexplicably covered with "animal hair" (60) when he appears at the Toussaints' house for dinner and he informs the gathering that sewers are backing up throughout the city, including at the rectory (62), but he makes no connections among these repugnant occurrences. Emma, her daughter Christine, and Claire see a seething mass of bleeding, biting, dying rats by the river (78), yet while there is coverage of an election on television, there is nothing about the rats. Civic indifference appears to be the order of the day, as exemplified by Emma, who remembers, "I had not, I thought guiltily, voted myself" (80).

The plague, for Emma, as for Camus's Tarrou in *The Plague,* provides an awakening from solipsism and from spiritually and morally deadening routines. Emma muses: "This was a force from the outside, an uproar in society, a collective panic that might render trivial problems like mine (whom to have sex with, whom to love, whom to give up) not only insoluble but inappropriate" (128). As her choice of words indicates ("inappropriate," "trivial," "whom to give up"), she is looking for an impetus to end her relationship with Pascal. Her resolve is stiffened by the fact that when the quarantine is imposed, her dwelling is within its confines while Pascal's home is outside the restricted zone. Separated from Pascal, Emma now spends much of her time helping others and in the company of Claire's confessor, Father Paine; Claire; and most importantly, her daughter Christine. When Pascal runs after Claire into the quarantined area and is consequently confined there, Emma once more surrenders to temptation, her final, nearly fatal, sexual encounter with Pascal, but "I thought of my daughter's innocent hand in mine, of Claire's innocent figure at my side" (168). Even after the quarantine is lifted and the plague appears to have passed, Emma does not return to Pascal.

In her use of the plague as a catalyst for communal awareness of the existential plight, Martin is also following the example of Walker Percy, whose protagonists awaken from spiritual torpor in and around New Orleans when various catastrophes, personal or communal, strike. Despite the facts that Emma's recovery from the plague of Pascal is couched in religious terms such as repentance, that the novel is full of references to saints, that Emma is influenced and heartened by a priest and a nun, that the daughter to whom she is devoted is named after Christ, that Emma makes a pilgrimage as she follows the route that led to Claire's death, and that the novel is entitled *A Recent Martyr*, in contrast to Percy's heroes, Emma finds a secular, not a religious meaning in her awakening. Emma does not convert to Catholicism because she cannot accept pain and misery as somehow right when emanating from a divinity. In particular, she rejects the slaughter of the innocents, the children dying of plague in the hospital where she volunteers, commenting, "I found the suffering of children hard to bear" (147). She does not believe that Claire performed miracles. She qualifies her "pilgrimage" to the site of Claire's death by saying "I had traveled as a pilgrim travels, for the love of the dead" (197), not for the love of Christ or "St. Claire." Emma revises this dense web of Christian, specifically Catholic, allusions, for her own purposes, to change the ending, a potential martyrdom for "love," to her own story of life and community.

For despite all of its religious trappings, *A Recent Martyr* is a decidedly secular and existential novel. Emma learns that religious contemplation and mysticism can be monitory correctives to the cynicism and materialism of modern life, but she rejects their divine emanations. Emma realizes that life matters, but she does not need the existence of a god to make it matter. Without Pascal's "twin filters of judgment and doubt" (172), his "deep and abiding cynicism" (172), Emma "enjoyed periods of intense receptivity when my senses were all on the alert and the world poured in freely" (172) and she "could contemplate the enormous suffering of all living things with something approaching the real sympathy that they deserve" (172). From her encounters with religious devotion, Emma begins to recognize the importance of spirituality, in the sense of an inner life with a striving for improvement and growth, as a necessary counterbalance to hedonistic materialism. After Claire's death, Emma reflects: "She possessed that quality we might make better use of in the future, an indomitable will turned inward. She cared to change no one else, but she would change herself, daily, hourly, into something better, stronger, paradoxically more obedient and more willful" (202).

In the course of the novel, Emma has been presented with two masochistic extremes: Pascal's self-deprecating reason and Claire's self-abnegating religion, as amalgamated in the novel's epigraph from Blaise Pascal's *Pensées*: "That we are in ourselves hateful, reason alone will convince us; and yet there is no religion but the Christian which teaches us to hate ourselves; wherefore no other religion can be entertained by those who know themselves to be worthy of nothing else but hatred." Both Pascal's and Claire's ways lead only to death, and death's imminence in the novel is reinforced by the plague and by New Orleans's perilous situation below sea level (a danger borne out by the bursting of the levees in the aftermath to Hurricane Katrina in 2005).

In the midst of death, Emma learns to treasure life, as represented by her daughter Christine and her fellow survivors of the plague. The last lines of the novel convey that only with the recognition of the inexorability of death can one recognize and savor the positive aspects of life. This is not a grandiose or romantic declaration like the poet Wallace Stevens's pronouncement that "death is the mother of beauty," but, as is characteristic of Martin, a modest and moderate attempt to find a manageable life with others. Emma has spoken in terms of herself, "I," throughout most of the novel, but in her final words to the reader she takes a collective point of view, "We": "The future holds a simple promise. We are well below sea level, and inundation is inevitable. We are content, for now, to have our heads above the water" (204).

Emma Miller has escaped the fatal extremes of the heedlessly romantic Emma Bovary and has survived with her child. Emma is more like the narrator of another novel based on *Madame Bovary* by a writer Martin greatly admires, Elizabeth Taylor. At end of *At Mrs. Lippincote's* (1945), Julia concludes, "I never wanted to be a Madame Bovary. That way forever—literature teaches us as much, if life doesn't—lies disillusionment and destruction. I would rather be a good mother, a fairly good wife, and at peace" (204). Emma also renounces the transient excitements that lead to destruction, but she wants more than a tranquil domesticity, and she will try to achieve it through cultivating her inner life, as in the written reflections, her art, that constitute the novel, and through mutually supportive relationships with others. *A Recent Martyr* actually ends, not on the last page, but in the first pages where Emma takes her daughter Christine downtown after the plague has ended, on a streetcar named, not desire or martyrdom, but perhaps compassion. Christine "whisper[s], 'Here we go'" (2), as they embark on their communal journey, the story they are writing together, despite and because of the constant risk of death.

4

The Consolation of Nature

WOMEN, NATURE, DEATH

*V*alerie Martin's next three books—*The Consolation of Nature and Other Stories* (1988), *Mary Reilly* (1990), and *The Great Divorce* (1994)—can be seen as a triptych exploring our cultural beliefs about humanity's place in the natural world. Martin's earlier motifs remain in evidence: female masochism in the context of gothic enclosure, the limited power of passivity, the future as revealed through the treatment of children, and the need for community, especially female fellowship. However, these themes are now transformed within the context of a greater emphasis on nature and what humans share with animals, particularly powerlessness in the face of death. Martin considers *Mary Reilly* a "connector novel" ("Transformations" 32), and it can be seen as the central panel in the triptych depicting perspectives on humanity within nature. As do the female protagonists in *The Consolation of Nature and Other Stories*, Mary must come to terms with nature as both the nurturing and nurtured garden associated with maternity at its best and with "nature red in tooth and claw" as embodied in the failed paternity of Dr. Jekyll, the bestial Mr. Hyde, and the drunken brutality of her father. Like the three female protagonists of the novel that follows *Mary Reilly*, *The Great Divorce*, Mary confronts the paradox that the more humans divorce themselves from nature by seeking to conquer it, the more they find themselves in nature's thrall. All three works use animals as representatives of the natural world and the ways that humans use and abuse it; aptly, since stereotypical views of nature regard women as inferior because closer to nature, the (mis) treatment of women and animals is repeatedly paralleled.

The stories in the first panel of the triptych, *The Consolation of Nature*, indicate that such romanticized human identification with animals is dangerous, and even fatal, for humans, particularly women, and for nature.

In these stories, Martin reveals various aspects of humanity within nature through her continued postmodern dialogue with her narrative predecessors, including philosophers and writers of various periods and places, but foremost through writers of the American Renaissance (American romanticism and transcendentalism), such as Edgar Allan Poe, Walt Whitman, and Emily Dickinson. Romanticism, Martin indicates, whether in regard to nature or to love, is a fatal attraction, especially for women. The stories in this collection comprise a female bildungsroman, as they move, with different protagonists, from immature self-deception about nature to the mature consolation of recognizing a bleak truth. In these critiques of her predecessors' romanticized view of nature, Martin paradoxically suggests that we must continue to create narratives, to create art whether in public form or in private meditations, in order to provide some meanings for our lives and resist the dangerously outmoded ideas which endanger our survival and that of the natural world.

The epigraph and dedications of *The Consolation of Nature* introduce the paradox that nature is both consolation and what causes the need for consolation. The epigraph is a stanza from Thomas Hardy's "The Subalterns" in which Death explains to the speaker, a "wanderer," that

> "I did not will a grave
> Should end thy pilgrimage to-day,
> But I, too, am a slave!"

Other forces of nature—"the leaden sky," "the North," and "Sickness"— also claim that they are powerless subalterns. At the conclusion of the poem,

> We smiled upon each other then,
> And life to me wore less
> That fell contour it wore ere when
> They owned their passiveness.

The "wanderer," Everyman or Everywoman, is consoled by fellow feeling with the natural elements when they recognize their mutual plight as tools of the natural order, not the powerful agents that they may appear to be.

Nature is a gothic enclosure in which humans are passive slaves; their consolation arises from their ability to imagine or construct a narrative of fellowship with other humans and with elements of nature: "We smiled upon each other."

Fellow feeling is also a source of consolation for Martin as two dedications within *The Consolation of Nature* indicate. The stories are "for my daughter, Adrienne," a child at the time of publication. Like the novel *A Recent Martyr*, which precedes this collection, the three books of Martin's triptych repeatedly return to another paradox of nature: the consolations of a daughter as an extension of self, but who is also a hostage to fortune, or, more precisely for Martin, to nature. The hostage to fortune in *A Recent Martyr* is Emma's daughter Christine who is menaced by the plague, and the first and title story of *The Consolation of Nature* concerns a daughter who is attacked by a rat, the plague bearer in *A Recent Martyr*, and is dedicated to another Christine, "to Chris Wiltz," a fellow New Orleans writer and friend. These comforts are mere mitigations because Martin's worldview, like that of Thomas Hardy, is stark: the only true consolation is a shared awareness of the human condition through the heuristics of art.

The consolations of art may be transient and fragile, what Robert Frost called "a momentary stay against confusion," but they are superior to the illusory and sometimes harmfully prescriptive consolations of philosophy and religion. In *A Recent Martyr*, Martin explores the escapist, self-justifying, and ultimately destructive false solace of religion. In *The Consolation of Nature and Other Stories*, she is weighing *The Consolation of Philosophy* and finding it wanting. The sixth-century Roman and Christian philosopher Boethius struggled with the idea that a good supreme being would permit evil; he wrote *The Consolation of Philosophy* as he faced execution at the behest of what he regarded as evil rulers although he considered himself a good man. Boethius concludes that human beings' limited capacities do not permit them to see the ultimate good that is served by what appears to them to be evil and injustice, such as death. For Martin, Boethius's solution, that we simply lack information about how good everything really is, can only be an illusory, somewhat romantic distraction from humans' subjection to the natural order and the inevitability of death. As she writes in "Elegy for Dead Animals," the last piece in the collection, "Death is not the end of life but the enemy of life. Death can be no friend to any creature that lives" (146).

What Martin regards as a detrimental divorce from the natural world, Boethius sees as a desirable goal. As God and his judgments are superior to man's, so, Boethius believes, are men superior to nature in that God "intended that the human race should be above other earthly beings." For Boethius what is a "great" divorce in the sense of grandeur and nobility is for Martin an enormous and detrimental dissociation that she will explore in *The Great Divorce*. Through her art, as in "Elegy for Dead Animals," Martin attempts to show her readers that awareness of the human condition as part of nature is at once its tragedy and consolation: "Before the shovel blow ended his [the rat's] ordeal, I saw, and clearly, that though rats may not suffer as I do, depressions, boredom, loneliness, jealous rage, we do share equally our tenacity to life, our terror of death" (146).

The ten stories in *The Consolation of Nature* comprise a fragmented female bildungsroman in which maturity is marked by an awareness of the tragedy and solace of the natural world. In contrast to a traditional bildungsroman, there is no consistent protagonist who is learning "the way of the world" (the title of the second story in the collection; instead the learner is the reader through the consciousness of the writer, as Boethius's reader is supposed to learn from his series of philosophical dialogues. The protagonist of the postmodernist penultimate story, "The Parallel World," makes the metafictional level and lesson of Martin's collection clear when she speculates that "she exists only inside the life of someone else" (133). As Boethius staged a conversation with Philosophia to illustrate his struggle with the concept of evil in a good world and his reconciliation with his limited point of view as a human being, so Martin uses her dialogue with canonical writers and her progression of female protagonists to gradually draw the reader to her own understanding that, with nature, we are "subalterns" to death.

Martin's use of the word "consolation" is more than an ironic play on Boethius; it suggests a source of comfort in a time of trouble, even though the comfort may arise from the very circumstances that caused the trouble. Cultural biases declare that women epitomize such paradoxes of nature: nature encompasses both birth and death so a woman may find comfort in the growth of her child while she herself ages toward death and fears the death of the child who is at once her solace and her hostage to fortune. Women may find power or consolation in their love and nurture of others, particularly children, as part of the natural order, but women also are confronted with a natural order of greater masculine size and strength and with the oppressive social structures that physical force allowed males to establish. For Martin, women survive, and sometimes thrive, through seeming subjection in gendered power struggles while remaining acutely aware that the ultimate power resides with death. Nature and society are mutually reinforcing gothic enclosures for women.

Lily, the eleven-year-old central consciousness of the first and title story, "The Consolation of Nature," learns her place in nature and society, for good or ill, when confronting a rat, the plague bearer of Martin's preceding book, *A Recent Martyr*. Thus far, Lily has only seen nature's beneficent side: the lizards that she likes (7), her mother's thriving and devotedly tended garden, and her mother's even more loving tending of Lily, named for a flower and whose "head rose and fell, like a flower on a stalk" (3) as her mother brushes her hair. Their carefully cultivated life is threatened by a large rat that appears in the kitchen. Lily and her mother demand that her father kill the rat, as if that were his job due to his greater strength in the natural order or to his gendered superiority in a patriarchal society.

Although the rat is a repugnant menace to her family, Lily learns that the rat, like her family, is a part of the natural order and is also trying to survive; her mother explains that the torrential rains have driven rats away from the river: "Lily felt a twinge of sympathy for the rat" (6). Even when the rat becomes tangled in her long hair when she is in bed, she realizes that the rat is acting in a "panic" (10) and that he wants to get away from her as soon as he can disentangle himself (10). When the cornered rat bares his teeth and springs at Lily's father, Lily sees that her father's "eyes opened wide in shock, his teeth bared too" (15), emphasizing his identity with the rat in their drive to live.

Lily is becoming "a reliable reporter on the natural scene" (12), what Martin would call a true artist who can recognize the paradoxical consolation of nature. After her father kills the rat, Lily is still afraid to sleep and decides to go out and view the rat's remains to assure herself that it is really dead before she returns to bed. She is consoled by nature through two memories, one of growth, and one of death. She sees her mother's burgeoning garden and remembers the joy of working amid the earth and flowers with her mother.[1] She then remembers the sight of the rat's corpse and realizes that "he would never seek her again in that particular form. His menace had quite gone out of that form" (19). Lily goes back to bed and "understood, for the first time, that she was safe" (19), the last line of the story. She needs to tell herself the story that "she was safe" in order to sleep and continue to grow and live, but she is beginning to realize that death is part of the natural order and will come in other forms, but so will opportunities for nurture and growth for her and for her mother's garden.

In "The Way of the World," another eleven-year-old girl begins to realize the harsh facts of the natural order, this time with regard to gender relations as indicated by Martin's use of the same title as William Congreve's play of 1700 about heterosexual power struggles masked as love and lust. Martin's story is also a woman artist's version of Walt Whitman's poetic and romantic *künstlerroman* "Out of the Cradle Endlessly Rocking," in which the narrator regards his youthful self, "a man, yet by these tears a little boy again." As the boy learns about true love and death from the song of a bird who has lost his beloved mate, he recognizes his destiny as an artist: "My own songs awaked from that hour." As in much romantic art, especially that of Poe, the death of a female is grist for the artistic mill since she can now be distanced as an inspiring muse. Martin reverses this trope through the use of a female adult narrator who simultaneously regards memories of her child-self through memory and her consciousness of her daughter, a link between past and future, making her revision of Whitman female and realistically prospective, instead of male and romantically nostalgic.

The narrator of Martin's "The Way of the World," now in her forties, provides a much more jaundiced and ironic version of the development of the artist when that artist is a woman. Her eleven-year-old self enjoys a "fantasy life" (24) that is "powerful" and allows her to tell dramatically

---

1. In an interview, Martin states that the "scene" of "digging in the soil" was one "that actually took place between me and my grandfather" (McCay and Wiltz 13).

tragic lies about herself to her fellow passengers on train journeys. On one journey, however, her imagination clashes with reality. She has a favorite gothic masochistic daydream in which she is a "beautiful, fair-haired, voluptuous, young woman, dressed in a robe of flowing white" (28) who is forced by men through a series of doors until she reaches "the black velvet chamber, and this time she would be forced to go inside whether she wanted to or not" (29). This fantasy is contrasted with the "sharp cold, unexpected finger of reality" (30) in the form of her seatmate on the train, an exhausted and hungry young woman whom the child realizes is "running away from a man" (27). The real version of her fantasy is much less attractive to the narrator's younger self, but like Lily believing she is safe from the rat, this unnamed girl is not ready to accept the reality of gendered power and continues to hope that her seatmate will serve as the "silent, blind, still . . . mysterious guide to the underworld" (27) of her fantasies.

In apparent contrast to her fantasy-ridden earlier self is the narrator's own daughter, now also eleven, whom she is waiting to meet at the train station. She imagines her daughter listening to the train whistle "with that unprejudiced sense of wonder, that deep, helpless listening, we forget over the years, listening to the train howling into the cold, black indifferent universe, listening down to the bones" (29). The narrator seems to condemn her earlier self as deafened by illusion, unlike her "listening" daughter when she states that "the other little girl, the one who lives in a dream . . . hardly ever listens to anything" (29–30). The narrator needs to console herself with her belief in her daughter's "unprejudiced" listening to the train's song of death, but that scenario may be as much a fantasy as the narrator's earlier self's "black velvet room." We don't know what her daughter actually hears or thinks. Both girls are projections of a woman's *künstlerroman* that reverses Whitman's in that the girls do not mature into a romantic universe where they participate in nature's songs of the life cycle. Unlike Whitman, Martin provides the song of the female bird, dominated by the male in life and death, and suggests a consolation in fellow feeling with women readers as the narrator forms a sympathetic bond with her younger self in the last line of the story: "Far away, down the years, I'm looking at her now" (30).

In the next story, "Sea Lovers," Martin continues her commentary on "Out of the Cradle Endlessly Rocking" since for Martin "the sea is full of death" (34). Whitman's narrator finds the sea's song of "Death, death, death, death, death" a "strong and delicious word" because he regards the cycle of life and death as a manifestation of a divine presence. In contrast, Martin regards the sea's message of death as the final word, unmitigated by divinity, or by love, as the story's three pairs of "sea lovers" demonstrate the dangers of blindly following cultural scripts. The first pair is comprised of "innocent, foolish lovers" (33) who are so busy embracing that they go too far from the shore and drown in service to the paradigm of romantic love. The second pair consists of a man who is killed by a mermaid whom he finds on shore and believes he is rescuing, reflecting his belief in the superiority of men to women and to nature, a notion proved wrong when the mermaid uses his testicles to fertilize her eggs. The third pair of lovers is oblivious to these deaths and "would like to make love in the sand, the water's edge" (42), the last line in the story, as if humans can never learn to resist the fatally alluring legend of romance.

While the five humans in the story exhibit a willed ignorance to their position as subalterns to nature's powers, the seemingly triumphant mermaid is equally subordinate to nature. "She is being driven toward land by a force stronger than her own will, and she hates that force as she gives into it" (36). Even mermaids are subject to female masochism as part of nature's reproductive dance: "It's useless to fight the waves," she realizes, and so, by following nature's dictates, she reproduces and lives. Her dealings with humanity are more problematic. She "turned toward shore" (34) after she was "nearly killed" (34) by the blades of a steamship, an early indication of an increasingly pronounced theme in Martin's work: man's abuse of nature will lead to his own destruction, as it does to the man whom the mermaid encounters on that shore. In Martin's hands, Whitman's transcendentally triumphant *künstlerroman* is transformed into a cautionary tale of dangerous illusions about humanity's subjection to nature and women's double subjection to men and nature. Martin presents the deceptive, fatal siren call of the sea much as does Kate Chopin in *The Awakening*: "The voice of the sea is seductive, never ceasing whispering, clamoring, murmuring, inviting the soul to wander in abysses of solitude"

(999). Edna Pontellier surrenders to the lure of romanticized nature as she walks into the sea at the end of *The Awakening,* thus ending her bondage to men and to nature.

The next two stories in the collection consider two extreme methods that humans use to cope with their subaltern status in the natural world, particularly their subjection to death. Like the protagonist of Henry James's "The Beast in the Jungle" (1903) and like Claude in Martin's *Alexandra,* Eva, "The Woman Who Was Never Satisfied," is always waiting for the event that will define her life and give it significance: "any moment could be the one" (46). She tries to fit herself into several cultural metanarratives: sex in the guise of romance; masochism; a secular peaceable kingdom; freedom in the sense of unfettered motion as in Martin's first novel, *Set in Motion*; and religion through the peaceable kingdom of a prelapsarian Eden.

Like the protagonists in Martin's first story collection, the ironically titled *Love,* Eva engages in meaningless sex and cuts herself to try to make herself feel something. She believes that her marriage to Lawrence, a veterinarian with a houseful of animals to tend, would fulfill "her persistent childhood fantasy, one in which she lived among wild animals and neither had nor desired human companionship" (52), a fantasy that Martin also examines in the collection's penultimate tale, "The Parallel World." When Eva tires of the peaceable kingdom and Lawrence dies, she sells everything, thinking that freedom is the answer, but "now her freedom sounded as hollow and useless as the inside of her own head" (49). Her freedom was purchased at the price of the life of two animals, the snakes that were in the car when Lawrence died in an accident, an ironic indication of how poorly the fantasy of the peaceable kingdom works out for the animals.

Despite her panaceas, Eva remains obsessed by death: Lawrence's death, the presumed death of the two snakes that were in the car during Lawrence's fatal accident, and the demise of a bird that died in her hand, but, like the unwary couples in "The Sea Lovers," she cannot accept the imminence and reality of death and returns to her unsatisfactory distractions of sex and cutting herself. At the end of the story, Eva turns to religion, "kneeling" and then "prostrate" (57) in a church. In accordance with the biblical narrative, Eva, like her near namesake Eve, is expelled from her paradisiacal illusion of harmony with nature through her dissatisfaction and curiosity as signified by the snakes, and she now attempts to join the Christian paradigm through repentance for her supposed sins. As the unsatisfactory nature of her earlier fantasies presages, the biblical story of redemption that Eva attempts to live as she grovels before an altar is just another distraction from death, and Eva will remain "The Woman Who Was Never Satisfied."

Eva may try anything to avoid the knowledge of death, but Atala, the protagonist of the next story, "Death Goes to a Party," chooses the other extreme and becomes unable to think of anything other than death, particularly the consolations of nature in growth and fellowship. Martin is parodying two male tales concerning the gothic dangers of romantic nature in the wilderness: Chateaubriand's short novel *Atala* (1801), in which an Indian maiden commits suicide rather than break her religious vow to remain a virgin, and Hawthorne's short story "Young Goodman Brown" (1835), in which the title character can see nothing but sin in his fellow creatures after he attends, or dreams he attended, a Black Mass in the forest. Like Chateaubriand's eponymous protagonist, Martin's Atala foolishly chooses death; she masks as death at a party and embraces Death in the form of a wolf-man whom she meets at the party and with whom she has masochistic sex until she believes she is dying as he chokes her. Like Young Goodman Brown, after her horrific experience, she can now see only one aspect of human existence, in her case, death in the form of the wolf-man: "in her sleep . . . and in her waking hours . . . behind every door, down every corridor, in the eyes of strangers, and when she consulted her reflection" (73).

Young Goodman Brown, the Indian maiden Atala, and Martin's Atala are all examples of the ways that intellectual pride or hubris produces a tunnel vision that excludes any beneficent aspects of nature or the consolations of fellow feeling in the face of death. Each believes that her or his individual decisions and knowledge are of overweening importance and gives her or him power; conversely, each lacks the humility that leads to fellow feeling and community. Young Goodman Brown thinks he can turn back from the forest and remain untainted by his experience, but he dies abhorring his family, friends, and community because he sees them only as sinners. Chateaubriand's Atala can only view the world from her religious perspective and cruelly leaves her lover to life as a solitary wanderer in the wilderness of Louisiana. The hubris of Martin's Atala is that of the failed artist and is mirrored in the eyes of the wolf-man: "the searching, anxious soul, the cynical, practical ego, the deep sense of irony, the persistent curiosity to know, the fear of being known, the inveterate will for power" (64). There is no true creativity here in the sense of imagining ways to live in the face of death; Atala can only "mask" her vulnerability by a monomaniacal preoccupation with death. The wolf-man, Martin's version of the Cajun werewolf of Louisiana lore, seeks replication, not creation. Although the Loup Garou makes his victims become like him, Martin's ironic twist is that Atala was already like him so that they were drawn to each other as kindred spirits at the party.

In the next three stories in *The Consolation of Nature,* humans attempt to enact their fantasies in ways that prove fatal to domestic animals, a dog and two cats; these deceptive daydreams are paralleled by male fantasies that injure women, all in a ruthless hierarchy of power: humans over animals and men over women. In "Spats," Lydia, a professional singer, has been left by her husband, Ivan, for another woman. Although "she sings better than she ever has" (82), she has been too acculturated by fantasies of heterosexual romance to believe in her independent creative powers as an artist. She misses "find[ing] herself in his eyes" (82) and believes that she cannot see herself without him: "She will sing like some blinded bird lost in a dark forest trying to find her way out by listening to the echo of her own voice" (82).

Instead of turning to the creation of her own meaning through art, Lydia turns to evasive fantasies to distract herself from her pain. She fantasizes about "accidentally" killing her husband when mistaking him for a home invader (80); even in fantasy, she will not recognize and take responsibility for what she really feels and relies on mistaken identity to mask her regicidal urges. Mainly, though, she tries to remedy her situation through using their pet dogs, Spats and Gretta, as surrogates.

> Before he [Spats] was half her size he had terrorized Gretta into the
> role that he and Ivan had worked out for her: dog-wife, mother to

his children. She would never have a moment's freedom as long as he lived, no sleep that could not be disturbed by his sudden desire for play, no meal that he did not oversee and covet. She was more intelligent than he, and his brutishness wore her down. She became a nervous, quiet animal who would rather be patted than fed, who barricaded herself under desks, behind chairs, wherever she could find space Spats couldn't occupy at the same time. (86–87)

Lydia is clearly describing herself and many other women who retreat into passive acquiescence in a world in which men wield power based on their physical strength. Lydia tries to help herself through helping Gretta, an identification that grows when Spats growls and bares his teeth at Lydia, who then tells him, "You just killed yourself" (85).

Killing Spats does not solve Lydia's human problems, but forces her to confront them through her further recognition that all creatures, animal and human, are subject to death. As she sits with Spats as the veterinarian euthanizes him, she does not feel joy or relief or revenge, but sorrow. As Mary Reilly will hold and mourn over the corpse of Dr. Jekyll, who dies when he can no longer control his vicious double, Mr. Hyde, so does Lydia mourn Spats, who "between these attacks . . . was normal, friendly, playful. . . . He was so full of energy, of such inexhaustible force, it was as if he embodied life, and death must stand back a little in awe of him" (87–88). Lydia recognizes that the natural order, as embodied in animals, is beyond morality, but that humans use animals, sometimes to their detriment, as anthropomorphized players in moral dramas that the animals do not recognize. As she gazes at Spats's lifeless body, there is some hope that through this fellowship, Lydia can begin to find her own constructive meanings for life as she "look[s] straight into the natural beauty that was his life, and she sees resting over it like a relentless cloud of doom, the empty lovelessness that is her own" (88).

"Empty lovelessness" is also characteristic of Sylvia, the wealthy and indulged protagonist of "The Cat in the Attic," and it produces a similarly fatal effect on a domestic animal used as a surrogate and who also represents the fate of women in a world organized according to male physical power. Sylvia, who "had a feline quality about her" (95), is coveted by her husband and her lover, both of whom want to tame and possess her like a pet in the name of love. She takes refuge from masculine needs and inadequacies in cocaine and in her love for her cat, Gino, "with his cool manner and athletic beauty" (97). Claiming that "no one loves me but Gino" (98), Sylvia decides to take him with her to their remote estate so that he can have a "yard" (98) of "one thousand acres of Virginia pine forest" (98); he will have the freedom that she cannot have.

Since Gino, like Sylvia, is not accustomed to freedom, he becomes inadvertently locked in the attic and eventually starves to death. When his "emaciated corpse" (101) is found, his "death-frozen jaws [are] coated with the plaster he'd chewed out of the wall in his futile struggle for life" (101), like the prematurely buried victims of Edgar Allan Poe's gothic tales. Her lover justly remarks that "you killed that cat yourself, Sylvia, as surely as if you had strangled him with your own hands" (103) since he, like Spats, died as part of a human sexual drama incomprehensible to him. Sylvia, like Gino attempting to claw his way out of the attic, or the eponymous madwomen in the attic of Victorian fiction, slashes with a knife her husband's favorite painting (his preferred view of life) and her "marriage bed" (103) in her futile attempt at escape, for she remains in thrall to the two men and the animal is collateral damage. She focuses on surrogates—the cat, the painting, the bed—and damages them, but is prematurely buried in cultural myths.

In "The Freeze," another cat is relegated to a cold premature burial due to a woman's preoccupation with romance as the source of her identity. In this story, though, the protagonist learns from her mistaken beliefs and from the fate of the cat. Forty-year-old, divorced Anne becomes infatuated with a college student, Aaron, who uses her to help type his medical school applications. Their relationship remains platonic until a party when she offers herself to him and he coolly responds, "No, thank you" (116); he has used her for clerical help and is through with her. The weather changes with a sudden freeze and Anne returns home to discover a changed perspective on her life. As she tries to sleep she hears a clinking noise in her yard but does not investigate. In the morning, she finds a cat who has died with his head wedged in a discarded salmon can and whose frantic attempts to free himself produced the noises that Anne ignored in her preoccupation with her own misery over what she, like the cat, was trying desperately to get; her treat, her salmon, was Aaron.

But Anne, unlike the cat, is still alive and, like the mother in "The Way of the World," has the consolation of nature in the form of a daughter with a firm grasp on reality. Anne is gratified that her young daughter Nell "was neither squeamish nor overimaginative when it came to death. She understood it already as in the nature of things" (126), as Lily in the collection's title story begins to learn after the death of the rat. Anne, like Emma in *A Recent Martyr*, tries to find a middle way that helps her while promoting the future through her daughter; she wants to become more like Nell, "neither squeamish nor overimaginative." Anne no longer sees death as an external gothic figure who "stalk[s]" his "prey" (138), but as an absence of the life force: "The great fluidity, the sinuousness that was in the nature of these animals, had simply gone out of this one" (138). Anne "lifted her hand, held it before her, and gazed down into her own palm. 'It comes from the inside,' she said" (138).

Anne has achieved a realistic view of death as part of the natural world and herself as part of nature. She does not evade her knowledge through religion, like Eva, or become obsessed with it, like Atala, or futilely fight it, like Sylvia. Anne disposes of the cat's body and gets on with her life and her daughter's, no longer fearful and dependent on men: "She was different now and better now. As a young woman she had been in constant fear, but that fear was gone. It was true that her loneliness was hard to bear; it made her foolish and because of it she imagined that rich, idle young men might be in love with her. It was time to face it, she told herself. Her own youth was gone; it was permanently, irretrievably gone. But it was worth that confession to be rid of the fear that, for her, had been the by-product of dependence" (127). Paradoxically, greater independence comes as the life force departs "from the inside" (138), presaging death's severance of links with the world, a consolation of nature, as is the freedom from the cultural imperative of living for and through a man in the name of love.

A poet who severed many of her links with the world and who shares Martin's preoccupations with nature and death, Emily Dickinson, presides over this collection's postmodern penultimate story, "The Parallel World." The story's central consciousness, an unnamed Everywoman, has been damaged in unexplained ways by her life in society until "an escape into a world of aliens could not result in deeper loneliness than she feels among beings of her own kind" (132). She wants to emulate Dickinson's discriminating "soul" and choose her own company:

> The soul selects her own society
> Then shuts the door.
> On her divine majority
> Obtrude no more.

Unlike Dickinson's goddess soul, Martin's central consciousness has lacked the power to choose: "Imagine that a woman *is allowed* to go away to perfect solitude" (italics mine; 131), a denial of agency that suggests her motive for shunning society and the demands for care that others, usually family, place upon most women.

Under this first layer of metafiction in which the author exhorts us to "imagine" this woman's situation, we find the layers of the woman's own attempted fictions. In a reversal, of Martin's usual consolation of nature as sympathy with others while confronting nature's indifference, the woman chooses instead to immerse herself in "the parallel world" that "lies between the ground and the tip of the long grasses" (131); there she initially finds relief: "It is the absence of anything resembling human emotion that renders this world cause for joy and, paradoxically, despair" (132). Although the protagonist surrenders herself to the parallel world to the point where insects run freely over her supine body and rain water pools in her crevices, her fiction of a peaceable, or at least soothingly indifferent, kingdom is threatened by death in the form of a snake, "as black as the death he leaves behind him, barreling toward her like an express train" (136). Like Dickinson's "narrow fellow in the grass" who leaves that narrator a premonition of death's chill, "zero at the bone," Martin's protagonist realizes that death will arrive as inexorably as a train to the station. When she can no longer find solace in nature, the protagonist then turns to a different parallel world, that of divinity or religion. She toys with the idea that "she exists only in the life of someone else" (133) and dreams that she is "dashed to the floor," much as she crushes the insects of the parallel world in the grass. She also tries the accepted narrative of modern science when she dreams that she wakes to find herself with "insect eyes" (139), suggesting human evolution from, and intrinsic identity with, ostensibly lower life forms.

In her ending to the story, Martin suggests that the fictions we create to give life meaning are worthless unless we recognize that part of our human nature is the need for others who provide the consolation of a mutual recognition of, and assistance in, the face of death's inexorability in nature. Escape to any of the parallel worlds that this Everywoman imagines, above or below her, offers no true consolation because she is denying her own level, her own world. She wakes to find herself "still alive" (139) and "the loneliness of being at last, fully conscious is intolerable"(139) while "outside, the grasses hum with activity and the cycles of life and death consume one another, closer and closer" (139), the final lines of the story. Without the fellowship of others, the "loneliness" of the human condition, the knowledge of death without the ability to evade it, is "intolerable."

The final piece in *The Consolation of Nature* is not a short story in any conventional sense but an "Elegy for Dead Animals." The narrator remembers and mourns the death of her own pets, of unknown animals like a bird crushed against a windshield, and of animals whose deaths she has heard of from others. She recognizes that, with the animals, "we do share equally our tenacity to life, our terror of death" (146), an identity that Martin will explore further in *Mary Reilly*. The narrator exhorts us to "mourn now for all the animals who have died at the hands of men, who have seen in the furious progress of our civilization over the earth only the great two-legged stride of death" (146), the environmental tragedy that Martin will delineate in *The Great Divorce*. Like Whitman's elegy for the death of animals and humans, "Out of the Cradle Endlessly Rocking," Martin's "Elegy" concludes with a paragraph that combines the child's growing awareness in the first stories of the collection with the artist's mature consciousness.

> As a child I conceived the dream of the animal life. In this dream no
> animals ever die. Nothing dies, yet the seasons change and the planet

teems with life. All the animals, lost and unknown, past and future, lift their eyes in the vast stillness of a starry night, deer and lions, snakes and birds, fish, lizards, frogs, even the innumerable insects, all gaze together for a moment at the starry dome and they hear the earth as it whirls softly in the black stillness of the universe, and for one moment there is no death on earth, no death possible, even in dreams. (147)

In these concluding lines of *The Consolation of Nature,* Martin evokes Vincent van Gogh's renowned painting *Starry Night* to suggest once more that the paradoxes of nature's consolations, beauty and terror, life and death, can be held in the temporary timelessness and fellow feeling of art as "all gaze together for a moment." In Robert Frost's words, art is "a momentary stay against confusion," and Martin's many allusions to artists in this collection evoke art as a consolation of nature, however temporary and fragile in its transcendence.

5

Mary Reilly

EMPATHY AS EPHEMERAL EMPOWERMENT

*A*lthough *Mary Reilly* (1990) could be read as a melodramatic recapitulation in Victorian costume of Valerie Martin's typical themes
and tropes, especially female masochism and rats, the novel is much more
than a quaintly historical and titillating thriller. Marta Miquel-Baldellou
correctly identifies *Mary Reilly* as "a neo-Victorian gothic text" (119), but
it can also be fruitfully regarded as a reversal of Martin's previous emphases: instead of a gothic plot of thwarted female development, *Mary Reilly*
is a female bildungsroman with strongly gothic overtones. Mary is more
than a passive and exploited victim; she learns and acts, and learns more
and acts again. What she learns is reflected in her writing, giving the novel
some overtones of a *künstlerroman*. Through Mary's cycle of reflection
and action, Martin continues to explore the existential and environmental themes suggested in the title of her preceding work, *The Consolation
of Nature* (1988): humanity's ambivalent and often self-deceptive relation
to nature, particularly the inevitability of death, and the ways that people
attempt to console themselves for their mortality through community and
art. Unlike *The Consolation of Nature,* though, *Mary Reilly* is not a collection of short stories that explores these issues in a variety of aspects, but
a novel that compellingly unites Martin's preoccupations and images in a
female bildungsroman.

Mary Reilly is the seemingly simple and engaging tale of the developing consciousness of the maidservant in the household of Robert Louis
Stevenson's Dr. Jekyll and Mr. Hyde,[1] but it is also a *künstlerroman,* for

---

1. Valerie Martin greatly admires the work of J. M. Coetzee and the idea of telling
Stevenson's tale through the eyes of the maidservant may have been inspired by Coetzee's
novel *Foe* (1986), in which Robinson Crusoe's tale is told by Susan Barton, a fellow castaway

Mary is an artist in words and writes her own tale in her own voice. As she develops a philosophy of life from her experiences, Mary expresses and tests what she learns in her writing. As is typical of Martin's work, however, the consolations of art, like those of nature, are limited, both in terms of her writing's contributions to Mary's growth and happiness and in terms of the sustained integrity and interpretation of her work. People and art may be valiant and valuable, yet they are perpetually vulnerable, as Martin suggests through her postmodern parodies, particularly her re-visioning of works by literary forebears.

As in the title story of *The Consolation of Nature,* in *Mary Reilly* humans are perpetually menaced by natural predators, like rats, but can exert only a limited control over nature in its beneficent aspects, as in gardens. Lily, the child in "The Consolation of Nature," is terrified of the large rat that appears and reappears in her home in New Orleans. The rat is eventually killed by her father, and Lily experiences a tentative solace from the sight of her mother's nurturing and nurtured garden and by her realization that the rat is dead. As a child, Mary Reilly is also threatened by a rat, but he actually does bite her, repeatedly, on her hands and neck, because, unlike the loved and protected Lily, Mary's mother does not defend her and her father locked her in a tiny closet with the rat in an act of inebriated sadism. Despite their terror, both Lily and Mary recognize that the rat is also a fellow creature struggling for survival; Lily characterizes it as in a "panic" (10), and Mary recalls him as "no doubt as frightened as I was" (6).

Nature's brutal aspects are never eradicated in Martin's universe despite human attempts to hold them in abeyance in gardens; both Lily and Mary fear meeting the rat again; Lily can't sleep and decides to go view the rat's corpse to convince herself that he is dead, but when she sees her mother's garden, she no longer feels the need to view the rat's body because she knows that "he would never seek her again in that particular form. His menace had quite gone out of that form" (19). We do not know what happens to Lily as an adult, but the adult Mary does meet the rat in another "form," that of Mr. Hyde, who also bites her on the neck and disturbs her

---

invented by Coetzee, and in which Daniel Defoe is treated as an obtuse editor, much like the editor of Mary Reilly's journals.

sleep: "A strange fear come to me, so strong that I sat up in bed holding the cover to my chest and that was this, he is not dead" (250). When Mary goes across the courtyard to prove to herself that Hyde is dead, she "note[s] the tips of the bulbs have broken through the soil" (251), but, unlike the young and loved Lily, the adult and solitary Mary's reassurance from her garden is undercut when she subsequently witnesses the death of her beloved Dr. Jekyll.

Gardens are associated with maternal nurturance in Martin's fiction, as they are for Lily and Mary, and are, as Barbara Braid has suggested about *Mary Reilly*, "a place of liberation for Mary and Mrs. Kent [the cook], the only space of female creativity and freedom" (77), though one might argue that cooking for Mrs. Kent and writing for Mary also present similarly liberating occasions. Lily has a mother who tends her child like the flower of her name and who also nurtures her garden and teaches Lily how to garden. Mary has no such experiences as a child, but seeks them in the maternal figure of "Cook" in Dr. Jekyll's household; Cook teaches her how to design and plant a garden. The adult Mary recognizes that maternal nurturance is at the mercy of the patriarchs in charge when she is forced to abandon her garden after Dr. Jekyll's horrific death, as her mother was forced to abandon Mary by putting her in service away from the horrors of her father. Rats replace serpents in the Garden, as Paradise is regained and then lost once again.

In contrast to the biblical story, through Mary's meditations on her garden Martin reinforces her theme of humans as part of, but not necessarily superior to, the natural world. Mary identifies with the plants' great efforts to survive: "I thought how all plants do struggle and seem to be longing to flourish no matter how badly they are treated and on what hard, unprofitable soil they fall" (32). When Mary began to "feel a little sad for the poor bushes" (32), Cook reminds her that fellowship is thwarted by the competition to survive: "Cook said they'd be the death of our herbs so up they mun come" (32). For Mary believes that human beings, unlike plants, often act in opposition to their own best interests, as one could argue that Jekyll does in evoking Hyde or that Mary does in supporting Dr. Jekyll despite her misgivings and suspicions about what he is doing: "I thought about the bulbs storing up food under the soil and waiting for the time when they knew it would be safe to push up. How odd it is that plants can have what we so often do without—good sense and judgment" (218).

Through Mary, Martin indicates that although the instinct to survive persists in the face of life's tribulations, darkness and brutality, what some would call evil, predominate in the natural world. As Dr. Jekyll points out when they look at the stars, there is "all blackness and only pinpoints of light" (242). Mary, with her own strong will for survival, focuses on the light, however small and wavering: "no matter how dark I feel I would never take my own life, because when the darkness is over, then what a blessing is the feeblest ray of light!" (36). Dim rays of light, like cultivated plants and domesticity, are perpetually menaced by untamed forces like darkness and weeds: "It seems that being wild, they have a greater will to life. . . . I think it's true of many things as is deprived, and children too . . . , that they grow strong when no one cares for them and seem to love whatever life they can eke out and will kill to keep it, while the pampered child sickens and dies" (57–58).

Mary reflects Martin's persistent theme that children, as representing life and the future, are one of the consolations of a nature that also encompasses death and termination, and that nurturing children is one way to find meaning in life through promoting what Mary calls the "good" in life. Mary wants to help all children, the "pampered children" along with the deprived. She loves to polish the fender for the fire in Dr. Jekyll's laboratory until the babies depicted on it are "like two children romping in the sun" (223). She tries to mother the "pampered" Dr. Jekyll's strength with fires, a comfortable bed, and food; she even spoon-feeds him when he is weak. Mary believes that chaotic destruction is nature's default state while orderly growth, which the privileged regard as the status quo, actually requires constant effort: "I was thinking that there never can be such a thing as a force for good. . . . That good is what always needs trying, as it is work for us, and don't seem to come natural, whereas havoc comes of its own accord. And also it does seem to me that the two words won't go together, as force can never do aught but evil" (78). To Mary, progress seems practically impossible: "But as for *doing* good, I confess I don't think of it. I only do what I mun to stay as I am" (78), which she defines as "safe"

(79). Any kind of order is Frost's "momentary stay against confusion": "I would tell myself, now be content while you can and be *good*, and maybe this time it will last. But it never did" (150).

Although *Mary Reilly* is generally considered a critique of a society based on class and gender privileges, Martin is actually more concerned with the way that the chaotic and brutal forces of nature are replicated in the social order. If the social order were a matter of choices, it might be possible to establish and maintain a more equitable society. But if social inequality is based on nature, equality and fairness are always threatened by "havoc" (78). If male dominance in society, an issue that Martin repeatedly explores, is based on physical strength in nature, then women in society must fall back on the power of passivity; any gains they make are endangered. In Martin's short story "Spats" in *The Consolation of Nature,* the male dog Spats dominates the female dog Gretta with his spasmodic fits of brutality: "She was more intelligent than he, and his brutishness wore her down. She became a nervous, quiet animal who would rather be patted than fed, who barricaded herself under desks, behind chairs, wherever she could find space Spats couldn't occupy at the same time" (86–87), much like Mary and her mother avoiding her brutal father, or Mary in her inability to relax or sleep when she believes Mr. Hyde is afoot in Dr. Jekyll's house. She compares Hyde to "a bad dog who might suddenly knock me sprawling" (99); Mrs. Farraday, Hyde's landlady, calls him "a mad dog" (125); and Mr. Poole, the butler, says "he has a wolfish way about him" (115). Mary also recognizes the feral dog in Hyde and she "did not want him to touch me or think of me for one moment as his prey, for I knew that if he did he would not be able to stop himself" (235). When Hyde does touch her, he cannot stop himself: he grabs her by the hair, puts his hands around her neck, and digs his teeth into her shoulder (238).

While this may sound like the usual scenario of female masochism from Martin's earlier works, there are significant differences. The encounter is based on wild and "natural" urges on the part of Hyde, not the mutually agreed-upon playing of social sex games. Unlike Martin's earlier protagonists, Mary does not want Hyde to continue; she does not feel erotic pleasure, but "terror," and begs, "Please, sir. Do not do this" (238). Mary has already been cut with teeth, the rat's, and does not want to be cut or to cut herself in order to feel more alive. Mary is not bored with the quotidian as are Martin's relatively privileged earlier protagonists because she sees mundane life as serene, not stagnant, and perpetually vulnerable to the forces of brutality and disorder. She enjoys her hard work and Cook's "simple" (35) companionship and tutelage; she wants to stay "safe" (79). She resents the crumbling of her haven, and despairs, "I thought, I cannot live if I am not to feel safe in *this* house, with *this* master, who has cared for me and talked to me, who values me as no one ever has. If I must cringe and weep in *this* house, then what will become of me?" (101).

Through Mary, Martin reveals the female longing, based on a patriarchal social order, for a good father, a benevolent despot. Yet Mary, despite the experiences of her past and the evidence of her present, remains in Jekyll's household and even goes on errands for him to Mrs. Farraday's den of blood and iniquity. Mary sees Jekyll as the good father that she believes her father was—when he did not drink his potion, alcohol, and turn into a Hyde-like beast. Indeed, Martin dedicates *Mary Reilly* to her own father and to Robert Louis Stevenson—as R. McClure Smith puts it, "the biological and the literary" fathers (254). While longing for a good father may be part of her reason for remaining in an increasingly dangerous household, Mary is, as Heidi Garner asserts, "pre-conditioned" to be "easy prey to a man like Dr. Jekyll" (195), but I would argue that she has been at least as much conditioned by her mother's acquiescence as her father's brutality. When she comments that her mother was absent the day that her father locked her in the closet with the rat, Mary makes this telling aside, "not that she ever dared to cross him" (4). After her mother's death, Mary learned that her father had recently been visiting her mother as if he were looking for a reconciliation: "So, I thought, she never got free of him and even as she left this life he was there. With his last strength he hunted her down and she was too weak herself to do aught but his will, as it was always between them, only now his will was that he should be forgiven" (201–2). Mary's mother ends up in a dark closet with the rats where her landlord stores her corpse before burial; Mary "heard the scurrying of some animal feet as we went down" (178) to the cupboard, a warning about what happens to women who decide to trust patriarchs.

In Mary's view of life, female passivity and compliance, but not masochism, comprise a survival mechanism in a society based on the superior physical strength of men and with social class based on the original strength of certain men; social order reinforces and calcifies natural order. "Order in a household is as important to us below stairs as above" (22), asserts Mary, because this order holds in check the brutality from both sides. Mary repeatedly admonishes herself about "how wrong it is ever to have fancies outside one's station as it always leads to misery" (15), but she protests too much. She says she needs to keep "remembering my place" (10) because her own inner wildness and strength cause her to repeatedly forget her place. When Dr. Jekyll sends her on one of his clean-up errands to the house of the rapacious Mrs. Farraday, Mary momentarily rebels: "I felt he hardly saw me, that I was some object to him, useful like his pen or his cheque, such as only exist to serve his will. A rush of anger came upon me, but I fought it down, remembering my place and my duty" (120–21). She will even obey Hyde since Jekyll has instructed the servants to do so: "Everything in me wanted to cry out, No, I will not serve you" (158), but she brings Hyde's tea. When Hyde breaks a teacup and smears his bloody fingers across Mary's mouth, she later reflects to her diary, "I will not stand for this, but I've stood for worse, that much is certain, and I've no right to speak now, nor have I ever" (162).

Through Mary, Martin delineates the ways that women are trained to acquiesce in the face of male physical violence. Mary has been well conditioned by the example of her parents to not only fear the male brutality used to keep women in their place, but to fear the wildness in herself that might provoke male violence against her. Mary does not want Hyde as her master: "I cannot bear to hear it—saying, *I* am your master. *I* am your master" (246), but she does not question the fact that she must have a master. She rejects Hyde's sadomasochistic advances, but she has erotic fantasies about Jekyll. "I fell on thinking of his cool fingers against my neck which was a thought I knew I had no business to be entertaining" (15). She longs for a lock of his hair, but writes that she is "shocked at my own strange whims, which it seems I never can control" (61). She admits to Jekyll that she is sometimes afraid of herself (142–43).

Martin ironically points out destructive aspects of two major cultural narratives through Mary's lack of education and acculturation. Mary does not employ the two usual Victorian means of repressing the natural man or woman: science and religion. She evinces little interest in or understanding of science, though she dislikes Jekyll's laboratory, "the workplace of a man of science" (223), on what she claims are aesthetic grounds: "There was not too many bottles and strange tubes upon the table, but what I found there I had washed up so they was sparkling, but the light they gave off was not pleasing. I wished I had a big vase of roses . . . to set in the middle of that table" (223). As Bette B. Roberts points out, "Her pleasure in polishing the laughing babies on the fireplace fender [in Jekyll's adjacent study] comments ironically on the unnaturalness of Jekyll's experiments" (42).

As in *The Consolation of Nature*, Martin suggests man's destructive hubris with regard to nature. Mary's response to the laboratory may have been influenced by what she hears about and from two scientists. Of Dr. Denman, the preceding owner of the operating theatre and laboratory, "they said he would find a reason to cut open a perfect well man out of his desire to have a look inside him" (50). Dr. Jekyll's version of science also disregards the human need for beauty, pleasure, and an improved quality of life: "My work doesn't have such pleasing results as yours. It may finally be of benefit to no one. It may only make the world more strange than it is already, and more frightening to those who haven't the courage to know the worst" (113). He places knowledge above humanity, or in the common trope of Victorianism, the head above the heart. Yet he admits that scientific knowledge is so limited and scientific ignorance so vast that science may be destroying nature, including humanity: "It is a world we know little about, one that may have no place for us in it, a world . . . we made ourselves but which is already beyond our control" (212). This hubristic, harmful, and foolhardy tinkering with nature is a theme that Martin explores fully in her next novel, *The Great Divorce*.

Martin also emphasizes Mary's lack of proper Victorian acculturation in order to deconstruct the powerful cultural influence of Christianity. While one might not expect a Victorian maidservant to have much knowledge of or interest in science, it is much more unusual that Mary evinces little indoctrination in or reliance upon a major pillar of the Victorian social order, religion. Many of Mary's references to Dr. Jekyll as her "Master" could double as allusions to God, for example, "like serving a ghost, who may see what you do or may not" (24). Mary thinks of Dr. Jekyll, shut away in his study, "as if he is in a tomb" (231) and as if she were a latter-day Mary, the Magdalene. She sometimes uses biblical language, like "trying to serve two masters" (23; Luke 16:13) in regard to the contradictory orders of Dr. Jekyll and his butler Poole, but without any apparent religious intent. Indeed, Mary is quite conscious of her lack of religious belief: "I wish I was one who could find solace in prayer, but I am not" (231).

To explain Mary's seemingly anomalous lack of belief in the supernatural, particularly Christianity, in a Victorian servant, James Washick asserts that Martin "effectively eliminates the religious quality which undergirds the previous [Stevenson's] text in favor of a Marxist tale of social morality" (170). Martin, however, is actually de-emphasizing both religion and society to stress that people use both religion and society to attempt to deny that they are part of nature; human beings want to believe that they are above nature and can control it. As David Cowart states, "Stevenson's story, especially as reimagined by Martin, encapsulates at once the demotion of humanity from its angelic aspirations and the recognition that the God who became a human being was never more than the projective fantasy of a reasoning but flawed animal" (101).

Although religion and science are not supportive systems of belief for Mary, she has two other, much more tentative and humanistic means of making sense of her world: the fortunate fall, as a secular version of the Christian story; and art, her writing as her non-scientific means of making observations and testing hypotheses. These structures of meaning are made even more provisional through Martin's postmodern uses of metafiction and the parodic re-visioning of precursor texts.

The fortunate fall (the Latin *felix culpa,* "happy fault") is the secular version of Christianity's basic story: Adam's fall was ultimately fortunate because it allowed God the Father to show his love for mankind by sending his only son to redeem them through his death by crucifixion. In that sense, mankind was "happier" than if Adam had not sinned and remained in Eden. In secular terms, it is the belief that while humans suffer pain and death from error, they also gain wisdom from their movement from innocence to experience, particularly sympathy for their fellow sufferers in the human condition. In *The Consolation of Nature,* Martin explored this theme in the story "Death Goes to a Party," which is her revision of one of literature's most renowned fortunate falls, that of Hawthorne's title character in his short story "Young Goodman Brown" (1835). Both Martin's protagonist, Atala, and Hawthorne's Goodman Brown are failed examples of the fortunate fall because their new knowledge of humanity's propensity for darkness and depravity make them paranoid and, for the rest of their lives, unable to bond with their fellows, whom they shun as repulsive threats.

A more successful example of the fortunate fall from *The Consolation of Nature* is Anne, the protagonist of "The Freeze," who learns to be more self-reliant and less fearful when she realizes that death is not an external threat but "comes from the inside" (138) for everyone; Anne does not shun humanity because of this but bonds more firmly with her daughter, her "consolation of nature." Mary Reilly's "consolation of nature" is the fellowship of the fortunate fall as limited to a bond with one person, not all of humanity. Mary Reilly, like Anne, finds fellowship with one human being, Jekyll, through her fall from innocence to experience, but she is much more sinned against than sinning, unlike the Christian and Hawthorne's versions of *felix culpa*.

Concepts like sin and guilt are not part of Martin's worldview because she sees people as part of nature. Mary did not sin, in the sense of the willful transgressions of Martin's Atala or Young Goodman Brown. As a child, Mary accidentally broke a teacup, providing her drunken and sadistic father with an excuse to "punish" her by locking her in a closet with a biting rat; children by their nature may accidentally break teacups at a greater rate than adults; it is not a matter for blame and retribution. Since young Mary did not intentionally "sin," her fall is not entirely "fortunate."

> I feel my father made me thus, or left me thus, with this sadness which has been hard to bear and will never likely leave no matter what fortune I have, and it sets me apart from my fellows who seem never to know it. While I can't forgive my father, neither can I regret what I am, and there are times when I would not give up the sadness and darkness because it do seem to me true that this is part of how we mun see life if we are to say we saw it, and it has to do with our being alone and dying alone, which we all mun do. (36)

Mary's "fall" from innocence to experience gives her greater knowledge, a more realistic view of life, but it does not initially provide her with the community or fellowship for which (unlike Atala and Young Goodman Brown) she longs: "It has been the bane of my life that I cannot be as light at heart as my fellows are" (175). Mary does find sympathetic community with one fellow initiate, Dr. Jekyll: "And this is truly something I see in Master and why I am so drawn to serve him and what I think he must see in me, and why he has wanted to look into my history, because we are both souls who knew this sadness and darkness inside and we have both of us learned to wait" (36).

Mary is partially deceived in Dr. Jekyll because while he shares her knowledge of the bestiality that is a part of humanity, he chooses to promote it through Hyde. As Laurie F. Leach observes, "Jekyll is not a good man led tragically astray by overindulgence in pardonable human weaknesses, but a dishonest, selfish, and ultimately abusive figure" (93). In contrast, Mary has not chosen brutality, but has been its victim and asserts, "I have no will to cause pain and suffering as some do" (78). Jekyll betrays their fellowship in his hubristic and selfish pursuit, through Hyde, of scientific knowledge and the pleasure of bestiality. Dr. Jekyll lies to Mary about what he is doing and why, and he thus attenuates the bond between them since she, his servant, is compelled to repress her suspicions and feels "sadness that Master should lie to me and I to him" (108). Mary recognizes that this lack of honesty is the real "fall" and it is neither redeemable nor fortunate: "I know he has said all will be well, but how can I believe it when I know that between us, nothing will ever be as it was again" (140). Martin is here echoing, through Mary, Kate Croy's declaration to her fellow conspirator against innocence, Merton Densher, in the last line of Henry James's *The Wings of the Dove* (1902): "We shall never be again as we were!" Like Kate Croy and Merton Densher, Mary and Dr. Jekyll can never regain their fellowship, but Mary, although she is not a Christian, decides to hate the sin but love the sinner, and she chooses Jekyll, even in death, over the rest of humanity:

> But you said you no longer care for the world's opinion . . . nor will I . . . and I lay down beside Master, covering us both with my cloak as

best I could, for the floor was cold. I rested my head upon his chest
and put my arms about his neck. I could hear my own heart in my ear
and it seemed to be beating against his still one.

That was how they found us. (256)

Mary's fellowship with Jekyll in their dark knowledge has paradoxically
removed her even further from community, but unlike Atala and Young
Goodman Brown, she acts from knowledge, not "the world's opinion,"
and from love, "my own heart." In this sense, she epitomizes the fortunate
fall because she has profoundly increased her capacity for compassion.

While the fortunate fall gives meaning to Mary's experiences, her writing gives it structure and expression, as she, like Emma in *A Recent Martyr*, ultimately writes the story she needs to survive. Mary writes first for
the solitary pleasure of her own companionship, then as a means of fellowship with Dr. Jekyll, then to record the truth of her past, and finally
to determine what is true in *The Strange Case of Dr. Jekyll and Mr. Hyde*
(Stevenson's complete title, 1886). Since her sadness removes her from her
fellows, "my journal which I do keep for my own pleasure" (16) serves as
outlet and companion, even before her arrival in Dr. Jekyll's household:
"It eases me to write what I do not say, for no one cares enough to hear
it" (204). It is also her substitute for prayer's place in Christianity: "I wish
I was one who could find solace in prayer, but I am not. To put things
down, that is my way" (231).

The need for fellowship, human companionship in the face of death,
is the solace Mary seeks. *Mary Reilly* does not begin with an excerpt from
Mary's journal, but with the pages she composed at Dr. Jekyll's request
to explain the scars on her neck and arms, the traumatic tale of the rat in
the closet. She welcomes the chance to share her writing with Dr. Jekyll:
"So I worked all day with the thought of giving my writing to Master in
the evening like the promise of a fine day out before me" (17). Mary is
rewarded for her writing with Jekyll's approbation, "Like many a good
storyteller . . . you raise more questions in your tale than you answer"
(26), also an apt description of Valerie Martin's artistry.

Mary, like Valerie Martin, is a realist, and any pleasure or relief in art
is secondary to the truth-value that is the salutary effect of realism. The

catalyst of Dr. Jekyll's fellow feeling leads Mary to explore some of these questions for herself in her journals, most importantly Dr. Jekyll's questions about her feelings toward her father. After her mother's funeral, Mary writes in her journal, "The undertaker gave me a remembrance card which was engraved with a willow at one corner, I thought a pretty picture though there was no such tree anywhere near that I could see" (200). Mary is determined that the passage of time or senility will not make "pretty" what her father had done to her: "Though I do not hate him I do not forgive him; and . . . if I write it now, then it cannot be denied in future. Will I ever be myself so muddled that I will soften the long horror that was my childhood and tell myself perhaps it was not so bad? Let this book serve as my memory" (204). Mary, however, is less in danger of falsifying her memories of her childhood than she is of rationalizing and softening what she witnesses in Dr. Jekyll's employ. When she sees the blood-covered room at Mrs. Farraday's, she writes, "I have made up some stories that might explain this part or that, but none that satisfy me" (137), until she accepts the truth that "there is one story as explains it all" (138), which at that point she takes to be that Mr. Hyde, Dr. Jekyll's assistant, is a murderer and Dr. Jekyll is covering for him. Still dissatisfied, Mary keeps trying: "So I write and write in my book, as if I could make the darkness come clear by setting it down on my page" (162). She is not satisfied because, unlike many people, she knows that what she wants to believe is not true to reality.

Martin not only stresses art's necessary truth-value, but its fragility in a world where distortion and destruction are inevitable. Mary cannot make clear the darkness through her writing, nor can she control her journals' survival, dissemination, or interpretation. As Elaine Showalter notes, "Martin ends with an afterword by an anonymous 'editor,' like the postscript to Margaret Atwood's 1985 *The Handmaid's Tale*" (586), another first-person account of an intelligent female servant in a patriarchal dystopia, which Martin read in manuscript form when Atwood finished it while they were both teaching at the University of Alabama. The editor of Mary's work renames what Mary calls her journal her "diaries" (257) and decides not to publish the preceding journal where Mary, according to the editor, learned from the housekeeper Mrs. Swit, "who filled her head with maxims about the proper relations of servants to masters and, importantly for our sake, encouraged Mary to keep a record of her life" (258). The editor does not see Mrs. Swit as a tutelary maternal figure, preceding Jekyll's Cook, who teaches Mary about domesticity as Cook does about gardening, and convinces her that her life is valuable enough to record. The editor sees Mary's journals as important only "for our sake" (258), not for their value to Mary herself, because the editor wants to solve the mystery of Jekyll and Hyde. The editor speculates that they were two separate men with Hyde as Jekyll's drug dealer or that maybe there really was a chemical that changed Jekyll into Hyde and vice versa (262): that is the important story for the editor, who consequently declares, "I have taken various liberties with Mary's text to prepare it for publication" (257). The editor does recognize, however briefly and offhandedly, Martin's theme of the basis of the social order in nature: "Who among us has not felt at some moment the press of an unconscious desire to create havoc? Is it not the fear of this impulse that drives us to insist upon social order?" (262). Through this aside, Martin points out the figure in this novel's carpet.

Martin is well aware that all art is subject to revision and reinterpretation, for she herself is, of course, revising Robert Louis Stevenson's *The Strange Case of Dr. Jekyll and Mr. Hyde* by telling the story from the maid's point of view.[2] More tellingly, Martin is also, somewhat like Mary's "editor," using the diaries of a Victorian female servant for her own ends, in this case, *The Diaries of Hannah Cullwick, Victorian Maidservant,* which were themselves edited in 1984 by Liz Stanley. To create Mary Reilly, Martin borrowed Hannah Cullwick's prodigious work ethic and zeal for cleaning; her getting "black" from her labors and then trying to remove the dirt before heading above stairs; her ability to read and write; her devotion and subservience to Alfred Munby, the man she calls her "Massa"; and her rejection of a lady's life because of its physical and mental stultification,[3] or as Mary Reilly puts it, "I've seen plenty of those and never envied them one moment, as it does seem their lives are full of mean spirit, if they are

2. For a consideration of this novel as "the intertextual play of a *textual unconscious*" (246), see R. M. Smith's "The Strange Case of Valerie Martin and *Mary Reilly.*"

3. Martin will deconstruct these paradigms of slaves and ladies in *The Great Divorce* and *Property.*

full of anything, because they are so idle" (48). Stanley points out that the "ubiquitous 'Mary'" was one of the "'stock names' for female servants" (32). The inspiration for the closet in which Mary is entrapped with the rat and the hole beneath the stairs in which Mary's mother is temporarily interred may have come from this passage in Hannah Cullwick's diary: "Swept the passage & took the things out of the hole under the stairs— Mary uses it for her dustpans and brushes. It's a dark hole & about 2 yards long & very low. I crawl'd in on my hands & knees & lay curl'd up in the dirt for a minute or so" (119).

Liz Stanley, Cullwick's editor, also shares Martin's belief in the power of female passivity, and she states of Hannah and Munby: "She used 'powerlessness' to achieve 'power' over him so as to confirm his need for her and thus the relationship" (14), much as Mary coddles Jekyll in his weakened state and runs the vital errands of concealment to Mrs. Farraday. Indeed, *Mary Reilly* could be read as Martin's answer to Stanley, who asserts, "The question that needs to be asked is whether strong, stubborn, independent, assured, and competent Hannah was powerless within the elements of her relationship that might be termed sado-masochistic" (14).

Martin may also have derived from Cullwick's diaries and Stanley's speculations about them her suggestion that the seemingly fantastic story of Jekyll and Hyde is simply the reality of patriarchal and class-ridden Victorian England writ large, and perhaps of other equally hierarchical patriarchies, such as the plantation South in Martin's *The Great Divorce* and *Property,* and contemporary America in her other novels, as well as Atwood's futurist dystopian United States in *The Handmaid's Tale.* Liz Stanley sees Munby's fetishes as ignored by a society that would not look too closely into the "private" activities of a man of his station; he was "someone who didn't want, or couldn't manage, close and demanding relationships, for whatever reason . . . he allowed no one to come too close to him, aided by an entire ideological structure which both justified and helped to create the way he behaved" (23), all of which could be said of both Stevenson's and Martin's Dr. Jekylls, depicted as bachelors only sporadically sociable with their male peers.

Despite the similarities between Hannah Cullwick and Mary Reilly, the major difference between these maidservants, one historical and one fictional, reinforces Martin's belief in the human need for expression and meaning through art. Unlike Mary's pleasure in her writing, Hannah wrote all her diaries at her Massa's behest, not simply a small portion like Mary's tale of the rat in the closet for Jekyll. Hannah found her writing a daily burdensome chore (21); she would quite literally have rather scrubbed filthy floors and grates. Stanley points out that "in the diaries Hannah gives us a partial view of what was going on in her life, for these focus on activities almost to the exclusion of feelings and assessments" (27), in contrast to Mary's use of her journals to clarify her feelings and attempt to ascertain the truth of nature and society. Mary, like an artist, must not only observe reality, but also try to emphasize salient details to suggest meaning.

Ultimately, Valerie Martin is very much a Jamesian in her view of art as a superior form of reality. The last line of the novel raises the possibility that Mary's journal "is now and always was intended to be nothing less serious than a work of fiction" (263), and it expresses Martin's credo about the value of art. In a letter to Edith Wharton on May 12, 1912, in which he mentions Stevenson, Henry James declare his belief in art's superior form of reality: "Form alone *takes,* and holds and preserves, substance—saves it from the welter of helpless verbiage that we swim in as a sea of tasteless tepid pudding" (*Letters,* IV, 615). For Martin as well, art selects, organizes, and interprets from the "welter" of unmediated reality.

Yet for all of art's selective and interpretive powers in the Jamesian sense, Martin finds it as vulnerable as the mortals who create it. Martin revises the creations of Robert Louis Stevenson and Hannah Cullwick, and her own work is revised in the sense of widely varying critical interpretations and through its revision in another medium. Stephen Frears's 1996 movie version of *Mary Reilly* stresses the romance of Mary's feelings for Dr. Jekyll and adds a strong erotic attraction to Mr. Hyde, making Martin's novel into a "love story," however dark and perverse. As Martin herself told an interviewer, "that is the thing about movies; they aren't the books they are taken from. Everything has to be more explicit. The subtleties of Mary's character are gone" (McCay and Wiltz 21).

When it leaves the artist, art is vulnerable not only due to various revisions and reinterpretations, but also because of the possibility that the novelist may not really be the creator, but is manipulated in the same way that she manipulates her characters. Martin raises the possibility that her "editor" is as fictive as Mary's journals. Within those journals, after Hyde runs his bloody fingers across her face, Mary sits in the park, "feeling I'd been thrown down on that bench from some high place and must wait to get my bearings before going on" (163). She later finds Hyde in the court-yard with "his arms stretched out at his sides as if he had been flung down there from a great height" (233). In her short story "The Parallel World" in *The Consolation of Nature,* Martin's female protagonist wonders if "she exists only in the life of someone else" (133) and dreams that, like someone else's toy, she is "dashed to the floor" (133) by a greater power. Postmodern art is like a series of encapsulated dolls with the kernel of truth getting smaller and smaller or like a sequence of mirrors facing each other with the subject regressing into the distance. Mary Reilly embodies the best of human responses to the fact that we cannot know who is "above" us, if anyone, and who made the first doll or put the mirrors together. As Martin explores in her next novel, *The Great Divorce,* our uneasy conscious-ness of our connection to what we consider "below" us, nature, is what paradoxically, gradually, and inexorably divorces us from nature.

6

The Great Divorce

THE CONSEQUENCES OF NATURE

*I*n *The Consolation of Nature* and *Mary Reilly,* Valerie Martin explores how women find consolation, however fragile, in nature's creative aspects, such as gardens, motherhood, and art. In *The Great Divorce* (1994), she delineates the positive and negative ways that women and men attempt to deal with the often-frightening realization that they are part of nature. As Martin explains in an interview: "I've always loved the idea of the wild, and I have more and more the sensation that in losing the wild, we live in a different way and that we're no longer animals. We're something else. That was the question that generated *The Great Divorce*: 'Are we animals or are we something else?'" (Biguenet Interview 50). The epigraph of the novel states its theme: "Those who identify with nature must live with the consequences." In *The Great Divorce,* some deal with these "consequences" through the illusions of the supernatural and madness, like Elisabeth and Camille, or through art misused for evasion rather than truth, like Paul; others, like the novel's protagonist Ellen Clayton and her daughter Celia, struggle to find ways to keep living and working despite the knowledge of nature's harsh realities.

As in *The Consolation of Nature* and *Mary Reilly,* Martin focuses in *The Great Divorce* on the ways that women cope with the seemingly unbearable knowledge of their especially disadvantaged state in the natural order as it is replicated in the social order, what Martin represented through gothic enclosures in her earlier works. As in *Mary Reilly* with its implied critique of Stevenson's *The Strange Case of Dr. Jekyll and Mr. Hyde,* Martin examines the way that the male artist's construction of reality can contribute to the control and abuse of women through the reification and augmentation of cultural fictions about "natural" and social hierarchies. In *The Great Divorce,* Martin delineates the many facets of this problem through two male artists—one real, Walter Inglis Anderson (1903–65), and one fictive, the historian Paul Clayton, and through three women—one of the nineteenth century, Elisabeth, and two contemporary, Camille and Ellen—who try to survive and make their lives meaningful under these malign cultural fictions.

The novel's epigraph comes from a 1955 logbook of the Mississippi artist Walter Anderson (quoted in Maurer 227). As Martin told an interviewer, "I was fascinated by him. . . . So I thought he was a good person to look to for a quote [for the epigraph], and when I read that quote . . . I said, 'That's it!'" ("Transformations" 35). Martin's fascination with Anderson arises from the "awful"—awe-inspiring and horrific—consequences of his identification with nature as demonstrated through his interactions with nature, through his art, and through his relationships with other people, especially women. After hospitalizations for mental illness in midlife, Anderson spent more and more time alone in his "cottage" on the Anderson family compound in Ocean Springs and on a nearby Gulf of Mexico barrier island, Horn Island, and less and less time with other people, including his family: his mother, his wife, his four children, and his two brothers and their families. On Horn Island, Anderson prolifically, obsessively, and masterfully painted and sketched the abundant and increasingly ecologically challenged flora and fauna that he found there.

Although Anderson could be seen as a latter-day St. Francis of Assisi, sharing his rice and other food with birds and raccoons, he was not the benevolent nature lover of a Disney movie. He often killed the creatures that he fed when he used them for models, separating young birds too soon from their mothers or leaving young frogs out too long in the sun. Although he expressed guilt over these negligent homicides, he justified them through his belief that while man was a part of nature, and not necessarily superior to the rest of nature, nature needed man's appreciation and recognition, particularly through art, to "realize" itself. According to Anderson's biographer, Christopher Maurer, "'Realization' was more than a psychological process in the creator; it was, metaphorically at least, a phase of nature itself, by which nature—and mankind—achieve a perfection they could not reach on their own" (215).

Anderson's realizations are truly remarkable in any number of media:

watercolors, oils, murals, sketches, prints, sculptures, and ceramics. While the quality of his artistry would certainly attract Martin, who viewed his work in New Orleans and Ocean Springs ("Transformations" 35), a particular technique that is characteristic of Anderson's late Horn Island work, "materialization," is remarkably close to Martin's own artistic technique. As Maurer explains:

> Many of the watercolors attempt to suggest the moment of confusion, of sensory "assemblage" immediately before "materialization"; one stares at the painting a few seconds before knowing what, exactly, it represents: hawk, alligator gar, squirrel hidden in a tree. The effect of materialization . . . is to defeat custom which blinds us to the beauty of the world, covering it, as De Chirico once said, as though under a veil. The momentary puzzlement, the visual groping toward unity which precedes "materialization," sparks wonder, and without wonder art—and even life—seemed to him hardly worth living. (219)

We, as readers, experience a similar "moment of confusion" before the welter of details about nature (human and animal) in *The Great Divorce*, including the separate yet interlocking stories of three Louisiana women, two contemporary (Ellen Clayton, veterinarian at the New Orleans zoo, and Camille, a keeper at the zoo who admires and often assists Ellen) and one antebellum (Elisabeth Boyer Schlaeger, a plantation mistress). Valerie Martin, like Walter Anderson, makes the mundane strange through her art, prods us to "wonder" through questioning and admiration, and compels us to work to see the novel's three stories "materialize" as a coherent whole.

In addition to Anderson's techniques, Martin may also be attracted to the paradox that while Anderson could share nature's realizations with his audience through his art, his other interactions with humanity, especially with women, were quite vexed. His identification with nature could have serious consequences, especially for his wife "Sissy," Agnes Grinstead Anderson. Walter Anderson seemed to regard sex as an immitigably natural act in which the male used his greater strength to satisfy himself whenever he wanted, with no consideration for the wishes of the female. In her journal, Sissy meditated on the word "tenderness," which seemed to have little meaning to her husband: "It connotes sympathy and understanding and thoughtfulness. Respect, too. For one who is tender is gentle, and gentleness asks leave" (quoted in Maurer 186). After leaving him because of his demands for rough sex and his violence toward her, Sissy wrote to Walter, "Don't you see that if I do everything you say in order not to make a scene, or not to be struck, or whatever it may be, that there will be no reason for you to want to change?" (quoted in Maurer 162). Yet Sissy could return to him and act as if such actions would never occur again; or as one of Walter Anderson's psychiatrists noted, his "wife is like a bewitched woman" (quoted in Maurer 171), much like Martin's acquiescently masochistic female protagonists.

Sissy Anderson's seeming passivity before superior physical strength masks the ability to repeatedly walk away, to be "set in motion," as is also characteristic of the female protagonists of Martin's early work. Her later heroines, such as Mary Reilly or the three Louisiana women of *The Great Divorce,* are no longer willing participants in violence as a sex game but attempt to escape their predators. If Anderson's words "those who identify with nature must live with the consequences" are to serve as a guide to this complex novel, it is necessary to understand how Martin uses nature and its consequences in the social order as focused through the novel's artist, writer Paul Clayton, and the ways that his interpretations of these cultural narratives intertwine with the stories of three women—Elisabeth, Camille, and his wife Ellen—in their struggles for survival and meaning.

Paul Clayton, the popular historian who is veterinarian Ellen Clayton's philandering husband, employs art both to reveal and to conceal the truth. To his credit, Paul discovers the mention of Elisabeth's execution in an old newspaper, intensively researches the case, and reaches the conclusion that an escaped leopard, baited by a slave, Charles, killed Elisabeth's husband, Hermann; thus, Elisabeth was innocent of the crime, her husband's murder, for which she was executed. Paul will use his art, writing, to reveal this probable truth, instead of spinning a sensational tale of a wife who turns into a leopard to avenge herself upon her husband, as in Elisabeth's insane delusions or in the plot of the 1943 classic horror film *Cat People.*

Paul is one of Martin's characters, such as Emma Miller in *A Recent*

Martyr, who, like Martin herself and one of her literary models, Flaubert, try to combat their romantic tendencies with the realism of hard facts. Martin told an interviewer, "I think Paul gets a lot of bad press, but he is not a bad guy. He is weak, he is a romantic, and, in some ways, he is me. He wants to make a leap. He wants to make a change. I know that is childish, but I understand it" (McCay and Wiltz 22). Unlike Emma Miller, Martin, or Flaubert, for Paul, in his writing and in his life, the romantic wins, as it does for Flaubert's Emma Bovary, but, since Paul is a man, the consequences for himself are pathetic rather than tragic as they are for Madame Bovary.

Paul wants to dwell on the beautiful and enlightening aspects of history. When he discovers the way the circus pitted animals, like the leopard, against one another in bloody battles, he reflects: "He rarely mentioned events of this kind in his evocations of the past. His readers had a vested interest, as he did himself, in the notion that the past had something to offer the present, that it was not merely the record of how vicious the human animal has always been" (317).[1] Here Paul comes close to Martin's own *raison d'art.* Martin's unflinching realism demonstrates the ways that human society replicates the brutal aspects of the natural order, but her writing also offers the aesthetic pleasures and discoveries of "realization," in Walter Anderson's sense of the word, in which the human sensibility joins with nature to form an artifact that is superior to both. Such realizations suggest ways that human beings can, though they often will not, rise above behaviors based on "nature, red in tooth and claw" (Tennyson's "In Memoriam").

Unlike Martin, however, Paul uses art to evade truth as well as to reveal and act upon it. Like the imprisoned Elisabeth with her obsessive piano playing, he takes refuge from life's vicissitudes in his passion for music, listening to it to avoid hearing less gratifying sounds. In his car, music keeps him "comfortably ensconced in his own perfectly controlled, intensely interesting, mobile little world" (318). He can be so wrapped up in music's sensory pleasures that he fails to consider its meanings. As he

1. In an interview, Martin notes that Paul is "modeled" on the author Lyle Saxon, "who used to write stories about Louisiana" (Martin, Smith interview, 8) that Martin read as a child ("Transformations" 26).

plots a meeting, suspected by his wife Ellen, with his current mistress, Donna, he sings a line from Puccini's *Tosca,* in which Tosca demands of God "Why do you pay me back like this?" (2), claiming that she lives for love and for art and hurts no one. Paul believes he lives for love and art and hurts no one since he is unaware that Ellen knows of his string of infidelities. Ellen, hearing Paul's song, feels that Tosca's aria about undeserved suffering belongs to her as the "Maligned Spouse" (3), an irony of which Paul remains blissfully unaware.

Like some of Martin's early male characters, especially Claude in *Alexandra,* Paul is another of Martin's sardonic versions of the heroes of Walker Percy's novels. Like them, Paul believes himself to be mired in the quotidian with "his fear of boredom, of being ordinary" (327). He tells himself that his adulteries help him escape the "death in life" (128) exemplified by his faithfully married friend and colleague, Joe. Paul the romantic believes that romance will give him freedom: "He required a secret life, in which he was different, at liberty, his ordinary existence at risk" (327), like Dr. Jekyll in *Mary Reilly.* Paul's notions of romantic liberty are fantasies since Paul uses these younger women as what Walker Percy would call "rotations," novelties that refresh without producing any significant changes in Paul's life—until he makes the decision to leave Ellen and their two daughters for Donna. As Paul resembles Claude in *Alexandra,* so is Donna another version of that novel's Diana: she is also "big, taller, than he was, but lean, graceful; she moved with unexpected ease" (53). He sees Donna as an idealized, almost mythic figure, the way that Claude perceives Diana. Again, to Ellen's ironic recognition, Paul "was humming over his work, a snatch from a duet she recognized, in which one man describes to another his vision of a goddess" (87).

Like Percy, Martin emphasizes that "rotations," a change of scenery or domestic partners, disrupt the lives of others while only offering temporary relief for the seeker. When Paul and Donna start a domestic and conjugal routine, Paul suspects that he has not liberated himself from "his ordinary existence" but just exchanged it for a nearly identical version: "Perhaps the routine into which [he and Donna] had so immediately fallen was disconcerting" (321), threatening his vision of himself as the tragic hero suffering for his freedom: "He knew he would pay a price for his actions, but this did not daunt him, as he believed it was liberty he wanted, and liberty, as we all agree, comes at a premium but is always worth the expense. Yet there was something lifeless in Paul's determination, something already dead in his eyes. Ellen thought of the zoo, where there was so much that was wild but none of it at liberty" (135). Paul, because he continues to deceive himself, remains in a "death in life" (128), trapped in a series of rotations, like the wild animals pacing their cages in the zoo.

Through Paul's wife Ellen, Martin significantly critiques Percy's endings of a second marriage with a nurturing, younger woman (*Love in the Ruins*, 1971, and *The Second Coming*, 1980) since Paul has actually left the woman who was willing to sacrifice herself for him. Ellen has followed a course antithetical to Paul's, repressing her emotions and needs in the interests of serving nature through science, and her family through domestic tranquility. In an interview, Valerie Martin commented: "Ellen is absorbed in science. She is in many ways unsympathetic to his [Paul's] need to be the center of his own romantic fantasies" (McCay and Wiltz 22). On an excursion with her daughters, she has told them that she wants an angel on her tombstone. Since angels are benign spirits who serve as messengers for and mediators between the divine and the human, Ellen has been discounting her own significance in favor of service to others. This modern scientist has relegated herself not only to the Victorian "angel in the house," but the angel in the zoo: in both realms, she places others before herself. Although she does not approach Camille's or Elisabeth's degrees of abjection before men, Ellen outwardly defers to men while unobtrusively trying to reach her own ends, as do many of Martin's female protagonists. With Paul, she uses "giving in, forgiving, smoothing over" (208), and she reflects, "Over the years she had often thought that marriage was largely a matter of holding one's tongue" (118).

Martin points out that since the social order, based on nature, favors the strong over the weak, men over women, Paul leaves Ellen for Donna because he not only wants to, but he can; he is following an approved cultural paradigm in which a powerful man can replace a "worn-out" wife with an attractive younger woman, despite the irony that the wife may have been worn away, physically and spiritually, by following the approved cultural script of domestic service. Instead, Paul uses Ellen's learned repression, her avoidance of conflict and unwillingness to challenge his infidelities, to rationalize his fantasies of his continuing youth through a romance with a younger woman. He muses: "Ellen was only forty, but she seemed already to be entering a resigned usefulness, ambitious still and certainly strong, but not as, as this young woman [Donna] was, excitable, capable of fire. Ellen had the patient look of one who has survived a great passion" (54). What he calls "a resigned usefulness" might also be the responsible behavior of maturity, and Martin employs Ellen's increasingly clear-eyed vision of reality, both natural and social, to counteract Paul's hazy romanticism. For Martin, a great passion is something women survive, if they are strong and lucky. Ellen is a survivor, and through her story, and those of two women who do not survive, Elisabeth and Camille, Martin dramatizes the epigraph to the novel, "those who identify with nature must live with the consequences," as she explores the meaning of nature, identification, and consequences for Ellen, Elisabeth, and Camille.

Ellen Clayton, a veterinarian at the New Orleans zoo, muses, "Natural. Another meaningless word, or a word that could mean anything, like love" (39). In the opening paragraphs of the novel, Ellen rejects the sentimental and romantic view of nature as consistently benevolent and nurturing. She is reading an article entitled "The Great Divorce" and agrees with its author that the "Zoo Eden" and its "expensive exhibits conjure up a world that never did, never will, exist, in which predator and prey gaze stupidly at one another across invisible but effective barriers" (1). When Ellen sees a reproduction of *The Peaceable Kingdom,* she picks out "boy and girl, and lion and lamb," paralleling the lion and the male, the lamb and the female. In the actual Zoo Eden, superior strength, not love, prevails: Paolo, the lion, dominates Antonella, his mate, who "gave way at once and followed him" (272), like Gretta the dog with her mate in the short story "Spats" in *The Consolation of Nature.* Humans are part of this natural world, clever and strong carnivores: "How given the canine teeth and close-set eyes that declare the human animal to be a predator, had we come up with the notion that oat bran is more natural to eat than chicken?" (39). As part of the natural order, the three female protagonists of the novel are in varying degrees subject to their men: Camille is mentally disturbed and easy prey; delicate and cultured Elisabeth is physically and psychologically broken by her brutal husband; and Ellen loses her husband to the physical allure of a younger mate.

In this brutal natural order, Martin again explores the consolation of nature through maternal love, especially of daughters who represent a woman's future, in nature and in society, as she did in *A Recent Martyr, The Consolations of Nature,* and *Mary Reilly.* Ellen remembers a "lioness fighting her starving cubs for a piece of meat" (40) and thinks, "what perverse twisting of what happens in nature had visited on women the notion that mothering is a natural instinct, that a woman who does not love her child is unnatural, when the most casual investigation of mothers in the wild reveals that only those with leisure and a plentiful food supply indulge themselves in the luxury of caring for their offspring" (40). In the animal world, even mother's love is a "luxury" in the struggle for survival, an order that seems replicated in much of society, present and past. In contemporary New Orleans, Camille's mother is too solitary and damaged by alcohol to do anything but verbally abuse her; her favorite room is "what she called the den, a word that always struck Camille as appropriate, the place where she lay in wait . . . ready to spring" (289). In nineteenth-century Louisiana, Elisabeth's mother won't help her escape her brutal husband because she is too afraid of her own husband, of Elisabeth's husband, and of the patriarchal laws that support them. Only Ellen, privileged by her material and educational circumstances and what she learns from her vocation as a veterinarian, has the physical and mental strength, the financial stability, and the time to care for her daughters, who are deeply hurt by their father's departure, to "indulge . . . in the luxury of caring for [her] offspring" (40).

As in *The Consolation of Nature,* Martin parallels the fates of captive animals with those of women. When animals are confined in the Zoo Eden, they may benefit in that they may live longer and healthier lives and their species, if endangered, may be preserved. However, they also may be damaged, frustrated, and bewildered by the environment that is supposed to save them, like the baby monkey whose mother bit off its finger (2, 4). The zoo animals are subject to a mysterious, usually fatal, virus that spreads quickly in the unnatural confines of the zoo and that Ellen is trying to identify and cure. As Martin has noted, "imprisonment"

(McCay and Wiltz 18) is a major theme of *The Great Divorce,* and the human animal is also imprisoned by society with similarly maddening and virulent effects. The Zoo Eden is another version of the gothic enclosure in Martin's earlier works that is supposed to protect women but sinisterly works to their psychological detriment since they are supposed to like it and feel grateful for it. Camille becomes locked within the masochistic view of women that she has now internalized and Elisabeth is literally locked up in the plantation house by her husband: both women go mad.

Society's replication of the dominance of the male over the female is one type of identification with nature that, in effect, imprisons the female who, like the zoo animals, turns to self-destructive behaviors in frustration. Since she fails to find assistance from a potential maternal figure, Ellen, who is preoccupied by the Clayton domestic dramas, Camille comes to believes that when men abuse her she can transform herself into the leopard Magda, whom she tends as part of her job as a keeper at the zoo. When Camille no longer believes in this fantasy, she has nothing left and she kills herself. Elisabeth believes that she turned into a leopard and killed her husband; she clings to this belief that leads to her destruction: hanging as a convicted murderess. Unlike Irena, the protagonist of the film *Cat People,* Camille and Elisabeth do not literally turn into black leopards when rejected by men, and by the women who collude with the men, but the intensity of their identification with black leopards attests to the depths of their confinement in despair and humiliation.

Through Ellen, Martin suggests a healthier balance or middle way in that Ellen selectively identifies with nature: she realizes that while she is an animal, she is a different kind of animal, one with a consciousness of time and so she tries to learn from nature and to plan for the future for herself and for her daughters. When her husband Paul leaves her and their daughters for the much younger Diana, Ellen, in her troubled sleep, dreams about her own Peaceable Kingdom in which she has sex with animals: "She had confidence in these dream animals, in their uncompromising devotion to her, a confidence she knew she would never have with a human lover again" (197). Ellen, however, unlike Camille and Elisabeth, can distinguish between fantasy and reality and act on that distinction while learning what she can from her kinship with animals: "Whether she was loved or not was a matter of indifference to the universe. The proper way to suffer was to treat her broken heart as an animal would a broken limb; use it if possible, stay off it if necessary" (115). She decides that "like a tired old lioness, she would turn her back on the new, the reigning couple [Paul and Donna], summon whatever dignity she could muster, and quietly walk away" (121), like many of Martin's early female protagonists. In contrast to Camille and Elisabeth, Ellen constructively uses what she has learned from nature, recognizes the limits of her identification, and survives.

Martin presents the human tendency to identify with nature as, in effect, natural; the deleterious consequences arise when the identification is a willed illusion, a lying and controlling narrative that imprisons humanity and nature in a viciously destructive, downward spiral. Ellen reflects on humanity's past and present views of nature: "This was a satisfactory attitude toward the wild: bring it down. Now that we have been successful in that quest we want to be told it isn't so, to see wild animals at a safe distance, healthy and strong, as if their existence is not threatened at all" (57). The supermarket is an even more horrifying illusion than the zoo, "with its wretched imitation of music piped in to keep shoppers from being able to think about the nightmare of the scene before them; whole aisles of poisonous cleaning products, the repulsive creatures grinning luridly on cereal boxes, the solid wall of meat" (111). As in *The Consolation of Nature*, where pets, to their destruction, are ostensibly loved as a link between humanity and nature, Ellen concludes that the human love of nature, based on a putative identification with it, is the biggest and most destructive delusion of all: "In spite of our protests, we don't really like nature at all. Why do we imagine that we can care for the planet when we measure the progress of our peculiar civilizations by how much they allow us to be free of it? (111). F. Scott Fitzgerald, in an essay tellingly titled "The Crack-Up," posited that "the test of a first-rate intelligence is the ability to hold two opposed ideas in the mind at the same time, and still retain the ability to function." In *The Great Divorce,* Martin applies this test to three Louisiana women with regard to their relations with nature as reified by society.

Camille's "ability to function" is highly tentative, constantly challenged, and ultimately overwhelmed. Of the three female protagonists,

Camille is the one whose childhood most resembles the gothic confining milieu of Mary Reilly because she also suffered constantly at the hands of an alcoholic. While Mary suffered physical abuse amounting to torture from her drunken father, Camille is verbally abused by her drinking and smoking mother. Mary feared the sound of her father's footsteps before he locked her into a closet with a rat, and, as an adult, she heard those footsteps again emanating from menacing Mr. Hyde. With a similar claustrophobia, Camille compares how she feels around men with the dread evoked by her mother. "She felt as she often did in her room at night when she heard her mother's footsteps in the hall, smothered in a suffocating darkness from which there was no escape" (100). Like Mary Reilly, Camille is at the mercy of an abusive parent because the other parent is missing, literally absent in the case of Camille's father and intermittently and ineffectually present in the case of Mary's mother.

Both Mary and Camille see nature in both its malevolent and benevolent aspects in parents and parent substitutes. After the hospitalization that followed her injuries from the rat in the closet, Mary escaped her abuser by going into service and, before entering the Jekyll household, was taught the values of order, decency, and industry by a housekeeper who functioned as a positive maternal figure by giving Mary standards by which she could succeed. Mary then learns to garden from another maternal figure, the cook in Dr. Jekyll's establishment. By nurturing Dr. Jekyll's household, Mary learns to nurture herself. She resists the violently bestial Mr. Hyde and, at the end of the novel, embraces the benevolent aspects of nature and human nature in the dying Dr. Jekyll. Mary survives through her choice of promoting the best in nature and through the encouragement of positive, if flawed, parental models.

In contrast, Camille continues to live with her mother as a young adult and transfers her sense of worthlessness to her relationships with men. On a blind date as a teenager, "she could not overcome her sense that it was degrading and disgusting to be treated in this way, yet she said nothing and stayed very still" (37), using passive acquiescence to stave off possible attacks from the more powerful, men. She then attempted to escape (like the protagonist of Martin's early short story "Surface Calm") by cutting herself in what may have been a suicide attempt: "It was marvelous then, for a few minutes; her sense of release, of relaxation was complete" (51). Like Mary Reilly, she initially finds a refuge in "her job, her salvation" (44), but it is based on a delusion. Like Irena in the movie *Cat People*, Camille believes that she metamorphoses into a ferocious black leopard when men humiliate her. Revenge is her motive, as it is for Irena. Camille even bites one sexual partner, the painter Jack, when she thinks she is Magda, the black leopard she tends at the zoo. Camille, in effect, wishes she could turn into Mr. Hyde: "I am vengeance" (78), she tells herself in the persona of Magda. Camille may be mad, but her powerlessness in the face of patriarchal society's realities makes madness seem desirable.

Like Mary Reilly through Dr. Jekyll, Camille wants to find a good father, a benevolent patriarch into whose care she can place herself since she believes she cannot survive on her own. Camille feels forced to choose a violent aspect of nature, her inner Mr. Hyde through Magda, but she is really looking for Dr. Jekyll. A potential father figure, her psychiatrist, Dr. Veider, is at worst a Darth Vader–like destructive father and at best "bizarre," which is the meaning of "veider" in Estonian. Seemingly undercutting the goals of his profession, he tells Camille that he does not believe that people can change, leading her to conclude that "if this was true, he had condemned her to a lifetime of servitude" (215). Camille wants her own version of the Christian cultural ideal, a Peaceable Kingdom, a Garden of Eden presided over by a benevolent god: an attractive, but destructively false, illusion. A "new world of felicity and peace" (105), perhaps even marriage, is what Camille hopes for in her relationship with her final lover, Eddie. He proves himself another Mr. Hyde when he turns out to be, is "transformed" into, a married man. After this revelation, she finds temporary sanctuary in "the pale light of the small cafe, which seemed to her a place of limitless possibility, freedom, and hope" (143), reminiscent of the cafe esteemed by the old waiter in Hemingway's short story "A Clean, Well-Lighted Place" (1926) who is also approaching life's end. Recognizing that there will be no "clean, well-lighted place for her," in a phallus-parodying and self-destructive form of vengeance, she commits suicide by using the gun and the apartment of an earlier sexual partner, the painter whom she bit in the persona of Magda.

Through demonstrating the consequences of older women's neglect or cowardice, Martin suggests that older female mentors are vital for younger women to survive and develop in a patriarchal society. During her childhood, Camille did not have the benevolent mother substitutes of Mary Reilly nor her sustained belief in the dignity and worth of her work, zoo-keeping, rather than housekeeping. At last, Camille apparently finds a positive female role model in Ellen Clayton, the veterinarian at the zoo, whom she watches stitching up an animal under her care. In her admiration for Ellen's calm competence, Camille briefly realizes that her Magda-identification is a delusion: "The lie of the hidden world had been exposed, and for a moment Camille knew she resembled the woman sewing more than the unconscious leopard under her hands. She had no wish to deny it; for the first time in her life she was not ashamed of her own kind" (161). Ellen, however, is wrapped up in the troubles of her recently arrested younger daughter, and she fails to reach out to Camille after Magda's death. To Camille, Ellen seems less like a role model and more like an impossibly competent member of another species. When Ellen tells Camille, "I don't want to give up. I don't like to make some of the compromises I have to make. But that's the deal" (288), Camille thinks, "so it must seem to someone like Ellen, who had, in fact, something, an ideal, a principle, some shred of dignity, that could be compromised. But Camille felt herself to be beyond that now. Perhaps this was a kind of liberty, she thought" (308). Much like the protagonist of Camus's *The Stranger* (1942), an influential work for Martin, Camille realizes her existential predicament as she faces death.

Without support and the example of women who manage to maintain their self-worth and a sense of meaning, a woman may not be able to survive in a man's natural and social world. With the death of Magda the leopard and Ellen's indifference, Camille loses her sense of "her job, her salvation" (44). Convinced of her permanent isolation and inability to make a meaningful contribution through work, Camille sits by the riverbank with its scurrying rats and remembers this line of poetry: "And I the while, the sole unbusy thing" (296), from Samuel Taylor Coleridge's sonnet of 1825 "Work without Hope." Coleridge's solitary speaker, though he is surrounded by nature in its springtime glory, laments, "And I, the while, the sole unbusy thing, / Nor honey make, nor pair, nor build, nor sing." The last lines of this sonnet, which Martin does not quote, presage Camille's suicide: "Work without Hope draws nectar in a sieve, / And Hope without an Object cannot live."

Martin shows that women can be destroyed in gilded gothic cages or prisons, as well as in less privileged dungeons, since both are controlled by cultural beliefs in male natural and social superiority. In contrast to Camille, Elisabeth Boyer Schlaeger, Martin's nineteenth-century protagonist, has been delicately nurtured, but like Camille, her upbringing has led to delusion. Elisabeth believes that she is loved and valued as a person in her Creole society; she does not yet see that her society replicates nature in the way that the physically stronger, the males, control the females. In fact, the Creole men treat women and slaves as if they were different and inferior species, like animals, not like humans. Elisabeth does not recognize that she is just another costly possession that her male owners have raised as an investment, like the slaves or the horses. Her father wants her to marry her dissolute cousin and keep property in the family, but he willingly changes his mind and transfers ownership of Elisabeth to Hermann Schlaeger, a German immigrant with no social, humane, or intellectual gifts to recommend him but with a great deal of money that he made in "clever, often shady, land speculation" (30). Elisabeth thinks she will live in a Peaceable Kingdom in which Hermann "was a big bull, but she would make a lamb of him" (96). He, however, recognizes the hierarchy of her gendered society and Elisabeth's place in it: like "a fine young filly he intended to own. . . . Once her high spirits were broken, she would suit him down to his shoes" (96). When she is "broken," without delusions or hopes, Elisabeth learns to dread Hermann's footsteps, "which she knew would follow her forever" (241), as Camille has learned to dread her mother's footsteps and Mary Reilly those of her father and Mr. Hyde.

Through Elisabeth, Martin demonstrates the way that women's acculturation, through teaching them to identify with their wardens, not their fellow prisoners, leads to their destruction, mental and physical. Although Hermann attempts to break Elisabeth by locking up her piano so she cannot play the music that is her passion, and by beating and crippling the maid Bessie who is her devoted slave, Elisabeth still refuses to recognize that she has more in common with the slaves than with the white males around her. She tells Hermann of Bessie, "She isn't yours. She's mine" (169) and thinks, "Surely she would never be reduced to begging for what was rightfully hers" (167). Elisabeth foreshadows Manon, the protagonist of Martin's 2003 Orange Prize–winning novel, *Property,* in her blindness to the similarities of her situation to that of the slaves and her consequent inability to make an ally of a clever and well-placed slave. As Manon haughtily declines to ally herself with the slave Sarah, who is her husband's mistress-under-duress, so Elisabeth will not swallow her pride to get help from the plantation's major domo, Charles, who sympathizes with Bessie and her mistress. By the time Charles does save her and the other slaves by luring the leopard into the house to kill Hermann, Elisabeth is too broken to profit from her liberation, or perhaps takes refuge in madness since she may have realized that only one patriarch is gone but the system remains. In some ways, Elisabeth's story could be seen as Martin's revision of Kate Chopin's "The Story of an Hour." When Mrs. Mallard learns of her husband's death in an accident, she proclaims to herself "Free! Body and soul free!" (354), only to drop dead of a heart attack upon his return. The report of his death was as erroneous as the prospect of escape from cultural imprisonment for Mrs. Mallard and Mrs. Schlaeger.

Martin also shows the way that a male's attractive surface of culture, manners, and apparent empathy is merely another trap, as Dr. Jekyll was for Mary Reilly. Someone who might seem a "natural" ally for Elisabeth, a seemingly sympathetic and cultured fellow Creole like Andre Davillier, master of a neighboring plantation, is too imbued with the system to help her. He is so certain of male ownership of females that he does nothing when he sees that "the light in her [Elisabeth's] eyes has gone out" and "he felt he was looking at a shell, a burned-out house in which all that remained of once elegant furnishings were a few charred sticks, bits of broken glass, and ashes" (261). Slaves, like women, are not fully human, and so like Manon's father in *Property,* Andre is too caught up in his system for managing slaves, which he thinks is benevolent and efficient (255–56), to challenge what he sees as the natural order. As with Hermann, who sees his wife as a "filly" to be "broken," "this analogy [of the slave] to the horse was the linchpin of Andre's argument" (256).

Again, Martin underlines the need for female mentors by the consequences of their absence. Like Camille, Elisabeth has female role models
who either are too blindly acculturated to help her or whose example
she is too acculturated to follow. Elisabeth's mother is not abusive like
Camille's but ineffectual like Mary Reilly's; those who are not among the
fittest survive by deferring to them and by raising female progeny who
are equally subservient. In the naturalistic terms of the novel, the Creoles
are "inbred" (6), and Elisabeth resembles Sonya, the exotic and much-
admired white tiger in Ellen's zoo, whom Ellen considers "a great disaster
of inbreeding" (111). Gardens and zoos may preserve and develop species,
but they may also render them incapable of survival outside of the protective space. Martin once again uses a garden analogy for the mother-
daughter relation in that Elisabeth was reared like a delicate, exotic plant.
In her imprisonment by Hermann, she comforts herself by "stroking her
cheek, as her mother had done when she was a child, remembering the
gentle, sweet, pleasure-laden life she had once enjoyed, detail by detail;
the scent of orange trees in her mother's garden" (310). When Elisabeth
flees to her parents' home in New Orleans to enlist their help against
Hermann, all her mother does is put flowers in her room and acquiesce in
sending Elisabeth back to her brutish husband; her gesture is loving and
lovely, but inefficacious.

Elisabeth is too acculturated to recognize or imitate women who have
used their wits to survive and thrive in a society that replicates a natural
order based on physical strength. When Elisabeth's aunt gives her the
money to make her unsuccessful journey to her parents' home, "Elisabeth sensed that her aunt knew exactly what she was up against, that the
proffered envelope represented the strong woman's sanction" (193), but
she does not pursue the logical implications. Elisabeth's aunt has been in
charge of her plantation herself since "her husband's untimely, acciden-
tal death" (193) a decade earlier. Since she has not remarried, one might
speculate, but Elisabeth does not, that her aunt helped her husband to his
sudden end and/or that she has never remarried because she relishes her
relative freedom without a husband. Unlike the New Orleans protagonist
of Martin's first novel, *Set in Motion* (1978; 105, 146), Elisabeth also seems
unaware of the example of another Louisiana contemporary, the Baron-

ess Pontalba, who triumphed over imprisonment by her husband and his family through surviving gunshot wounds from her father-in-law in 1834 and escaping to build a fortune in real estate in Paris and New Orleans, including the Pontalba buildings on Jackson Square.

Elisabeth has been bred and trained to be incapable of helping herself so she turns to the *super*natural, to voodoo, to which she believes she is entitled as a human being "above" ("super") the natural. As Ellen Clayton speculates in a different context, "People who believed they could summon the spirits of animals to set them free had already accepted that they were, in an important way—something having to do with volition—not animals" (337). Elisabeth, however, also cannot profit from the example of two black women, Lucinde and Mambo Pitou, who manipulate society's version of the natural order to their own ends; instead, Elisabeth attributes their success to the supernatural. Elisabeth's New Orleans hairdresser, the free woman of color Lucinde, has the necessary attributes for the survival of the fittest: "her sharp features alert to every movement around her, posed like a great raptor with the power to tear out hearts if necessary, and no shred of pity or mercy for anything weaker than herself" (242). Like Ellen's aunt, Lucinde has achieved independence: she "had her tidy, charming bungalow" (244). When Lucinde takes Elisabeth to the voodoo priestess Mambo Pitou for help, Elisabeth is surprised that Mambo Pitou can describe Hermann so well: "How could this woman who had never seen him know so much about him?" (249). As in the case of her aunt, Elisabeth cannot follow the logical implications: either Mambo Pitou has been briefed by Lucinde and/or Mambo Pitou has probably been approached by many women with husbands like Hermann. When Mambo Pitou unleashes what she calls "the spirit of rage against imprisonment" (254), Elisabeth swoons. She cannot act in her own interest like these canny and autonomous women.

Lucinde, Mambo Pitou, probably Elisabeth's aunt, and the enslaved butler Charles all can invoke the "spirit of rage against imprisonment" to free themselves. Even the leopard displayed liberating rage by escaping the circus where it was cruelly treated. Because Elisabeth belongs to a privileged race and species, she is too acculturated to follow an instinct for survival; she did not really believe in the reality of her imprisonment and is incapable of saving herself. By the time that she realizes her plight and Charles has Hermann killed, she is too sunk in madness to profit. As her husband's corpse lies bleeding on the staircase, Elisabeth rushes to her piano to play Mendelssohn's "Songs without Words" "with the pure concentration of a mind and soul at peace, entirely and perfectly free" (315), like Paul evading reality through music. She is comforted by her delusion that she was the man-eating leopard; she believes in her own autonomy and retains "her insistence on her own guilt, and her calm, proud demeanor" (319) until her execution in April of 1846.

When confronted with nature's preference for brute strength as replicated in society, Elisabeth uses three futile means of coping: the supernatural, madness, and culture or art. In *The Great Divorce,* Martin begins an interrogation of art—its purposes, contexts, uses, and misuses—that she pursues in most of her later novels and short stories. Ellen Clayton is unresponsive to art in many ways, but one aspect of her attitude is resonant with Martin's questioning of dominant cultural narratives: Ellen "was suspicious of culture, of its ability to disguise or even glorify destruction and tyranny" (68). Paul uses his supposedly artistic and romantic sensibility to leave Ellen and their daughters. Jack the painter uses his pretensions as an artist as a justification for his humiliation of Camille, who is not an artist. Elisabeth plays Mendelssohn's popular piano pieces to ignore tyranny and deny her own destruction.

Ironically, Elisabeth and her fellow Creoles' devotion to culture, and indeed their entire culture, actually leads to her destruction. Hermann's surname is Schlaeger, which means "basher" in German, and he is intrinsically antagonistic to culture. He literally, as well as figuratively, does not speak the Creoles' language, French, "the sound of the language he found so unnerving; its very softness and fluidity suggested weakness to him, a language for women and slaves" (33), those two "naturally" inferior species. He dislikes dancing and finds Elisabeth's passion for "music was a peculiar trial to him" (91), so he uses it as a means of breaking her, imprisoning the piano in the locked drawing room away from Elisabeth the way he imprisons Elisabeth in the plantation house away from any friends or allies.

Since Hermann is killed by "the spirit of rage against imprisonment" in the form of the leopard manipulated by a slave, Martin suggests that nature does have a higher value than brute force, such as freedom, particularly the freedom of expression of art. In the sense of Walter Anderson's "realizations," art is not opposed to nature, but helps nature "realize" itself to the utmost if the art is used to reveal and emphasize, not conceal, the truth. A truth that Martin wants to emphasize here is that both nature and society need women to survive, and that motherhood, biological or through mentorship and example, is crucial for the future in many aspects.

Through maternal feeling, women fight for the future of society, of the species, and of the natural world. Although Ellen resigns herself to Paul's departure "like a tired old lioness" (121) who will "quietly walk away" (121), she refuses to acquiesce in the mistreatment of her teenage daughters, Lillian and Celia, and she is angry with Paul on their behalf. Lillian shares Ellen's equable temperament, but Celia, whose personality resembles Paul's, is greatly affected by her father's leaving. Ellen agonizes on Celia's behalf, "Being abandoned by a father was the same as being abandoned by God; nothing ever filled the gap" (119). Celia becomes increasingly alienated and troubled, culminating in her arrest on a drug charge. When Ellen hears from Celia about the way the two young men in the next cell verbally and visually sexually harassed her daughter, Ellen's ruminations no longer sound like those of a selflessly ministering angel.

> Her thoughts veered to the two teenage boys who had threatened Celia. She gave herself over to a few minutes of castigating men. Their passion for liberty knew no bounds, and it never occurred to them that their freedom always came at someone else's expense. They raped, women, countries, the planet, all in service of their passion to be pulled forward by the force between their legs, like murderous teenage boys on motorbikes. They thought women were sly and calculating, but that was because they never spent a minute contemplating the consequences of their actions. They felt scared, trapped; they ran from pillar to post, woman to woman; they wanted to be in control of something, anything, everything but themselves. (239)

In her rage to protect her daughter, Ellen finds the passion to indict Paul and other men for their untrammeled, misogynistic, and destructive impulses. She no longer wants an angel on her tombstone, but "a woman blindfolded, and holding a scale. *Justice*" (235–36).

In a striking deployment of Martin's maternal garden imagery, Ellen dreams of digging in a garden and unearthing a human hand that she thinks is Camille's: "I was trying to get her back" (331). As Ellen awakens and "as she swung her legs over the side of the bed, she had another thought. It was me, buried alive" (331). Ellen recognizes that despite her strength and her many privileges, she shares with Camille and other women the "death in life" that society assigns to females. When she attends Camille's funeral, her empathy for Camille's mother spurs her to action on behalf of her daughters: "She wanted to get home, to see her own daughters, to reassure herself that she might not ever share this woman's unbearable fate" (332–33).

Martin's belief in the salutary nature of realism is evident as Ellen encourages Celia's interest in helping her at the zoo, particularly Celia's passion for taking x-rays. Indeed, Celia has the impulses of the true artist, one who wants to "realize" nature; she tells her mother: "I like seeing what ordinarily can't be seen. . . . And I like getting a good, clear picture" (336). In the last lines of the novel, mother and daughter save themselves and their relationship as they work to save a new jaguar named Minx from the viral epidemic at the zoo. "Here was a small, a pitiful triumph, Ellen thought. Of course she knew that. In the face of what was coming it was laughable, a joke, like struggling to scoop out a thimbleful of water from a sinking ship, from the *Titanic*. . . . So why did this little victory feel so satisfying, so important? Ellen put her arm around her daughter. . . . Why did she feel such joy, such unexpected and overwhelming joy? . . . 'I think,' she said firmly, 'this time, we win'" (340). In the great divorce between humanity and nature, Ellen is fighting for justice. She has made a choice for good the way that C. S. Lewis insisted that every person must choose between good and evil in his moral parable *The Great Divorce* (1945, a work known to Martin, "Transformations" 34). Unlike Lewis, Martin does not posit a heavenly reward; her existential dilemma and its hellish consequences, the annihilation of the environment, are before us in this world.

As in the ending of *A Recent Martyr,* a woman does what she can to help her community, her society, and the future through her daughter; there are no romantic transformations or male saviors. All that Ellen can realistically desire is what she has at that very moment: the satisfaction of acting for justice and the fellowship that she feels with her daughter, who is her hope for an earthly, not heavenly, future. In this moment, Ellen has met F. Scott Fitzgerald's challenge: "The test of a first-rate intelligence is the ability to hold two opposed ideas in the mind at the same time and still retain the ability to function" ("The Crack-Up"). Martin herself may have surpassed that standard. In *The Great Divorce,* she has, in Walter Anderson's terms, "materialized" the stories of *three* seemingly disparate women into a "realization" of nature at its most profound.

7

Italian Fever

ART FOR LIFE OR LIFE FOR ART?

*I*n *The Great Divorce,* Valerie Martin explored the tragic consequences of that novel's epigraph: "Those who identify with nature must live with the consequences." For *Italian Fever* (1999) that maxim could be revised thus: "Those who identify with art must live with the consequences." Martin's sojourn in Italy from 1994 to 1997 resulted in a shift in focus: "The Roman's constant preoccupation with art ultimately resulted in my thinking about what artists are, especially painters, and what they do" (Biguenet Interview 52). Art, like nature and love in Martin's earlier works, provides other cultural narratives that humans use either to learn to live more fully or to avoid confronting the knowledge of death, but, like all illusions, they present traps as well as liberations. Learning to distinguish between the two is the task of *Italian Fever*'s protagonist, Lucy Stark, a challenge made more difficult by the sensory overload of art, culture, and history that is Italy. Martin's novel itself is a parodic, humorous riot of literary and artistic allusions, but as Linda Hutcheon asserts, "To include irony and play is *never,* necessarily to exclude seriousness and purpose in postmodern art" (27). The reader, like Lucy, must not be overly distracted by the rich and entertaining Italian milieu, but must attempt to discern what Martin believes art can tell us about life, death, and ourselves, whether we are actual artists, or artists in life, those who use the imagination to create more meaningful lives and reject pernicious cultural prescriptions.

In *Italian Fever,* Martin punctures the gothic narrative of female religious masochism through humor, rather than horror, since Lucy Stark can be considered the comic version of Emma Miller of Martin's *A Recent Martyr.* As Avril Horner and Sue Zlosnick note, gothic texts often contain "the juxtaposition of incongruous textual effects" that "opens up the possibility of a comic turn in the presence of horror or terror" (3). When

Lucy's host at dinner, Antonio Cini, "hummed a familiar musical phrase" from the popular Neapolitan boat song "Santa Lucia" upon learning her name, Lucy tells him that St. Lucy is "always shown carrying her eyes on a plate" (58), a ridiculously unappetizing vision at a dinner party. Yet the allusion to the patron saint of vision is also serious, suggesting that Lucy Stark should look beyond appearances, and she does, as her relationship with the initially repulsive Antonio develops over the course of the novel from suspicion to friendship. In another grotesque depiction of female bodily parts offered up for male consumption that is at once ludicrous and serious, when Lucy puts on a push-up bra for an assignation with her Italian lover, Massimo, she has "the unsettling sensation that she was standing behind her breasts, as if she was presenting them for inspection" (178). St. Agatha, an intercessor in cases of sexual assault, is often depicted carrying her breasts before her on a plate, while St. Lucy is also one of many virgin martyrs whose refusal of sex cost them their lives. Lucy Stark needs to decide the importance of sex in her life and find a middle ground between abstention and obsession. She must take charge herself, not merely respond to the actions of men like a saintly and passive martyr.

Martin suggests that slow martyrdoms are just as destructive as rapid executions. Lucy needs to avoid the protracted martyrdom of another Lucy Stark, from Martin's home state of Louisiana. In Robert Penn Warren's novel *All the King's Men* (1946), Lucy Stark is the long-suffering wife of Willie Stark, the "King," based on Louisiana's populist governor Huey Long. Warren's Lucy Stark supports her husband by teaching school as he studies law and enters politics; remains faithful to him as he strays from his ideals and hers, both politically and sexually; and is ready to take him back when he announces his return to rectitude. This final display of wifely sacrifice is obviated by his assassination, but Lucy Stark manages to continue her career of self-abnegation by caring for their paraplegic son Tom and a baby who may or may not have been fathered out of wedlock by Tom.

Like many of Martin's female protagonists, her Lucy Stark started along a similarly self-sacrificial path: "That was what her husband had been drawn to: a pleasant, friendly young woman, resourceful and competent, who could support him while he went through law school, which was exactly what she had done" (84). Unlike Warren's, Martin's Lucy Stark rejects such romanticism and divorces her leech; she swings from the romantic to the pragmatic and uses her organizational talents to become the administrative assistant of a popular writer, DV. As is usual in Martin's fiction, Lucy must learn to balance romanticism and realism, but in a reversal of Martin's usual pattern, Lucy begins the novel at the realistic extreme. She learned too well how to separate her caretaking skills from caring, to the point of denying her heart. When she learns of DV's unexpected death at the beginning of the novel, she is not overcome by grief, but goes into action by planning her trip to wind up his affairs in Tuscany. Like Charlotte Brontë's self-deprecatory Jane Eyre, "Passion had never been one of her options, nor was it ever likely to be" (86), and so, as Lucy tries to persuade herself, "she had come to prefer liberty to passion" (85).

Martin revises other "Lucy tales" of passion and liberty as well. In another novel by Charlotte Brontë, *Villette* (1853), Lucy Snow, plain and unobtrusive, chooses a life of seemingly contradictory independence and self-denial as a paid companion to an elderly invalid and then as a teacher in a continental school for girls. At the school, she meets and gradually falls in love with a fellow teacher, Monsieur Paul, a native who tries to interpret her character and dictate a more healthful way of life for her. Following a fever in which she realizes her loneliness and need, they eventually agree to wed, but their union is thwarted by his sudden death. Martin's Lucy is also alone in a foreign country when she, due to a debilitating fever, falls passionately in love with and becomes dependent on handsome Massimo Compitelli, the publisher's representative delegated to assist her with DV's literary and personal remains. In contrast to the deaths of the lovers of Warren's Lucy Stark and Brontë's Lucy Snow, Massimo remains alive, but returns to his wife. Martin's Lucy will miss him, but she has known all along that Massimo is married and that their affair can only be a passionate interlude: "They both knew she was having an adventure that must come to an end when she returned to her old life in her own country" (123). Neither is devastated, and Lucy plans her return to America with equanimity. Perhaps like E. M. Forster's Lucy in Italy, Lucy Honeychurch of *A Room with a View* (1908), she will apply the knowledge of passion that she gained in Italy to a fervent and committed relationship in her native land.

The title of Martin's novel, like Lucy's name, is highly parodic, in this instance of the repeated narrative of passion as a fatal attraction for women. Before the discovery that malaria was caused by mosquitoes, it was thought to occur from exposures to "miasmas" that made the Italian night dangerous as well as romantic. *Italian Fever* evokes two literary masterpieces that explore the fatal attractions of American women in Italy, Henry James's novella *Daisy Miller* (1878) and Edith Wharton's short story "Roman Fever" (1934). James's expatriate Winterbourne has become too bound by European mores to pursue an alluring but unconventional American girl, Daisy Miller. With suicidal defiance, Daisy contracts the fever in the Roman Forum at night, where health and decorum dictate that she should not be, and dies of "Roman Fever," from her fevered passion. In Wharton's "Roman Fever," the supposed fever contracted at night masks a pregnancy contracted from another woman's fiancé. Decades later, when the two women meet as mature matrons, they learn the results of their youthful and stunted passions. Both James and Wharton use the "Italian fever" to signify the lethal nature of nineteenth-century social conventions. In contrast, the twentieth century had few, if any, social conventions regarding passion in Western civilization, never mind conventions that were death-dealing to those who defied them, but neither did contemporary society offer warnings about dangerous men and situations. Martin's Lucy must learn to discern realities among romantic appearances without either dire warnings or dire consequences, for, despite her demurrals, she has a passionate nature and a predilection for the romantic as symbolized by her own "Italian fever."

Martin provides Lucy with a saint—unlike Saints Lucy and Agnes, or James's and Wharton's martyrs to society—one who addresses both sides of her nature, the realistic and the romantic. Teresa of Avila was renowned for her practical common sense as an administrator as well as for her mystical raptures, which are often characterized in terms of sexual ecstasy. On the plane to Italy, Lucy is carrying *The Art of Ecstasy: Teresa, Bernini, and Crashaw,* an actual work, not one invented by Martin, published by the scholar Robert T. Petersson in 1970. However, "after a brief perusal of the excellent photographs of Bernini's *St. Teresa,* her thoughts began to wander" (17) to her job and other practical concerns; she is still avoiding her passions, the ecstasy that Bernini so compellingly creates in his sculpture of St. Teresa in a mystical transport, reproduced in Petersson's book. Early in her stay in Italy, when Lucy enters the Cinis' dining room, "she recall[s] St. Teresa of Avila's comparison of heaven to the Duchess of Alba's drawing room" (59), an ironic stance that helps Lucy distance herself from St. Teresa's ecstasy, from the people around her at the dinner party, and from her own passionate nature.

Through Lucy, Martin, like Bernini, is suggesting that the spiritual cannot be divided from the material, the spirit from the body. Only after the fever that leads to her intensely sexual affair with Massimo can Lucy recognize her own sensual fervor. She describes it to Massimo as an "*incendium amoris*" (205), a term from the fourteenth-century mystic Richard Rolle: "[Lucy] was hot, it was true, but this was no ordinary fever. She told [Massimo] a few stories of saints who evidenced unnaturally high temperatures; of one who when she drank water, was reported to emit a sound like sizzling coals while steam issued from her mouth and nostrils, and another, an Italian, whose temperature could not be recorded because he routinely burst thermometers" (205). Tellingly, Lucy hales from Concord, Massachusetts, home of America's romantics, the transcendentalists. Like Ralph Waldo Emerson and Henry David Thoreau, she now finds the spiritual in the material, God in nature, including the body.

But if one is not a saint, or even a martyr to social conventions like James's and Wharton's heroines, modern life can seem banal and boring, leading to the seductions of gothic melodrama that Martin parodied in her second novel, *Alexandra* (1979). In *Italian Fever,* Martin's paradigm is Jane Austen's comic gothic, *Northanger Abbey* (1817), in which the ordinary but charming Catherine Morland becomes an avid reader of gothic romances. When she is invited to stay at Northanger Abbey, the home of the young man, Henry Tilney, with whom she is forming a mutual attachment, she concocts a story of gothic horror about the Tilney family from her own imaginings and is proven, to her great embarrassment, quite wrong. Catherine is not raped, immured in a convent, or killed, but learns to control her imagination and marries the sympathetic and wise Henry Tilney.

Unlike Austen's Catherine, who finds a male savior, Lucy, as is typical of Martin's female protagonists, must learn to save herself or perish, at least spiritually, if not physically. Her story begins like that of Catherine Morland: Lucy Stark considers herself a practical and sensible young woman, but is similarly bored by the quotidian and imagines that DV's landlords, the aristocratic Cini family, are quite sinister and may be responsible for the disappearance of DV's lover, Catherine Bultman, and even for DV's sudden death. Lucy finds the Cini scion, Antonio, particularly cold and creepy. She, like Austen's comic heroine, becomes disabused of her extravagant suspicions: Catherine Bultman is alive and thriving in Rome; a drunken DV accidentally fell into a septic tank and drowned; and Antonio becomes Lucy's caring and discerning friend who, like Henry Tilney, helps free her from her delusions—though Martin feels no compunction to have Lucy marry Antonio in order to provide a happy ending; indeed, Martin's version of a comic ending is not the traditional one of marriage, but of the heroine's affirmed independence.

As Martin rewrites the stories of some of literature's most famous heroines, she is, of course, commenting on the greater freedoms and opportunities for women at the end of the twentieth century. Unlike the suicidal heroine of one of Martin's favorite novels, *Madame Bovary,* or that of Martin's fellow Louisiana writer Kate Chopin's *The Awakening,* or perhaps the young female suicide whose grave Lucy notices near DV's, Lucy Stark is not punished for her desires, sexual or imaginative, nor does she punish herself. She does not become mad, bad, or sad, but like Catherine Morland, wiser and more compassionate to others and to herself.

> She had not, as Massimo observed, really known all that much about what was "in" her character. And now she did. She sat under the stars on a perfect night, alone in a romantic setting, struggling to come to terms with this new view of herself, which allowed her, among other unthought-of liberties, to admit that she still longed for the embraces of a man she did not particularly like. Such wisdom as this led directly to cynicism; she recognized this possibility and set herself against it. She knew that when we prove small to ourselves, it is an easy matter to assume the world is smaller still. (239–40)

Lucy tries to find a middle ground, a happy medium, and she does not limit her quest to her relatively "small" personal realizations about romance, but continues to augment her "world" with large questions about art, death, and life.

For within the comic and pleasurable female bildungsroman of Lucy Stark's Italian adventures, Martin embeds deeply serious questions about the use of the imagination for good or ill, for both art lovers and artists. In the literary tradition of American innocents abroad, she sets her explorations of art in Italy, as did Henry James, who wrote in *Italian Hours* (1909): "how couldn't it be the very essence of the truth. . . . Italy is really so much the most beautiful country in the world, taking all things together, that others must stand off and be hushed while she speaks? Seen thus in great comprehensive iridescent stretches, it is the incomparable wrought *fusion*, fusion of human history and mortal passion with the elements of earth and air, of colour, composition and form, that constitutes her appeal and gives it the supreme heroic grace" (VII, K4854). The welter of culture that James calls "fusion" could also be termed "confusion." Martin, like Walter Inglis Anderson, the nature painter with whom Martin is in postmodern dialogue in *The Great Divorce*, suggests that the writer helps both nature and society "realize" a useful coherence or order among the welter, however temporary and tentative: that is the kind of metanarrative that Lucy Stark is seeking. As Linda Hutcheon puts it in her study of postmodern parody, "The local, the limited, the temporary, the provisional are what define postmodern 'truth'. . . . The point is not exactly that the world is meaningless . . . , but that any meaning that exists is our own creation" (43).

As Italy teaches Lucy Stark to distinguish the constructive from the destructive uses of the imagination, appearances from reality, Martin attempts to disentangle the uses and abuses of art, particularly the glamorous yet often pernicious myth of the romantic artist. Lucy devotes as much consideration to artists and their works as she does to saints because they have become more recent eras' models and martyrs, such as the romantic myth of the unappreciated artist starving in his garret like Chatterton. The artist suffers for humanity's redemption through truth, much as Christ and the saints sacrificed for mankind's salvation through grace. Also like saints, artists are supposed to be above mundane concerns; their art putatively takes precedence over the human claims of non-artists.

Martin punctures this myth through her references to a great artist who preceded the Romantics, Gian Lorenzo Bernini (1598–1680), originator of the baroque, and through some contemporary artists whom Lucy meets. Martin, through Lucy's encounter with Bernini's *Apollo and Daphne,* reveals that the legend of the romantic artist can be just as pernicious to women as any other patriarchal narrative. Lucy speculates about Daphne, and the model who sat for her: "Over every inch of her body he had lavished his miraculous attention. . . . And then, one day, he was finished with her" (187). Although Lucy is greatly moved by Bernini's works, she cannot accept the claim made by DV's former lover, the painter Catherine Bultman, that "an artist can't really care about anything but the work. The work comes first" (197). "Lucy sat in silence, considering the implications of this sweeping and grandiose statement. She was willing to admit that art must be a powerful calling, a vocation, like the religious life, but did it really release its disciples from the ordinary obligations of affection and trust? It was true that artists were often cads. Bernini was famous for his irritability and bad temper" (197–98). As she contemplates Catherine's artistic credo or artistic egotism, Lucy toys with the idea that art matters more than transient humanity because art can speak to humanity. "She had half-framed the thought that it didn't matter what Bernini was like, whether he was a saint or a monster—the agonized cry that filled the still and chilly air around the marble face of Daphne proved that he knew what it was to be betrayed. In that moment, Lucy had peered tremulously into a world where only art has value and no moral laws apply" (198). While with the distancing of the past, the figure of an artist like Bernini may have an attractive glamour, from contemporary artists Catherine and DV, Lucy learns that she *does* care if an artist is "a saint or a monster" as Martin continues to parody the trope of the romantic artist.

Thus far in her life, Lucy has chosen mundane practicality to evade a martyrdom to love, so she is initially captivated by a more active and glamorous counter-narrative of female vengeance in the person of Catherine when she first appears in a doorway "like the figure of a stained-glass saint illuminated by a sudden shaft of light" (165). Catherine, however, is much more "a monster" than a saint or avenging angel; she is a monster of selfishness, who resembles, physically and morally, similar characters in Martin's earlier works, Diana in *Alexandra* and Donna in *The Great Divorce:* "some beautiful animal, a thoroughbred horse, or a lion, something sudden, dangerous, and bursting with health and life" (165). Catherine also resembles another member of this Martin subspecies: the "fair," "fierce and merciless" (230) Elena who, during the Second World War, divided the Cini brothers because of their love for her. All of these women gain the love of men to the men's detriment just as Catherine's rejection leads to DV's death.

Lack of empathy characterizes Martin's leonine femme fatales and her failed artists. Like Bernini, Catherine can depict human suffering as in her sketch of a DV flayed open "from the neck to the abdomen" (48) with an understandably "agonized expression" (48) on his face. Unlike Bernini, however, Catherine did not depict DV's suffering through memories of her own, as Bernini "knew what it was to be betrayed" (198), but through her own betrayal of DV. Catherine exploited DV and then left him for a wealthy patron who set her up with her own gallery in Rome. Her sketch was not accurate at the time she made it; it was prophetic of DV's torments after she left him. Catherine would not admit her own selfish purposes, but justified herself by telling DV that she was leaving him because he was not a true artist. Except in the prescient sketch of the flayed DV, her art is as dishonest as she is, and Lucy realizes, "There was something academic about Catherine's painting. It was skillful, even facile" (234). Catherine's declaration that "I've never been in love" (197) explains her lack of depth; she cannot truly feel; she can only imitate a true artist's depictions of feeling. Ironically, what Catherine told DV about himself as an artist actually applies to her: "I told him he was a hack, a prostitute, that he should do something else, sell real estate, or just something useful, like gardening" (173). In a sense, Catherine murders DV with her words, instead of a gothic dagger, since she sets off the chain of events that leads to his death.

As Catherine resembles the magnificent and egotistical Diana of Martin's gothic parody *Alexandra,* so DV is a version of that novel's Claude, another male instead of a female as the overwhelmed gothic protagonist. Like Claude, DV is an older man dominated by a younger woman in an unfamiliar setting, abandoned by her, and irrevocably and fatally changed.

As part of the gothic spoof, DV is trapped in his Italian villa (by his inability to drive), is haunted by a ghost of a dead partisan (probably a living boar hunter), and meets an untimely end (in a septic tank). The reverse gothic in *Italian Fever* is clearly the subplot, not ostensibly the main plot as it is in *Alexandra*; the main plot here is what Lucy learns from this reverse gothic and the competing cultural scripts that surround her.

Italian Fever is also a tribute to another one of E. M. Forster's Italian novels, *Where Angels Fear to Tread* (1905), in which Forster rejects the sinister trappings of classic gothics set in Italy, like *The Monk* (1796) or *The Italian* (1797), in favor of a bracing, ironic, and sometimes grotesque realism. An English widow, Lilia Herriton, goes to Italy; marries a handsome younger Italian; becomes bored, neglected, and unhappy; and dies in childbirth. The lines from *Where Angels Fear to Tread* that Martin uses as the epigraph for *Italian Fever* are spoken by the widow's English brother-in-law, Philip Herriton: "'Let her go to Italy!' he cried. 'Let her meddle with what she does not understand!'" Like Forster's widow, DV goes to Italy; meddles with what he does not understand; suffers unrequited love, isolation, and ennui; and dies.

Through DV, Martin shows that even not very talented artists can learn from their art because they are creating their own stories to give their lives meaning; what differentiates the great from the mediocre is the ability to perceive truth in the welter of experience, not simply repeat cultural clichés. Early in the novel, Lucy notes with chagrin that in his latest manuscript "DV had gone Gothic" (11) with the ghost of a dead partisan haunting the writer-protagonist in his Tuscan villa, but she does not yet recognize the change from DV's earlier hackneyed work. DV has a resource that Lilia Herriton does not: he is an artist of sorts who sees his experiences as material for fiction, but what he writes before his trip to Italy is the male equivalent of the gothic potboiler for women.

> Under different names, in different settings, the narrators of DV's novels were all the same man: a self-absorbed, pretentious bore, always involved in a tragic but passionate relationship with a neurotic, artistic, beautiful woman, always caught up in some far-fetched rescue adventure, dipping occasionally into the dark underworld of thugs

and hired murderers, or rising to the empyrean abodes, the glitter-
ing palaces of the wealthy and the elite. The whole absurd mess was
glazed over with a sticky treacle of trite homilies and tributes by the
narrator to himself for being so strong and wise and brave when everyone around him was scarcely able to get out of bed. He was usually
a writer or a journalist; sometimes he traveled. When he traveled, he
was always recovering from an emotional crisis and he was always
alone. (10–11)

A bestselling author, DV writes the airport-novel version of an Ernest
Hemingway or Norman Mailer work: macho male for the masses. Although at his funeral Lucy smiles incredulously at his publisher's comparison of DV to Henry James (54), she discovers in Italy that DV and his
writing have changed for the better because DV has become interested in
something beyond himself: the Cini family's story of fraternal love and
betrayal in Italy during World War II in the town of Ugolino, a reference
to the treacherous Count Ugolino who was condemned to the circle of
political traitors in Dante's *Inferno*.

Through DV, Martin holds out the possibility of positive change
through authentic experience as opposed to experience filtered through
clichés. As DV's initials suggest, his story is a parody of Dante's *Divine
Comedy*, where *D*ante is guided by *V*irgil. Ironically, the end of DV's story
is the beginning of Dante's tale: DV loses himself in the dark wood, takes
the wrong fork, and dies, unlike Dante who is found and guided by Virgil. Yet DV did at least temporarily have his Virgil. "Gradually, with Antonio as his guide, DV had begun to imagine a world he knew nothing
about [the Cini family history]. . . . This was how he intended to get
Catherine back" (247–48); she was his muse, his Beatrice, however unworthy. DV's initials also evoke the Latin phrase Deo Volente, or "God
willing," which suggests that DV's art can improve when he lets go of his
own selfish will and lets himself sympathetically identify with other sufferers whose lives he cannot control.

Lucy proves that she has learned a similar lesson about empathy and
compassion when she can shed her dismissively judgmental attitude toward DV and tell herself a new story about him:

DV was not an artist—that was his tragedy—but did that mean he had no right to love beauty?

So Lucy came through jealousy and self-pity to a state of sympathetic identification with her dead employer. . . . Their situations were not dissimilar; they had both fallen in love with beauty, and beauty had briefly toyed with them. But beauty was inviolable, like great art; it both excited and resisted the passion for possession. That was why she always had the sensation that she could not break through Massimo's self-possession, and it was exactly that sense of exclusion that made their lovemaking so constantly tantalizing. Beauty is a cruel mother, Lucy thought sleepily. She draws us in and then rejects us. Irresistible, unobtainable. (213)

As this passage suggests, Martin uses art as a touchstone for character: both for what characters reveal about themselves through their responses to a work of art, and also to reveal what characters are capable of learning from art. For Martin, the ability to learn from art and from others may be what distinguishes gold from gilt. As American innocent abroad Maggie Verver smashes the gilt-covered ostensibly "golden bowl" in Henry James's *The Golden Bowl* (1904), recognizes her beautiful Italian husband Prince Amerigo for the flawed and bedizened object that he is, and continues their marriage, so Lucy can appraise Massimo for what he is worth. Unlike nineteenth-century Maggie Verver, twentieth-century Lucy moves on.

Knowledge about self and others, Martin suggests, is meaningful because it is dangerous, not in the sense of a gothic death, but as the death of comforting illusions. When Lucy compares Massimo's beauty to that of a work of art near the end of their affair, she is drawing her conclusion from her responses to the many works of art that she has viewed in Italy. Even at the beginning of her Italian sojourn, she recognized that art in Italy—"The Real Thing" (1892) in Henry James's phrase—is much more than a pleasant diversion; it can be a dangerous adventure: "Art in its home, she thought, at ease in its natural habitat. It was like encountering the tiger, seen previously stalking behind iron bars at a zoo, sleeping peacefully in its own lair" (16). In contrast, Lucy compares Massimo to a domestic cat (215, 216), and while he has furthered her self-knowledge, only her encounters with art, confrontations about life and death as with Henry James's "The Beast in the Jungle" (1903), can really awaken her.

Martin indicates how invaluable a moral touchstone art can be as Lucy learns to apply it to others and to herself. She has "mixed feelings about Caravaggio": "Those awful simpering boys, that boring fruit" (161). When she begins to fathom Catherine's true shallowness, "Catherine, Lucy recalled, was a fan of Caravaggio" (198). Lucy is equally, but oppositely, undeceived about Antonio Cini, who is not the "snake" (56) and "liar" (70) that she had presumed as part of her gothic fantasy about the sinister Cini family abducting Catherine and murdering DV. Antonio, like Henry Tilney in *Northanger Abbey*, is Lucy's true friend in that he reveals the truth to her. He informs her that Catherine is alive and in Rome; that his father, not himself, is Catherine's lover and patron; that Massimo schemes for money and social advancement; and that DV met his ignominious end in a septic tank. Of equal importance, Antonio talks with Lucy, authentically and self-revealingly, about art.

Antonio can discuss art truthfully with Lucy because he has put his own ego and aspirations aside and loves art for what it is, not for what he would like to be in its service. Although Lucy initially compares Antonio's stare to that of a cat (71), he is much more than a domestic feline since he is affiliated with larger cats such as the tiger of art: he carries a walking stick with the head of a leopard and asserts to Lucy that "the only novel worth reading in the last hundred years was Giuseppe Tomasi di Lampedusa's *Il Gattopardo* [*The Leopard*]" (70). In their clinging to the past, Antonio and his family resemble the decaying aristocrats in *The Leopard* (1958); Antonio tells Lucy, "The painters I admire have all been dead for five hundred years" (141). With a sort of tragic clarity, Antonio, like Lampedusa's Prince, can perceive the truth, though he feels himself powerless to change it or take an active part in the tawdry modern world. As his family name, "Cini," suggests, Antonio is reduced to "embers."

Although Antonio will never strike a blaze in this world, he contributes his warmth to a kindred spirit in need, as Martin presents him as the Virgil to Lucy's Dante. Neither is an artist in the aesthetic sense, but Antonio teaches Lucy to create her life as if it were a work of art. In addition to disabusing Lucy of her fantasies about DV's last days, he lends her his leopard-headed walking stick when she injures her ankle from a fall during her fever. He helps her move forward in an even more important way when he tells her the story of his youthful ambition. He aspired to be an artist, trained hard, and modeled himself upon Piero della Francesca, but renounced art as his vocation when he perceived that his work would never be more than "competent" (227) and "dead" (227), unlike the dead but living and risen Christ in Della Francesca's *The Resurrection,* which he takes Lucy to see. Through their conversation, Antonio helps Lucy formulate her own ideas about the relation of art to life for those who are not artists themselves. Lucy tells Antonio how she felt when she stood before Bernini's *Apollo and Daphne*: "I had the sensation—I think most people feel this in some way—that this statue was speaking somehow to me. To me personally. . . . But then I realized what a crass reaction that is. How dull and vain it is to think that I have anything to do with Bernini, or he with me" (220). Martin, however, does not dismiss Lucy's identification with the sculpture as trivial. In *The Great Divorce,* Martin explored the ways that, according to the artist Walter Anderson, nature needs the viewer in order to "realize" itself fully. Or, in the words of Robert T. Petersson, whose book on St. Teresa Lucy carries on the plane to Italy, "The way a painting or poem is perceived depends very much on the viewer's or reader's knowledge, memory, expectations, and personal predilections" (46), so that "the work of art is fulfilled by the beholder" (x).

Similarly, for Martin, great art requires an appreciative audience to realize meaning, though that meaning will change from viewer to viewer; and the viewer, like Lucy, also gains. For Lucy, the meaning of *Apollo and Daphne* enlarges her: "Because of him [Bernini] I can see a little, just a little, into the past, and I felt grateful to him, just for having lived, and that gratitude was so big, it was so strong, it made me sad. It brought tears to my eyes" (221). What makes Lucy sad is the realization of her own death: "'Because when we see something that stops us'—she paused, not liking the conclusion that beckoned at the end of her conjecture—'something that really holds us still, it reminds us how empty and short our lives are, and that is truly unbearable'" (222). This realization does not bring Lucy to despair, but strengthens her appetite for learning and life. As she tells Antonio a moment later when he asks her if she is hungry, "I'm always hungry, actually" (222).

Martin tests Lucy's resolve to live fully by presenting her with a gothic dilemma, a specter of art and death as manifested in the ghost of DV. Despite the view that Lucy shared with DV that "all notions of an after-life were wishful thinking" (54), she repeatedly experiences DV's ghostly presence in the villa where he lived and where she suffers her life-changing "Italian fever." While the early manifestations of DV's spirit through his voice and her sense that he is shaking her could be dismissed as delirium from her high fever, Lucy sees DV once more while fully recovered, calm and collected, as she prepares to leave the villa for her plane back to America. He is "ravaged almost past recognition" (256) as he sits at his table writing and reaches for a piece of paper that he has dropped. "He held her in his gaze for a moment with an expression of such mute and eloquent pleading that her fear evaporated and she understood he was incapable of harm. He was incapable of everything but suffering. And when she under-stood this, he released her. . . . Then he took up his pen again, bent over the table, and resumed the interminable labor of his composition" (257). He is the specter of the artist as one of Dante's eternally frustrated sinners in the *Inferno*. Lucy, in contrast to DV, can move forward as she rushes for the daylight and the front door: "It was behind her now, this thing, this horror, whatever it was; it was gone and she would never speak of it to anyone as long as she lived" (258).

Martin gives no explanation for this ghastly manifestation, but her reading in William James's *Varieties of Religious Experience* (quoted in *Salvation: Sketches from the Life of St. Francis*, 2001) suggests a hypothesis. Among many suppositions that William James considers about the na-ture of religious experiences, he posits that an individual's subconscious or subliminal need for change reaches a point where it can no longer be contained and manifests itself in some kind of dramatic or seemingly su-pernatural experience which then produces the change that the individual urgently needed. DV's ghost could be read as the manifestation of Lucy's need to put "behind her" (258) the seductive romantic illusions about suffering for love and suffering for art that killed DV so that she can continue to live and enjoy life.

Lucy can also be seen as a modern, secular, female St. Francis of Assisi who learns from her demons. In Martin's next book, *Salvation: Scenes from the Life of St. Francis,* she quotes St. Isidore of Seville's *Differentiae:* "Demons unsettle the senses, stir low passions, disorder life, cause alarms in sleep, bring diseases, fill the mind with terror, distort the limbs, control the way lots are cast, make a pretense of oracles by their tricks, arouse the passion of love, create the heat of cupidity, lurk in consecrated images" (113). St. Francis, in contrast, regards them more favorably: "Demons are God's constables. . . . Just as the *podesta* [magistrate], when someone offends, sends his constable to punish him, so God chastises and corrects those he loves through his police" (116–17). In *Salvation,* St. Francis believes that the demons have been sent to warn him against scandalizing his brethren by living relatively comfortably, instead of ascetically, in a tower provided for him by a cardinal. He "laughed" (117) and leaves the tower and its demons, saying, "Lo, demons have thrown me out of my cell" (117).

Italian Fever ends with Lucy thrown out of her "cell" of passions, delirium, fever, and messages in "consecrated illness" by her own guardian demon, DV. She, like Francis, rejoices in her expulsion as she watches the arrival of the car that will take her to the airport: "She was overcome with a powerful exultation. DV would be here forever, but she did not have to stay. '*Andiamo,*' she said, striding purposefully away from the house and down the drive to welcome her deliverer" (258). "Exultation" is another word for "ecstasy," but Lucy's ecstasy is not of the sexual or supernatural variety, but one of anticipation. "Andiamo" can be translated as "let's go" or "hurry up," but in the context of Martin's work, it can mean "I want to be set in motion." Lucy, like so many of Martin's female protagonists, keeps moving to avoid the suffering inherent in societal expectations of female passivity and paralysis as depicted in Bernini's Daphne or the many literary heroines to whom Martin alludes. Perhaps what Lucy anticipates so "purposefully" is her ability to compose her own life, make herself an artist of life. Motion is life and motion is also Lucy's "deliverer." "Deliverance" is another word for "salvation," which Martin explores in her next book about life, death, religion, and art, *Salvation: Sketches from the Life of St. Francis,* as she continues her colloquy with the varieties of the ecstatic experience.

8

Salvation: Scenes from the Life of St. Francis

THE ART OF LIFE AND DEATH

*V*alerie Martin's sojourn in Italy from 1994 to 1997 inspired two atypical works, the comic *Italian Fever* (1999) and what Martin terms a "biography," *Salvation: Scenes from the Life of St. Francis* (2001).[1] The respective protagonists, Lucy Stark and Francesco Bernardone (better known as St. Francis of Assisi), are both artists in life in that they come to regard the potential of their lives with the seriousness with which an artist confronts her or his canvas. In *Salvation,* Martin, an artist in words, uses the extremes of San Francesco's life to explore the relationship between the spiritual and the material. Reflection upon a life, like the contemplation of a work of art, evokes questions about how to live with, and despite, death's inevitability, questions that are the essential concerns of religion and philosophy. If in *Italian Fever* and many of Martin's other works, the magisterial influence of the novelist Henry James is manifest, in *Salvation,* his philosopher brother William James is a constantly hovering and inter-rogating presence. Through quotations and ideas from the latter's *Varieties of Religious Experience* (1902), Martin engages in postmodern dialogue with William James as well as with other writers and artists.

Salvation is not a conventional biography presenting detailed informa-tion in a chronological sequence of chapters from San Francesco's birth in 1181 through his death in 1226. As her "Notes" and "Sources" demonstrate, Martin performed the extensive research necessary for a conventional bi-ography, but *Salvation* is closer in many ways to her two well-researched historical novels, *Mary Reilly* (1990) and *Property* (2003). In *Salvation,* Martin uses her novelistic techniques to select and present her "Scenes":

---

1. Martin refers to *Salvation* on her website as a "biography" and that is also the clas-sification that her publisher put on the cover.

salient and representative incidents and characters in a vividly colored, aesthetically satisfying setting. Because there is relatively little documentation about San Francesco—and what does exist is often revised, contradictory, and speculative—Martin has the imaginative space to construct a thematically coherent interpretation of the saint's life. Also as in her historical fiction, *Salvation* is as much or more a commentary about contemporary life as it is about the Middle Ages.

Also unlike the usual biography, *Salvation* is not a sequence of chapters whose continuities are facilitated by transitions and foreshadowings. Instead, Martin presents for contemplation a series of discrete scenes, each of which could stand alone, as in the frescoes Martin so admired. She states in her introduction, "When I moved to Italy in 1994, I made it a practice to visit any church or monastery that was reputed to have good frescoes of San Francesco" (8). She was intrigued by the way the painters were "unconcerned with meaning, [as] they throw their energy into a personal vision, concentrating on atmosphere" (7). Martin's "scenes" stress atmosphere through her painterly use of color and detail, but unlike the frescoists, Martin is vitally concerned with meaning, as the order of her "scenes" indicates.

Strikingly unconventional for a biography is Martin's decision to present her thirty-one *Scenes from the Life of St. Francis* in reverse chronological order.[2] *Salvation* starts with Francesco's death and ends, not with his birth, but his rebirth, his conversion to the ascetic spirituality he regarded as his salvation. Martin regards Francesco's life as exemplary of an "extraordinary course that will result in a coherent and meaningful confrontation with one's own death" (13). Keeping death in the foreground "provides perspective, orders the chaos of experience, and is the proper object and goal of life" (13). As Ellen Babinsky notes, "To read Francis's story 'backwards' is to read his life well" (33).

The reverse chronological order is also a homage to "the cycle painted by Benozzo Gozzoli in Montelfalco," to which Martin says she was "particularly drawn" (8). Art historian Diane Cole Ahl explains the order of

---

2. The fact that there are 31 scenes may be chance or it may point to another "coherent and meaningful" artistic progression: the thirty-one parts of an octave in music.

Gozzoli's Franciscan cycle: "In contrast to many fresco cycles that begin at the top, the early scenes in the saint's life occupy the bottom tier with later events depicted in the upper registers. This 'ascending narrative' is a hallmark of Franciscan cycles. . . . As if to denote spiritual ascension, this narrative mode leads us from the unenlightened early life of the *poverello* [poor little man] to the upper register in which the Lord's will is served and his sanctity proven" (197). Gozzoli's cycle also manifests one of Martin's most cherished beliefs, "that the material and spiritual realms are intimately connected" (12) in that "the saint moves through a world that is both ordinary and magical" (8).

Like William James, Martin does not proffer an explanation for the connection between the "ordinary" and the "magical," the material and the spiritual; also like James, she remains open to possibilities. For example, the reader is told nothing about how Francesco's stigmata appeared. On a mountain during a storm, Francesco is standing in the posture of the crucifixion, arms outstretched. When the storm is over, he is depicted as "absorbed in wrapping a few strips of wool he has torn from his breeches around the wounds in his bleeding feet" (71). Martin declares in her introduction, "I am not a believer in miracles; rather, I hold that the laws of nature apply even to those who know nothing about them" (13), but she seems to share Hamlet's belief that "there are more things in heaven and earth, Horatio, than are dreamt of in your philosophy" (*Hamlet*, I, 5, 166–67).

Several passages from William James's *Varieties of Religious Experience* are crucial to Martin's approach to the supernatural: "It is one of the peculiarities of invasions from the subconscious region to take on objective appearances, and to suggest to the Subject an external control" (K7045), so that for James, "Even the stigmata of the cross on Saint Francis's hands and feet may not be a fable" (K881), or, in James's sense, that the apparition of DV to Lucy in *Italian Fever* or Elisabeth and Lucy becoming leopards in *The Great Divorce* are not wholly fantasies. William James further speculates: "The whole drift of my education goes to persuade me that the world of our present consciousness is only one out of many worlds of consciousness that exist, and that those other worlds must contain experiences which have a meaning for our life also; and that although in the main their experiences and those of this world keep discrete, yet the two become continuous at certain points, and higher energies filter in" (K7138–39). Martin is similarly open to the unknown when she says, in her introduction to *Salvation*, "spirituality, by which I mean the apprehension of another (not necessarily an after-) life, offers egress from a prison" (13), and one such "egress" is death, which she places first, not last, in Francesco's life.

While the order of scenes in *Salvation* is both meaningful and effective, it presents difficulties for readers that a conventional biography would not. Reviewer Patrick Jordan comments that "Martin's time inversion forces her to run a two-page chronology before she even begins her introduction. It is a good thing, however, for readers will need to backtrack to the chronology repeatedly to reestablish their bearings" (25). Another reviewer, Geoffrey Moorhouse, speculates that Martin "wished to create suspense, starting with what everybody knows (that Francis was a fully certified saint) and working toward the much less familiar. In a sense, it is a progression from darkness to light, which is a very spiritual approach, and it is brilliantly done, even if the effect is sometimes puzzling" (13). Patrick Jordan considers the scenes a contemplative technique similar to "the Ignatian method of meditation. She [Martin] stares intensely at a scene, immersing herself in it fully, and suddenly she and the whole thing take flight" (25). Martin makes the reader work for insight, in a literary recapitulation of San Francesco's struggle for salvation, or Martin's version of Louisiana artist Walter Inglis Anderson's credo that the viewer helps "realize" the work of art (see chap. 6).

In *Salvation*, Martin chooses the technique that most effectively presents her themes, much as she would in fiction. But because *Salvation* is labeled a "biography," Martin is compelled to assist readers whose primary motivation is seeking information about St. Francis, not the pleasures of another masterful work by Valerie Martin, so she includes a chronology and an introduction, as well as notes and sources. Martin uses these factual aids as occasions for postmodern dialogue. For example, she prefaces each "scene" with an epigraph that highlights its possible meanings (functioning much like the inscriptions beneath the scenes in Gozzoli's Franciscan cycle), thus causing the reader to construct her or his own meanings.

Aficionados of Martin's fiction thus receive in this generic hybrid a figure, or meaning, which is much less hidden in the carpet than in her fiction because Martin here more explicitly invites readers into the dialogic construction of meaning. Although she asserts that "San Francesco's life . . . requires neither defense nor interpretation" (14), Martin boldly delineates her beliefs about life and about death in her introduction and illustrates them through her *Scenes from the Life of St. Francis.* By presenting these beliefs in fragmentary quotations and scenes, she challenges her readers to create their own meaningful narratives from them.

Martin is well aware that historical fiction is an implicit commentary on the present, and she strives to avoid creating a past that reinforces twenty-first-century complacency about progress. Her San Francesco is not the plaster saint surrounded by cute, Disneyesque small animals who presides over back gardens and veterinary hospitals. She does not include among her scenes the hackneyed portrait of St. Francis preaching to the birds. Instead, she stresses in her introduction, "He was not so much a nature lover (he was certainly neither an environmentalist nor a vegetarian) as a man who saw no distinction between himself and the natural world" (14). "Those who identify with nature must live with the consequences" is the line from artist Walter Anderson that serves as the epigraph to her novel *The Great Divorce* (1994). Martin vividly depicts these consequences as Francesco rolls naked in the snow (122) or stands with his hands outstretched on a mountain in a pelting rain (69–71), but she also shows Francis exhibiting his gratitude and respect for "Brother Body's" care of him by caring, however minimally and ascetically, for "Brother Body" ("Brother Body Wins the Day," 57–61). Martin's San Francesco is the antithesis of the late twentieth-century characters of *The Great Divorce* who, through all kinds of illusory thinking, try to evade the knowledge that they are a part of nature and consequently are mortal.

In *Salvation,* Martin excoriates a strategy to repress knowledge of death's inevitability: materialism, or the sense that what we own—money, possessions, real estate—will somehow save us from nature and death. She portrays a San Francesco who not only gives away all his possessions, to the point of standing naked in the street, but who remains wary of the human tendency to covetousness. He renounces a sheepskin to which he had clung when running away from a fire (110–11), for Francesco recognizes the addictive allure of possessions. As he tells a young friar on another occasion: "If you have a psalter . . . then you will want a breviary. And when you have a breviary, you will sit in your stall like a grand prelate and say to your brother, 'Hand me my breviary'" (97). As Martin comments to an interviewer about St. Francis, "The more I found out about him, the more he interested me because he was obsessed with something that I was becoming obsessed with, which is how, when you own something, it owns you" (Biguenet Interview 53).

More striking than Francesco's positive example are the negative examples of other people regarding themselves and others as material objects or commodities. A "grand prelate" such as Pope Innocent is seen in life as "a small mound of gold, brocade, and jewels" (166), whose body after death is abandoned as "rotting flesh" (183) and a "naked corpse" (183). Francesco himself was posthumously in danger of becoming not only a "grand prelate" but also a commodity. Martin depicts the efforts of Francesco's brethren to protect the saint's body from avid relic hunters and from the rivalry of cities for possession of his corpse ("On His Death"). This ownership of a human being is foreshadowed early in Francesco's life (hindsight in Martin's narrative order) when his father resolves that "he will lock up his wayward son, just as he locks up his grain, and his bolts of fine linen, wool, and silk, and his house and all his furniture and everything that is his" (213).

"The St. Francis book was the beginning of my own preoccupation with property, which carried me through several books," Martin noted to an interviewer (Biguenet Interview 53). One such chilling classification of people with inanimate objects is the subject of Martin's next novel, the aptly titled *Property* (2003), as illustrated through slavery in the American South, but Martin does not see such soulless materialism as safely in the past. In modern Assisi she finds "hundreds of shops selling all manner of atrocious trinkets" (4), a city ruled by the "cold, relentless, insatiable, furious spirit of commerce" (4). With William James, she views this materialism as rooted in fear, the seeming vulnerability of the body without its fortress of possessions. As James puts it, "it is certain that the prevalent fear of poverty among the educated classes is the worst moral disease from which our civilization suffers" (K5053), so that "we have grown literally afraid to be poor" (K5036). In Martin's words: "The connection between destitution and virtue is largely lost upon us now, especially, it seems to me, in America, where poverty is so clearly unconstitutional that we once declared war upon it" (12). The modern crusade for prosperity replaces the medieval crusade for the Holy Land, but the zeal for possession remains constant.

Martin sees the life-affirming religious spirit as too readily calcified into property in the form of religious institutions. The scene "A Convocation of Friars" is preceded by this epigraph from James's *Varieties of Religious Experience*:

> A genuine first-hand religious experience . . . is bound to be a heterodoxy to its witnesses, the prophet appearing as a mere lonely madman. If his doctrine appears contagious enough to spread to any others, it becomes a definite and labeled heresy. But then if it then still prove contagious enough to triumph over persecution, it becomes itself an orthodoxy; and when a religion has become an orthodoxy, its day of inwardness is over: the spring is dry; the faithful live at second hand exclusively and stone the prophets in their turn. (quoted in *Salvation* 169)

A mere decade after founding his ascetic order, Francesco hurls the tiles from the roof of a house in which some members of his order live. As "he pulls up and smashes the hard, cold evidence that his bright dream has ended" (173), he chants, "We do not live in *houses*. We do not live in *houses*" (172). The bishop then reproaches him for "destroying the property of the Commune" (173).

A "legion of humorless administrators" (170) like the bishop, who put property before spirituality, is epitomized in *Salvation* by Francis's early colleague, then nemesis, the "reptilian" (144) Brother Elia. The Fratres Minores that Francesco founded on principles of extreme asceticism are to Elia a means of advancement, power, and comfort under the guise of imposing bureaucracy for the order's own good. Before taking over the order, Elia announces Francesco's death in a letter to the Fratres Minores depicting paradise as a celestial bank: Francesco "went away to the market of heaven, carrying with him a purse full of money (his merits)" (34). Martin presents Elia as a Judas-figure to Francesco's Christ. Francesco had recognized Elia's true character early in their association. In the scene "A Friar Damned," Francesco had refused to look at Elia, ostracizing him before the Fratres Minores, because "it has been revealed to me that you are damned" (102), and only after copious tears and pleadings from the rejected Elia will Francesco consent to pray for him (103).

As William James characterizes it, "The saintly temper is a moral temper, and a moral temper has often to be cruel. It is a partisan temper, and that is cruel" (K4686). Francesco's cruelty to Elia is further explained by the scene's epigraph, once again from *The Varieties of Religious Experience.*

> When the craving for moral consistency and purity is developed to this degree, the subject may well find the outer world too full of shocks to dwell in, and can unify his life and keep his soul unspotted only by withdrawing from it. That law which impels the artist to achieve harmony in his composition by simply dropping out whatever jars, or suggests a discord, rules also in the spiritual life. . . . So monasteries and communities of sympathetic devotees open their doors, and in their changeless order, characterized by omissions quite as much as constituted by actions, the holy-minded person finds that inner smoothness and cleanness which it is torture to him to feel violated at every turn by the discordancy and brutality of secular existence. (Quoted in *Salvation* 99)

The same need for purifying omissions that causes Francesco to reject materialism makes him also refuse to acknowledge the existence of a human being who might threaten his purity, much like the postulant nun Claire who is the title character of Martin's *A Recent Martyr*. In other words, Francesco and Claire create the stories or versions of themselves that they need and then defend these versions to the detriment of the needs and feelings of others—in Francesco's case, especially at the expense of women. For Martin, the greatest example of such a rejected threat to Francesco's chosen life narrative is Santa Chiara, or St. Clare of Assisi, founder of the order of the Poor Clares.

Through Chiara, Martin depicts the way that a woman can success-fully evade a number of patriarchal plots, only to be snagged by the most alluring one, romantic love. Chiara is a rebellious young woman who "refuses to marry anyone, refuses to live at home, refuses the established convents, refuses to eat" (192). When she escaped from her home to be-come an ascetic, "Chiara felt her heart throbbing with the joy of the es-cape, and the wide prospect of liberty" (188). She believes that she and other women will "live as the brothers do, to walk with them into the towns, preaching and begging, or they will live among the lepers and the sick and nurse them" (190). The Church, however, will only permit female asceticism in the confinement of a cloistered convent with prayer as the Sisters' sole means of changing the world. "The heady joy of flight has passed, and Chiara has plummeted back to earth like a wounded dove, struggling all the way" (190). As the first epigraph to "On the Poor Ladies" suggests, the initial crippling of Chiara's aspirations comes from patriar-chal misogyny in that the Church "Fathers were inclined by experience to anti-feminism" (187), as Carrolly Erickson asserts in *The Medieval Vision* as quoted by Martin.

While such misogyny is certainly real, Martin indicates that at least part of the problem is Chiara's internalization of a subordinate role through her romantic hero-worship of Francesco: "She will follow his way, take his rule as her own, and she will be answerable to no judgment but his" (190). The narrative voice inquires, "Does she imagine that she will see him often thus, leaning in her window [at the convent] in the soft morn-ing light?" (192). This Juliet-like hope is also disappointed since Chiara sees Francesco only once more before he dies. When she hears that Francis will visit her convent, "Chiara was nearly transported by this news" (194) because "she has so much to show him, to tell him, about the progress of their order and about the interior of her own well-scoured soul" (195). The much-anticipated encounter is unsatisfactory and scanty:

> He bends upon her a look of such affection and tenderness that her heart expands in the warmth of it. "How beautifully you have kept it all," he says.
> But the moment is fleeting. (196)

Instead of the personal attention that Chiara so desired, Francesco preached a sermon to the Poor Ladies in which he "said what he thinks the Poor Ladies need to hear" (198), using as his text a Psalm (chap. 51) in which David begs the Lord for purification after sex with Bathsheba, the wife of Uriah. As William James observes, "Only those who have no private interests can follow an ideal straight away" (K4389), and Francesco wants to reject any occasion of sin. While the other Poor Ladies cry and implore the Lord for deliverance, Chiara "does not call upon God to save her" (198). Neither male, God nor saint, truly cares for her as an individual; in the highest reaches of the religious spirit there seems to be no place for love as humans know it.

Martin suggests, though, that the sense of a shared humanity, subject to nature and death, does have a place in counteracting cruel scripts of religious purity. Francesco leaves the convent, but brother Elia, who has brought a chicken for the Poor Ladies' dinner, remains. Francesco, the heroic ascetic, regards Chiara as a potential pollution; the "damned" Brother Elia is willing to visit and share; yet between them nothing feeds Chiara's need for love. Martin hints at an admirable and admirably human stance between that of the renunciatory Francesco and the grasping Elia, both of whom are selfish and egotistical in their very different ways. When Chiara views Francesco's corpse, she kisses "the wound," the stigmata, on his palm and "tastes the dried blood liquefying in her tears" (204). Brother Leone has had a similar experience while tending the wounds of the living Francesco, "and it seems to him that his whole body and soul are bathed and refreshed in this blood" (82) from the stigmata.[3] This scene, "Brother Leone Is Transported," is introduced by an epigraph from *The Ascetical Works of St. Basil:* "Charity seeks not her own; but the solitary life removed from all others only has one aim, that of serving the ends of the individual concerned . . . if you live alone, whose feet will you wash?" (79). Martin suggests that the real *via salutis* may be the love for another human being that tries to alleviate her or his suffering. This theme of a compassionate community runs through many of Martin's works from the

3. The scenes may be suggested by Margaritone of Arezzo's fresco of *St. Francis Kissing the Feet of Christ,* in which blood streams from the wounds on Christ's feet onto St. Francis (Frugoni 172–73, 190).

assistance for the quarantined victims of the plague in *A Recent Martyr* to Mary's tending of Dr. Jekyll in *Mary Reilly* to Massimo and Antonio's very different ways of caring for Lucy Stark in *Italian Fever.*

This realization of the love of God through the love of fellow humans is only made clear to the reader at the end of Martin's book, which is the beginning of Francesco's story. As Patrick Jordan states, "Arriving at the final episode—Francis's youthful embrace of a leper—one is suddenly hit by a sense of all that motivated and preceded it (that is, what historically followed it). What had seemed obscure and viewed from afar finally becomes illuminated from within" (25). In the last lines of the book, the reader and Francesco experience what Jordan calls "a compelling sense of the whole" (25):

> Tenderly he takes the leper's hand, tenderly he brings it to his lips. At once his mouth is flooded with an unearthly sweetness, which pours over his tongue, sweet and hot, burning his throat, and bringing sudden tears to his eyes. These tears moisten the corrupted hand he presses to his mouth. His ears are filled with the sound of wind, and he can feel the wind chilling his face, a cold harsh wind, blowing toward him from the future, blowing away everything that has come before this moment, which he has longed for and dreaded, as if he thought he might not live through it. . . . Then the two men clutch each other, their faces pressed close together, their arms entwined. The sun beats down, the air is hot and still, yet they appear to be caught in a whirlwind. Their clothes whip about; their hair stands on end; they hold on to each other for dear life. (241)

The seizing of the leper's wounded hand recalls for the reader, and prefigures for Francesco, Chiara's and Leone's embraces of Francesco's stigmata. Such weeping as Francesco's over the leper William James finds typical of conversion experiences: "Our tears broke through an inveterate inner dam, and let all sorts of ancient peccancies and moral stagnancies drain away, leaving us now washed and soft of heart and open to every nobler leading" (K3668). After such a melting and cleansing experience, James notes, "With most of us the customary hardness quickly returns, but not so with saintly persons" (K3668), and it is not so with Francesco, who constructs his "dear life" (241) from this moment.

Martin asserts that Francesco's "great work, as much a work of art as the many paintings and statues that celebrate it, was his life" (14). In her introduction to *Salvation,* Martin reveals her "lifelong interest in hagiography" (8), a curiosity that stems from the affinities she perceives between saints and artists, such as the need for an ascetic or undistracted life. In her introduction to *Salvation,* Martin discloses that she "had for many years a framed detail of the [Il Sassetta's] panel entitled *The Mystical Marriage of St. Francis* over my desk; it shows St. Francis exchanging wedding rings with Lady Poverty, a pretty barefoot girl with a wooden yoke over her shoulders. (I thought, as a young writer, I might profit from a daily colloquy with this lady.)" (8). Like saints, artists must remain mindful of the fact that there is much more to life than materialism.

Saints and artists also present carefully constructed lives for meditation and for possible emulation. The emotions and reflections that such "Scenes from the Life" evoke from their audience can "set in motion" potentially life-altering actions, as Martin herself experienced as she contemplated various frescoes of St. Francis's life: "The ragged beggar cried out to me: This is what I made of my life! Now go out and change your own!" (14). Martin, with St. Francis, suggests that through creative and life-enhancing uses of our imaginations, we can be the artists of our own lives if we resist the confining clichés of *Property,* the title and subject of her next novel.

9

Property

THE OWNER OWNED

*F*rom *Salvation: Scenes from the Life of St. Francis* (2001) to the Orange Prize–winning novel *Property* (2003), Valerie Martin's exploration of the pernicious effects of materialism swings from one extreme to the other, from a saint trying to found an ascetic order with no property to a society, the antebellum South, that is based on the tenet that human beings can be property. In *Salvation,* Martin demonstrated the results, not entirely salubrious, of the striving for purity without possessions; in *Property,* she emphasizes the consequences of ownership on the owners, a detriment less obvious than the indefensible suffering of the owned. To do so, she uses the methods of postmodern parody as part of the dialogue with the gothic that runs throughout her works, but Martin also returns to the South as a setting and to continue her dialogue with a range of southern fiction.

Martin formulates her own "southern gothic" as she sees the South as a gothic enclosure for women, white and black. As Teresa Goddu has aptly observed, "The gothic, like race, seems to become most visible in a southern locale. Indeed, the South's 'peculiar' identity has not only been defined by its particular racial history, but has also often been depicted in gothic terms: the South is a benighted landscape, heavy with history and haunted with the ghosts of slavery" (147). Martin clearly delineates her own nightmarish sense of slavery as southern gothic enclosure when she describes how the first sentence of *Property,* "It never ends," came to her on waking "from a bad dream":

> I got up and wrote it down. I had this feeling of dissatisfaction, and I thought—that's it. That's the voice. Very shortly, I realized it was, in fact, an interior monologue; it takes place inside the confines of the

narrator's skull. I wanted this novel to be intensely claustrophobic because everything I read about slavery, the institution, for everybody,
white, black, in between, the institution controlled them all. It was a
constricted and perverted world. It must have been like having your
head in a vice twenty-four hours a day. (Biguenet Interview 55)

Prison does not bring out the best in human beings, and like the cornered
rats of Martin's earlier fiction, the enclosed southerners, black and white,
respond with vicious defenses, even the seemingly sacrosanct southern lady.

Through her portrait of the southern lady, Martin achieves her most
important revision of not only southern gothic fiction, but also the caricature of the South in the national imaginary, As Tara McPherson explains
in *Reconstructing Dixie*:

> The region remains at once the site of the trauma of slavery and also
> the mythic location of a vast nostalgia industry. In many ways, Ameri-
> cans can't seem to get enough of the horrors of slavery, and yet we
> remain unable to connect this past to the romanticized history of the
> plantation, unable or unwilling to process the emotional registers still
> echoing from the eras of slavery and Jim Crow. The brutalities of those
> periods remain dissociated from our representations of the material
> site of those atrocities, the plantation home. . . . The white southern
> lady—as mythologized image of innocence and purity—floats free
> from the violence for which she was the cover story [lynching]. (3)

Martin associates the dissociated and anchors the southern lady to slavery through Manon Gaudet, a Louisiana plantation mistress who believes
herself enslaved in her marriage and in her social role of lady, but who,
unlike St. Francis, does not propose a revolution in society's tenets, nor
does she walk to her death in the sea like Kate Chopin's Edna Pontellier
in *The Awakening;* instead, she tries to beat white males at their own game
by espousing their values and their methods. She cannot understand that,
in the words of the twentieth-century African American poet Audre Lord,
"The Master's Tools Will Never Dismantle the Master's House."

If William James's speculations on the varieties of religious experience
were an important context for *Salvation,* William Faulkner's depictions

of the twisted lives of white southerners are the warp on which Martin weaves her tale of possession by possessions. She evokes some of Faulkner's greatest works—*The Sound and the Fury* (1929), *Absalom, Absalom!* (1936), and *The Bear* (1942)—as she delineates the psychological contortions necessary to live in intimate daily contact with human beings who cannot be acknowledged as fully human. Although Martin rivals Faulkner in her thematic complexities, she does not emulate his convoluted, though rich, rhetoric. *Property* is deceptively simple and easy to read: a clear and readily comprehensible account by a single narrator over a short span of time. It is a tribute to Martin's technical mastery of point of view and her pellucid style that she can suggest the profound and complex stories of other characters and times, as well as the complex literary history of the South, through the single and singular narration of Manon Gaudet.

Property evokes some of the major genres of and about the South: plantation fiction like *Gone with the Wind* (1936) and its nineteenth-century predecessors; anti-plantation or anti-slavery fiction such as *Uncle Tom's Cabin* (1852); a number of slave narratives, particularly that of William and Ellen Craft (1860); neo-slave narratives like Toni Morrison's *Beloved* (1987); the plantation diary of a slave owner, Bennet H. Barrow's (not published until 1967); Willa Cather's *Sapphira and the Slave Girl* (1940); Kate Chopin's *The Awakening* (1899); and a hybrid Caribbean novel, Caryll Phillips's *Cambridge* (1981), which includes the narratives of a white plantation mistress and a black male slave who are both destroyed by the slave system.[1] The novelty and horror of Martin's novel arises from the

---

1. One reviewer, Maya Jaggi, finds *Property* "neither wholly original nor wholly convincing" and believes that "the similarities with Phillips's novel are sometimes troubling" (27). The main similarity is that both novels show white women as willfully blind to the injustices of the slavery system. *Cambridge*'s Emily Cartwright, with some abolitionist sympathies, is newly arrived from England at her father's Caribbean plantation so that much of her narration is a detailed description of the novelties of plantation society, including whipping. Manon Gaudet's account leaves out all such explanatory material since Martin's theme is that Manon, like others raised in the slave system, is so inured to it that she sees nothing worth describing ethnographically. Emily becomes the mistress of the plantation overseer, who had previously had a sexual relationship with an *obeah*, a conjure woman named Christiana, who becomes unbalanced in her jealousy of Emily. This "triangle" is not considered important by Emily, who rarely sees Christiana, while Manon is tormented by Sarah's constant presence as her lady's maid.

reader's gothic imprisonment through restriction to Manon's calloused and willfully limited perspective.

Interestingly, an important negative text for Martin's postmodern parody came from Martin's reading of Toni Morrison's exploration of race in American literature, *Playing in the Dark* (1992). Morrison attributes the failure of *Sapphira and the Slave Girl* to Cather's "struggle to address an almost completely buried subject: the interdependent working of power, race, and sexuality in a white woman's battle for coherence," so that "the real fugitive, the text asserts, is the slave mistress" (K335–340). These comments by Morrison led Martin to read *Sapphira* and conclude: "It was very useful in a cautionary sense. When I read it, I thought, No, I don't want to do that. It wasn't that it wasn't good, but I just didn't want to do that" (Biguenet Interview 54). And Martin didn't "do that," namely, present and reify Cather's view of the slave mistress as victim of a system that existed for happy, childlike blacks (a view similar to Kate Chopin's in her extensive body of Louisiana fiction), but instead created her own genre within the context of southern fiction. In "Telling Forgotten Stories of Slaveries in the Postmodern South," Susan V. Donaldson explores the ways that *Property* can be considered historical fiction, postmodern fiction, and historiographic metafiction. These comparisons and classifications are apt and valid, but one could, in addition, argue that Martin is creating her own genre here: the ascetic feminist novel by negative example. An intelligent, discerning, dryly witty woman becomes a simplistic fiend as her patriarchal and materialist society progressively cripples her consciousness, puts blinders on her perceptions, and deadens her recognition of irony. As in *Mary Reilly*, a complex Dr. Jekyll is reduced to the monster Mr(s). Hyde.

Martin provides the context for her ascetic feminist tale by evoking the ways that southern culture became barrenly inhumane in its defensive obsession with retaining slaves as property. In this understated novel, Martin does not provide us with a foreground of horrific whippings, backbreaking labors, and dismemberments. Instead, she shows—as does Frederick Douglass in his *Narrative* (1845) of his life as a slave—how even relatively mild slave owners who consider themselves beneficent can become self-deceiving brutes. This comparatively temperate experience is in some ways more chilling to readers than repeated depictions of gruesome violence since most of us prefer to believe that we could never act like that, and so we can be lured into empathizing with the "benevolent" slave owners as we would not with the overtly monstrous, much as readers do with Margaret Mitchell's lastingly popular novel and the resultant film *Gone with the Wind* (1936; 1939, respectively). The horror here is that readers can empathize with the corruption of characters who would be considered reasonably pleasant, decent, and respectable characters in another social structure. As Kathryn Harrison observes, Martin "forces the reader into the complicity and discomfort of a voyeur" (10).

One of her methods is a parody of the ultimate gothic hero of southern fiction, Rhett Butler of *Gone with the Wind.* As the novel opens, Manon, from a distance and through a window, routinely watches her husband play sadistically erotic games with slave boys. The reader later learns that he has fathered two children by Manon's maid Sarah after selling away her first child, also selling the slave butler who was that child's father. Mr. Gaudet is not insensitive in every circumstance. He does not want to have sex with Manon when she drugs herself into a state of insensibility before the act: "I've not much interest in making love to a corpse" (56). In this respect, Mr. Gaudet's attitude can be compared to that of the morally ambiguous Rhett Butler rejecting sex with his equally self-contradictory wife, Scarlett. Rhett saves Scarlett from burning Atlanta but abandons her to join the Confederate army, ostensibly due to his love of the South, but possibly for fear he would miss a good fight; Scarlett is left to, somewhat improbably, save herself from both armies and various marauders. In a more plausible reversal, after escaping from the plantation during a slave revolt, Mr. Gaudet returns to save Manon but dies in the attempt, leaving her to escape the enraged slaves on her own. Martin, through Mr. Gaudet, gives us the darker half of the southern gentleman as the leader of an often-crumbling slave system that Mitchell only suggests through Rhett as a titillating "bad boy" imbued with the glamor of the Lost Cause. Eschewing Mitchell's romantic trappings, Martin shows that while Mr. Gaudet may not be entirely bad or self-centered, he is, like his wife, desensitized by the slave system. Unlike Mitchell, Martin leaves room for the reality of ambiguity.

As is characteristic of Martin's postmodern dialogues and her complex analyses of human motivations, Mr. Gaudet's seemingly altruistic actions can also be read simultaneously as evidence of his egotism (she should at least pretend that she likes it) and an attempt to retain a valued possession (the slaves cannot have my pretty, elegant wife). Manon's treatment of her husband can be seen as justifiable repugnance and an independent spirit, while concurrently, as for reviewer Kathryn Harrison, "overtures that Manon rejects as self-serving might also be interpreted as clumsy attempts at showing affection. In any case, the bedroom scenarios Manon presents damn her more than they do Mr. Gaudet" (10). To Martin, a character can be at once selfish and compassionate: Mr. Hyde remains one with Dr. Jekyll, and no simplistic judgment is possible. As she states in an interview, novelists are "not trying to create models for people to live by, but to try to understand why all human character is flawed" (McHenry Interview).

Ownership promotes sins of omission as well as commission; some are simply so cocooned in comfort that they cannot recognize the true nature of the perverted system that provides their materialistic pleasures as it warps their capacity to benefit from the higher fellowship of equals. The neighboring plantation master, Joel Borden, is too busy enjoying himself in New Orleans with his quadroon mistress to ensure the welfare of his plantation slaves. Mr. Gaudet tells Manon that Joel "doesn't half-feed his negroes and his overseer is the meanest man on earth" (10). As in her early works, Martin stresses the way ostensibly pleasurable sexual games can mask a pattern of cruelty and neglect, but, like Mr. Gaudet, Joel Borden is not an unmitigated villain. He is charming to ladies, a favorite of Manon and her mother, who "wanted Joel to marry me," Manon relates, "though we all knew it was impossible because Joel needs money and I have none" (25). After Mr. Gaudet's death, Joel begins to court Manon, ostensibly a well-off widow, but backs off to pursue an heiress when he learns of Mr. Gaudet's debts. Manon concludes, "It seemed that happiness must always be just beyond me and I should always stand gazing at it as through a shopwindow where everything glittered and appealed to me, but I had not enough money to enter. It was money, only money, that would keep Joel from ever being more than my friendly admirer" (148). Manon's observations are astute in a society based on property, but she fails to realize that she would not have found "happiness" with Joel, any more than she had with her husband, because none of them understand that "happiness" evaporates when equated with possessions; an exalted human emotion is ironically devalued and diminished when Manon and Joel think that it can be bought.

Like many of Martin's female protagonists, especially the title character of *Mary Reilly*, Manon tries desperately to maintain her belief in an ultimately benevolent patriarchy by creating an idealized father for herself, thus making her sadistic husband only an aberration, not the ineluctable product of the slave system. Manon idolized her father and believed that he was "strong, loving, stern, and fair" (23), in other words, somehow uncorrupted by owning slaves. Because he used "the whip sparingly" (22), Manon considers him a good master. She approvingly cites his system for runaways: he did not assign a number of lashes corresponding to the length of time they were missing, but nonviolently sold them immediately (128–29). Manon is incapable of perceiving that separation from home, family, and friends could be a far worse punishment than a whipping. Her father also did not permit a slave to "marry off the farm" (21), visit other farms, or have an individual garden plot: the slaves are possessions and can own neither themselves nor a few vegetables; they must constantly recognize that they owe everything to their owner. Manon cannot see that her father's "benevolent" treatment of the slaves resembles society's "protection" of white ladies: all are gothic prisoners, no matter how relatively pleasant the enclosure.

Like Elisabeth in *The Great Divorce*, Manon is mainly bereft of female mentoring and thus seems incapable of appreciating or using it on the rare occasions she gets it. Her aunt, Mrs. Gray, tries to tell Manon the truth about her father in order to give Manon a more balanced view of her parents that would show her mother in a better light. After the death of Manon's two small brothers in an epidemic, her father, according to Mrs. Gray, "became obsessed with the negroes. . . . He wrote treatise after treatise on the management of the negro. . . . He seemed to think somehow he was going to make the negroes believe he was God and his farm was Eden, and they'd all be happy and grateful, which, you know, they never are" (174–75). Her father ceased to have sexual relations with her mother because he "decided to have no more children" (175), according to Manon's aunt, who tells her that "your mother came to feel your father cared more about the negroes than he did about his family" (175). He becomes like Ike McCaslin in Faulkner's *The Bear,* who after reading of his grandfather's incest and miscegenation in the plantation ledger, relinquishes the plantation in favor of his maternal cousin; eventually drives off his uncomprehending and resentful wife; and chooses to live celibate and without heirs. Although Ike is sustained to old age by his connection with the wilderness beyond society's corruptions, Manon's father has no comparable consolations, not even Manon and her mother, and follows his withdrawal from life to its logical conclusion: suicide. In his blind neglect of the women nearest to him, he is an extreme version of Andre Davillier, the plantation owner in *The Great Divorce* who is proud of "his system for managing slaves which he thinks is benevolent and efficient" (255–56), but who will not attempt to alleviate the misery he sees in the deterioration of Elisabeth, the mistress of a neighboring plantation, at the hands of her brutal husband.

Manon, too, resembles Ike McCaslin in that she discovers the truth about her paternal heritage by reading old documents: "I thought of his [her father's] journal, those banal entries about cotton and weather and disease, and no mention of me, as if I didn't exist, or he wished I didn't" (181).[2] She now regards her father as an "impostor" (181) and "Hypocrite" (182): "My aunt was right, he was obsessed by the negroes, he wanted them to admire him, to adore him, and my mother was right as well; they had killed him" (182). Manon is consumed with jealousy that she did not "own" her father's attention the way that the slaves paradoxically did; he possessed her admiration and adoration, but he did not value them. Manon can see neither that her father was destroyed by the hopeless effort

---

2. Bennet H. Barrow's plantation diary is Martin's "inspiration" (McHenry) for Manon's father, and Martin cites it in her acknowledgments. In an interview, she comments on his "distinctive management system of slaves," which in details is quite close to that of Manon's father. Martin also finds Barrow, like Manon's father, deeply concerned about his slaves: "There was no doubt in [my] mind that he knew that these black people were human, because they are constantly on his mind" (McHenry).

of making a materialistic system into a spiritual good nor that her love for her father had deteriorated into a struggle to possess him as her exclusive property.

Manon has learned from the examples of white women of her own class to treat marital love and husbands as property for which they compete with the blacks whom they legally own. Manon remembers her mother's strategically subservient advice to follow her example and "show more warmth to my husband even if I do not feel it" (58). Manon's mother may be hoping that Mr. Gaudet might emulate Mr. Perot, a member of their social circle who "at last acceded to his wife's wishes" (162) by renouncing his "yellow" (162) mistress, whom Manon finds "impressive" (161) as she storms Mrs. Perot's drawing room in protest at her rejection. In her intelligence, her speech, and her self-possession, Mr. Perot's mistress makes Manon uncomfortably cognizant of her own husband's coerced mistress, Sarah, and of the quadroon whom Joel Borden keeps. Consequently, Manon can only feel "sick with the recollection of this vengeful madwoman" (161), who, like Sarah, can act angrily and decisively for herself in a way that Manon has been taught is impossible for her as a lady.

Manon's aunt retains her proprietary interest in her husband through covert stratagems, not overt protest, and in this acts like slaves who must silently maneuver because they know the brutal consequences of open revolt. She gives Sarah to Manon as a "wedding gift" (19) when her husband "lost his head when a free man of color [Mr. Roget] offered to buy Sarah so that he might free her and marry her" (19). Mr. Gray re-asserted his ownership when he "had Sarah tied up in the kitchen and whipped her himself" (19). With a selfish denial of female fellowship, Manon's aunt has passed the attractive Sarah to Manon, precipitating the conflict between Manon and her husband. For Mrs. Gray herself, the result of her strategic deployment of Sarah is this scene of apparent domestic warmth that Manon witnesses during a card game: "My aunt took a card and sighed. Uncle Emile, resting his hand upon her shoulder, leaned down to whisper a word of advice into her ear. She smiled, adjusted her cards, then absently raised her hand to tap affectionately at his fingers. I looked away; it seemed such an intimate gesture I felt embarrassed to have seen it" (158). Manon cannot conceive that her aunt and uncle may still feel affection for each other because she is even more invested in questions of ownership than they are. She wants complete ownership of her husband, but above all, she wants to own herself freely and openly.

Manon sees a possible means to such independence in the example of Sally Pemberly and her husband: "She divorced him some years ago, because he was so cruel even the servants pitied her. He then ran up large gambling debts, bankrupting himself as well as his family. Sally sued to have her marriage portion, which was considerable, exempted from his creditors and restored to her. By some miracle, she had won. Now she has her own income and she is free of her detestable husband. Fortunate woman!" (44). Manon is so imbued in a system that equates identity with property that she can only see freedom as having her own property under her sole control. Consequently, she pursues the runaway Sarah "to recover what is mine" (171), unable to see that Sarah is her döppelganger, or double,[3] a more intensely enslaved version of herself.

Sally Pemberly is inspired by the famous New Orleans legend of Madame Pontalba. Her biography, *Intimate Enemies* by Christina Vella, is listed in Martin's "Acknowledgments" for *Property* (195). Baroness Micaela Almonester de Pontalba (1795–1874) managed to wrest from her husband and his grasping family some of the considerable property that she brought to her marriage. She then proceeded to make even more money through properties like the Pontalba buildings that she built on Jackson Square in New Orleans. As was the case with Manon, escaping her marriage crippled Baroness Pontalba, when, before her flight and the restitution of her property, her father-in-law shot her arm. Sally Pemberly, Madame Pontalba, and Manon can only buy their freedom with money after they are freed of husbands through widowhood or divorce, although they can never be freed of the maiming consequences of their marriages.

Although Martin focuses on the way that valuing humanity as property coarsens white sensibilities, male and female, she does not shy away from the ways that a brutal system can also make African Americans violent and hardened as they try to regain ownership of themselves. The

---

3. In an interview, Valerie Martin characterizes Sarah as Manon's double (S. Martin R3), as does Susan Donaldson (274).

Gaudets and their circle are constantly busy with fearing, thwarting, or putting down slave rebellions in which whites are killed. They listen avidly to tales of masters poisoned by their slaves, and Mr. Gaudet even suspects that Delphine, his cook, is trying to poison him (5). Mr. Gaudet does not die from what goes down his throat, however, but from the knife that slits it when held by one of the slave rebels who temporarily take over his plantation. Manon shows no emotion at this sight, but reacts quite differently when the rebels cut into her dining table while slicing a ham: "They've destroyed that table, I thought, which made me angry" (108). Some possessions are more valuable than others, and Manon shows no comprehension of the rebels' motivations in destroying property as they temporarily "steal" themselves and briefly stop being property.

The word "possessed" has another resonance in that Martin also demonstrates how the potentially "possessed" become "possessed" by the same values that oppress them. After Sarah takes advantage of the insurrection to free herself, Mr. Roget, a free man of color, provides her with the funds that she needs to escape to the North and again tries to buy her freedom, this time from the widowed Manon. "What possessed the man?" (170), Manon wonders, since she herself is now incapable of being possessed by love or of recognizing it in those she regards as beneath her. She is also irked by that fact that Mr. Roget is not "possessed" by a white person since she considers "free negroes . . . arrogant and supercilious" (155). When Mr. Roget entered Manon's parlor to make an offer for Sarah, "his eyes darted confidently over the cornices, the mantel, the baseboards then settled upon me with much the same quality of appraisal and assurance" (166), as if Manon were also property to be assessed. Manon speculates that he has performed a similar "appraisal" of Sarah for her value to his social ambitions: he wants "a wife lighter than he was but no free quadroon would have him" (167) and consequently attempts to buy Sarah for more than Manon thinks she is "worth."

In contrast to the timid and passive "slave girl" of Cather's *Sapphira*, Sarah may be seen as a piece of property by her Louisiana contacts, both black and white, but she displays considerable agency. She assists the slave rebels, points out Mr. Gaudet's location to them so that they can kill him, and escapes with her baby by pushing Manon away from the only available horse. Sarah even manages to make it all the way to the North with her baby before a slave hunter captures her in Philadelphia.

"But as any master-slave relationship illustrates," Kathryn Harrison points out, "victims have their own peculiar power, a forgiveness to withhold, a silence to impose: the currency of martyrdom" (10), the theme of female power through passivity that is so prevalent in Martin's early fiction. Sarah's character is strong enough even to serve as a model for Manon's behavior toward her husband. When on the Gaudet plantation, Sarah manipulates those around her with her silences.[4] Manon ironically imitates her when she looks at her husband "for a few moments blankly, without comment, as if he were speaking a foreign language. This unnerves him. It's a trick I learned from Sarah" (8). Manon is quite conscious of, and annoyed by, the fact that Sarah does not act like a piece of insentient property, but, indeed, has a sense of irony to match her own.[5] When Sarah escapes, she travels north in the guise of a white man called Maître ("Master" in English) and accompanied by a young female slave, as if she is mocking her former relationship with Mr. Gaudet.[6]

In Sarah and Manon's relationship, we see a mockery of maternal nurturing, whether from biological mothers or female mentors, that Martin believes so important to women's development amid patriarchal restrictions. When Sarah is captured and returned, she picks the very anecdote of freedom that would most enrage Manon: "When you gets to the North . . . they invites you to the dining room, and they asks you to sit at the table. Then they offers you a cup of tea, and they asks, 'Does you want cream and sugar?'" (192). Sarah is not only telling Manon that she too can be regarded as a lady, but she is also mockingly referring to the scene

4. In an unpublished essay, Alaina Kaus perceptively explores Sarah's skilled manipulation of speech and silence (Kaus).

5. Joyce Carol Oates believes that Manon is obsessed with Sarah in an erotic sense: "She is unwittingly in love with her servant Sarah" (139) and so her annoyance with Sarah stems from "thwarted passion" (139). Amy K. King also perceives the eroticism, but justly sees it based on power relations: "Manon feels pleasure not because she *shares* pleasure with another woman but rather because she *takes* it" (76).

6. Sarah's disguise may be inspired by the escape from slavery of William and Ellen Craft, which Martin cites in her acknowledgments. Ellen disguised herself as an invalid white man and William acted as her slave servant.

of degradation earlier in the novel when Manon sucks the milk from Sarah's breast, a scene reminiscent of Toni Morrison's *Beloved,* in which white boys similarly humiliate the slave Sethe. With the tale of the tea party, Sarah is telling Manon that she can be respected as a human being and offered milk, associated with maternal love and nurturance, instead of being drained like a domestic animal; she finds the taste of freedom as sweet as sugar.

Sarah's and the rebels' strong agency is quite different from the depiction of slaves in the nineteenth-century Louisiana tale embedded in Martin's contemporary novel, *The Great Divorce.* Elisabeth Boyer Schlaeger is also a plantation mistress in a loveless marriage, but with a much more brutal husband. He cripples Elisabeth's enslaved lady's maid, Bessie, whose name, a diminutive of Elisabeth, suggests that she is Elisabeth's döppelganger and foreshadows Elisabeth's destruction. Bessie is Elisabeth's wavering shadow, much more like the slave girl Nancy of Cather's novel, while Sarah is Manon's scheming and active döppelganger. Unlike Manon, Elisabeth is assisted, perhaps for monetary motives or perhaps coincidentally, by slaves. Her New Orleans hairdresser, a free woman of color named Lucinde, takes her to a voodoo priestess, Mambo Pitou, who may have conjured the leopard who tears out Mr. Schlaeger's throat. His death resembles that of Mr. Gaudet since both men have their throats lacerated, suggesting that their voices will no longer dominate (a reversal of the masochistic scenario in Martin's early novels in which the throats of women are menaced). Alternately, or additionally, Elisabeth is freed from her husband by their slave butler Charles, who lures the leopard into the house to end Mr. Schlaeger's cruelty and avenge Bessie, much as Sarah helps the slave insurrectionists into the Gaudet house. It is too late for Elisabeth, who by this point is quite mad and believes that she is the ravenous leopard. Similarly, Manon may be freed from her husband by his death, but the slave system has, physically and mentally, so crippled and scarred her that she is also somewhat mad, as obsessed with her leopard-like double, Sarah, as Elisabeth is with hers, the leopard.

The narrative mode is crucial to the variations of Cather's and Martin's novels upon the theme of slavery's effects. Cather's novel is told nostalgically from the point of view of an adult narrator who, as a child, heard the tale of Sapphira and her slave girl and seems to believe it had a happy ending since Nancy had a successful career as a housekeeper in the North; she cannot recognize the pain of Nancy's decades-long separation from her Virginia family. Elisabeth's tale is speculatively pieced together by a romantic and romanticizing twentieth-century historian, Paul Clayton, who probably wants to see slaves like Charles, who lured the leopard into the Schlaeger house to kill Hermann, as showing helpful affection to their relatively beneficent owners like Elisabeth. In contrast, Manon tells her tale as she lives it, without any softening by the mists of time and minus the sentimental lenses of plantation fiction in which slaves are devoted to their masters, as with the loyal bodyservant Sam in Thomas Nelson Page's "Marse Chan" (1884) or Mammy in Margaret Mitchell's *Gone with the Wind.* Sarah clearly does not feel self-sacrificing love and devotion toward Manon, and Manon knows it.

Yet despite her triumphs and her ironically self-possessed manner, Sarah, like all the other characters in the novel, is involuntarily and inevitably tainted by the violence and degradation of the slave system. Sarah is not content to escape during the slave insurrection, but makes sure her "owners" will be captured and presumably killed by the rebels, an understandable act of vengeance. More ambiguous, though, is her attitude toward her deaf son, Walter, who is also the son of Mr. Gaudet and has inherited his red hair and green eyes. At the time of the insurrection, Walter is seven years old and cannot speak except for a few phrases like "poo-poo," quite apt for the situation at the Gaudet plantation. He is hit across his head by the rebel captain shortly after another rebel characterizes him as "a little yellow monkey" (109), and then receives another shove of repulsion for his white blood from his mother. When Sarah is about to escape on the horse, Manon relates, "Walter collided with Sarah and clung to her skirt. I saw her face, her rage and desperation as she struggled to free herself. 'Let me go,' she cried, kicking the creature, who released her, wailing in distress" (114). Sarah leaves Walter behind, but takes her dark-skinned baby. Sarah can only see Walter as another vestige of her bondage by whites, a smaller and equally incomprehensible version of Mr. Gaudet and his repugnant embraces, from which she must "free herself" (114). She cannot see him as human, but only as a tool of slavery, another piece of property owned and used against her by Mr. Gaudet. Sarah's attitude is quite different from that of *Beloved*'s Sethe, who kills her child rather than let her be enslaved, or, at the other end of the spectrum, the title character of Kate Chopin's "Desirée's Baby," who kills herself and her child out of shame for their supposedly black blood; all are corrupted by slavery, including its victims like Sarah, Sethe, and Desirée.

Through Sarah, Martin is also raising some vexed questions about the nature of, and social expectations for, maternity. To what extent, is a child the "property" of the mother, to be disposed of as she will, and to what extent is the mother owned by the child in the sense that she is defined by her maternity (or lack thereof) and, if a mother, must she conform to the child's needs, not her own? What makes a mother: consanguinity, propinquity, or affinity? Who is the proprietor and who is the property? When is maternity a bond and when is it bondage? When is it nurturing and when is it noxious?

Both Sarah and Manon are largely defined by their ability to breed for the needs of the patriarchy, represented by Mr. Gaudet, and both must subject themselves to unwanted sexual relations with him. As Manon's enslaved lady's maid, Sarah is forced to nurture Manon to the point of suckling, but decisively rejects the role of "Mammy" by heading North. Upon her capture and return, Sarah needles Manon by reminding her that she is not her "Mammy" and was considered worthy of nurture herself by the abolitionists who served her tea at their table. Sarah has lost one child, her son by Bam the butler, who was sold by Mr. Gaudet. She abandons Walter, who looks like Mr. Gaudet. She takes the child who resembles her, a dark infant girl, to the North, but does not bring her back to Louisiana, so she presumably managed to free one part of herself. Indeed, one could speculate that Sarah's escape may have been as much or more for her daughter's freedom as for her own since Sarah carefully handed her daughter down from Manon's window to waiting arms at the beginning of the slave revolt. To the restricted extent that she can, Sarah chooses who and how she will mother: in the slave system, motherhood is a series of painful exigencies and choices.

Maternity under the other system of patriarchal enslavement, matrimony, is also toxic, as Manon learns from her aunt and her mother. Mrs. Gray is willing to potentially sacrifice her niece's happiness by giving the attractive Sarah to Manon as a wedding present despite the fact that she will be a constant temptation to Manon's new husband. Mrs. Gray does so to preserve her own family for herself and for her children. For Manon's mother, the death of Manon's two young brothers was not only a crushing blow in itself, but led to the loss of any further children because, as Mrs. Gray told Manon, her father was so "devastated" (174) that "in their marriage bed, he turned away" (176). Consequently, Manon's mother advocates that Manon, for the sake of producing children, starve her own needs and tastes and "show more warmth to my husband, even if I do not feel it" (58). This poisonous maternity is physically manifested when, at her mother's death, "from her [mother's] mouth, nose, eyes, and ears, a black fluid gushed forth" (69). That very evening, Manon forces Sarah to suckle her, the negative image of the black fluid gushing from her white mother, as if by so doing she could own and manipulate a mother's love at will, while she is only deepening Sarah's hatred. In a system in which both mothers and children are a form of property, mother's milk can be venomous.

In her invaluable psychological and literary study of the ways that women cope with oppression, *In the Name of Love, Women, Masochism, and the Gothic* (1992), Michelle Massé delineates the metanarratives that reinforce women's blindness to the forces that keep them enslaved: "The web of authority that constructs their social reality is first perceptible to most in family relationships, but they discover it to be finely and inextricably linked to religious, legal, medical and educational systems as well. All reverberate when any one point is touched and, needless to say, no neat sweeping away is possible" (36). Manon is caught in that web as she confronts the issue of maternity for herself. She tries to evade her status as breeder, but, after five years of childless marriage, capitulates to her mother and husband and agrees to see Dr. Sanchez in the hope that he "might find some physical reason for my failure to conceive, thereby freeing me of my detested conjugal duties, and putting an end to my mother's tiresome queries" (35). At the doctor's office, she is surrounded by coercive symbols of painful, fruitless marriage and sex: two canaries in a "large-wrought cage hanging from a chain near the open window," one singing "plaintively" (36), and a plantain tree's "big bruised purple pod of unripe fruit" with a fallen leaf "like a fold of impossibly bright satin" (37). Regardless of these ill omens, Manon finds Dr. Sanchez sympathetic; he even asks her if she wants children. Manon, brainwashed by her society, reflects, "I had assumed I would have children, the question of whether I wanted them had never occurred to me" (37). She wonders if she would reply affirmatively if she were married to someone "calm" and "patient" (37) like Dr. Sanchez, but she answers, "No" (37). Manon cannot see children as anything more than additional marital chains and cages; she is as imprisoned in her point of view as the canaries are in their cages. In *The Awakening*, Kate Chopin's Edna Pontellier holds similar views of matrimony and maternity, and she also fails to receive anything other than meaningless palliatives from her doctor, who believes that the natural and social order is more powerful than either of them.

Similarly, despite his compassionate manner, Dr. Sanchez can perceive Manon only as her husband's property, much as Manon can see Sarah only as hers. Manon is blind to everything but her own oppression, and the doctor views Manon's oppression as a requisite part of the social order; consequently, Manon remains part of the web that has captured her. Although Manon tells him that she "despise[s]" Mr. Gaudet because of his relations with Sarah and that Walter, having more freedom than she does, is "allowed to run loose in the house like a wild animal" (38), Dr. Sanchez complies with the system and refuses to lie for her so that she can avoid sex with her husband. In her misery and disappointment, Manon begs for something to alleviate her headaches and insomnia, and Dr. Sanchez acknowledges the limits of his role as her physician when he replies, "That much I can do for you" (39). Manon uses one of the strategies that Massé finds characteristic of gothic heroines: "self-conscious subversion that mimes cultural expectations of femininity to achieve the protagonist's freedom" (240). Manon uses these tinctures from Dr. Sanchez and alcohol to anesthetize herself against her encounters with her husband and eventually succeeds in repelling his sexual advances with her parodic corpse-like state of female passivity and acquiescence of which she says, "I was there and not there at the same time" (56).

With these words, Martin is parodically reversing the opening line of Ernest Gaines's 1993 novel *A Lesson before Dying*: "I was not there, and yet

I was there." Grant Wiggins, a black man in 1940s Louisiana, is relating how he could not avoid hearing about the trial and death sentence of his double, the condemned Jefferson, no matter how much he tried to avoid it. Not until Grant faces Jefferson can he break through the ice surrounding his heart and engage with his community and his fiancée. With this allusion to Gaines, Martin is pointing out the legacy of the slave system in Louisiana, reinforcing *Property*'s opening line, "It never ends." Or, as Faulkner put it, "The past is never dead, it's not even past" (*Requiem for a Nun*). Indeed, for Manon, it cannot end or die, leaving her in a sort of purgatory, "there and not there," as long as she, in contrast to Gaines's Grant, refuses to understand her double and nemesis, Sarah.

For Martin, "Mammy" belongs in the realm of sentimental plantation fiction as white wish fulfillment; thus she depicts a state of war, not loving mutual devotion, between mistress and maid. In Manon's willed incomprehension of Sarah, she resembles Miss Rosa in Faulkner's *Absalom, Absalom!* who pushes away but cannot bear to release the mulatta Clytie, who is the daughter of Miss Rosa's brother-in-law, Thomas Sutpen, by a slave woman. Miss Rosa regards Clytie as a threat to her ownership of the Sutpen family and its story. Yet Clytie, not Miss Rosa, tends the last Sutpen descendant, the mulatto "idiot" Jim Bond, until Clytie herself is immolated in the family mansion along with the other remaining Sutpen descendant. Howling, Jim Bond roams the deserted grounds, ending the family in "a tale told by an idiot, full of sound and fury, signifying nothing" (*Macbeth* 5.5, 26–28) as spoken by Shakespeare's solitary and childless Macbeth. Faulkner's most famous "idiot," though, is Benjy of *The Sound and the Fury*, the white scion of the decaying Compson family who never develops mentally beyond toddlerhood and cannot speak, only babble, cry, and howl. He is tended with compassion and perseverance by the Compsons' devoted black housekeeper, Dilsey. In contrast to Faulkner's depictions of Clytie and Dilsey, Martin, through Sarah, decidedly refutes the notion that a black woman would sincerely "mother" the scion, Walter, of a white family, even if that scion is also of her own blood; as Kathryn Harrison puts it, "Beautiful Sarah is no Mammy figure" (10).

Martin also reverses the Faulknerian paradigm by having, not the black woman, but the white woman, Manon, inextricably linked to the mulatto who is considered an "idiot," Walter. After Sarah escapes during the slave rebellion, the wounded Manon hides in a swamp, like a runaway slave, and awakens to see a "black hand" (117) that she eventually realizes is her own hand covered with black mud, without realizing the irony of her identity with escaped slaves. She also finds that the abused and abandoned Walter has followed her there. With the rigidly maintained blinders of her self-pity, Manon sees herself as the justly complaining victim: "A world of idiots and monsters, I thought, and I left to tell the tale" (119). Unlike the childless Lady Macbeth endlessly trying to wash the blood from her hands, Manon refuses to acknowledge her guilt, the blackness on her hands from the slave system. She will not recognize that she shares the "blackness" of her victimhood with the slaves in a world run by white patriarchs. As Susan Donaldson astutely notes, Manon "is increasingly diminished by her growing hatred for all black women (not just Sarah), and her own inability to recognize how tightly her identity is interwoven with Sarah's, whose dependence and subordination define Manon's very sense of self" (279).

Like one of Shakespeare's fools, particularly Lear's, Walter is a perpetual reminder of what Manon wants to forget: her common humanity and plight with the slaves. When Manon returns to the plantation, Walter sits by her feet and begins playing with the "dried mud" (121) between her toes until she tells him to "stop that" (121) and moves her feet away. As Kathryn Harrison puts it, "His role . . . is that of the holy fool, an innocent who alerts us to the sins of those we might mistakenly assume to be humane, or even civilized" (10). As Donaldson observes, Walter's deafness "emblematizes Manon's refusal to hear any words uttered by her slaves" (274): this is Manon's "sin," to use Kathryn Harrison's term.

Walter is also Manon's savior, in deed and in potential. During the insurrection, Walter, Manon relates, "threw himself at my husband's legs with such force that he stumbled" (113), lost his pistol, and was captured and killed by the slaves: Walter inadvertently managed to free Manon from her tormentor, her enslaver. The question now—which Martin leaves open—is if he can save her from herself, from her path of increased callousness and inhumanity. He simply will not leave Manon, no matter how contemptuously and continually she and Sarah reject him. Walter is like the initially uncontrollable Topsy, in Harriet Beecher Stowe's *Uncle Tom's Cabin,* who is devoted to her new mistress despite Miss Ophelia's repugnance toward her black skin. Like a cat and like Topsy, Walter has the uncanny ability to attach himself to the one person in the room who dislikes or fears him. Another slave, Rose, observes to Manon, "He always want to be where you are" (184).

Through Manon's ambivalent attitude toward Walter, Martin suggests a faint hope for both captives of the slave system. In a characteristically postmodern move, Martin makes Manon capable of simultaneously hating and loving Walter in that although Manon cannot get rid of Walter, it becomes increasingly doubtful that she really wants him gone. Manon's refusal of Mr. Roget's offer to buy Sarah and take Walter can readily be considered part of Manon's obsession with maintaining Sarah as her property since she uses Walter as a collateral means of reinforcing Sarah's sense of servitude: "If I have to live with Walter . . . so does she" (140); her "hatred" (the original title of the novel; Donaldson 274) is vengeful and self-destructive. Manon treats Walter like a pet when she moves to New Orleans after the insurrection:[7] she has him walked on a leash and lets him sleep on the hearth in the parlor while she is there. While such dog-like treatment is demeaning, Walter is the only one whom Manon bothers to care for; he is a major exception to her growing solitude. Keeping Walter close to her, instead of selling him or relegating him to servants' quarters, may indicate a soft spot in her increasingly callous heart for the only "creature" (as she repeatedly calls him) in this novel who seems capable of love. In two Christ-like displays of loving one's enemy, Walter cries upon finding his dead father, Mr. Gaudet, and remains devoted to Manon. Christ also asserted that the meek shall inherit the earth, and Martin, in an interview, held out a similar hope for Walter: "I think Walter is going to inherit the house" (McHenry).

In addition to Walter, Martin holds out a few other signs of hope for Manon's redemption as a human being. Manon fears that she "actually turned into my mother" (173), a plump widow giving modest dinners

---

7. In an interview with Sandra Martin, Valerie Martin cites Rachel O'Connor's Evergreen Plantation diary: O'Connor, states Martin, "became very attached to little boy slaves and kept them in the house, almost like pets" (S. Martin R3).

from her small New Orleans cottage. Manon's apprehension can be read as a positive sign in that Manon could become her own mother in the sense that she will think for herself and nurture herself. One indication of such possible self-redemption is that Manon looks for the truth behind powerful patriarchal imperatives, for example, when she genuinely ponders Dr. Sanchez's question about desiring children instead of automatically assuming that she does (37). She does not believe in conventional Christianity: "Everyone . . . felt the need to assure me that Mother's death was part of God's plan. Exactly, I wanted to shout after reading this sentiment half a dozen times—his plan is to kill us all, and if an innocent child dies in agony, and a wicked man breathes his last at an advanced age in his sleep, who are we to call it injustice?" (136). As she expresses her jealousy of white male slave owners' "fascination with these creatures" (180), she also refuses to believe in the beneficence of the slave system: "It was the lie at the center of everything, the great lie we all supported, tended, and worshiped as if our lives depended upon it, as if, should one person ever speak honestly, the whole world would crack open and send us all tumbling into a flaming pit" (179). Falling into hell begins to seem less terrible than the continued purgatory of a society built on mass self-delusion.

Manon begins to recognize these "lies" as the bars of her gothic prison. She fervently wishes, "Let me just live quietly, without illusions" (183), and she does appear to be moving toward some truths by the end of the novel. She realizes that it is not Sarah's now-defunct relationship with her husband that she so envies, but Sarah's independence, however brief. As Manon points out to her aunt, Sarah "has tasted a freedom you and I will never know. . . . She has traveled about the country as a free white man" (189). When Sarah tells Manon that in the North she was served tea by whites, Manon, in the last line of the novel, wonders, "What on earth did they think they were doing?" (193). Her question can be interpreted two ways simultaneously in a postmodern dialogue. She could be sardonic: how could these Yankees treat a piece of property as a human being? But her question also could be the beginning of a genuine revelation nudging her toward empathy. As she had imagined Sarah's "tast[e] of freedom" (189), she could now be trying to imagine what these abolitionists were thinking, the reasons and sentiments behind their actions: that slaves are human beings and thus entitled to freedom.

As Martin told an interviewer about the setting of *Property,* "To live in such a world . . . you have to lie to yourself and that makes everything poisoned and it stifles any impulse toward humanity. If you ever admit the truth, you have to do a wholesale rethinking of everything that you are and everything that you believe about the people around you" (Sandra Martin R3). Because Manon has questioned religion, maternity, and the role of women, she may be starting to take her "wholesale rethinking" to its logical conclusion in examining her hatred-filled perception of Sarah as her property. The novel begins with an epigraph from "a letter from A.B.C. of Halifax City to the *Richmond Whig* on January 28, 1832" in which the writer asserts, "be that property an evil, a curse, or what not, we intend to hold it." *Property* ends with Manon's possibly beginning to question the abolitionist recognition of the human dignity to which Sarah is entitled, but not with the willfully blind and determined grasping of "A.B.C." Manon's questioning indicates a fragile hope, undercut by, or held in postmodern dialogic tension with, the novel's first line: "It never ends." In her next novel, *Trespass* (2007), Martin explores the seemingly never-ending curse of property in the late twentieth century, where, even without the institution of slavery, people still seem compelled to draw boundaries around their relatives and relationships and repel trespassers from their "property."

Trespass

ELECTING ENCROACHMENT OR EMPATHY

*I*n *Trespass* (2007), Martin returns to the contemporary world to reexamine the deadening materialism and failed empathy she so sardonically dissected in the antebellum South in the novel *Property* (2003) and
in medieval Italy in *Salvation: Scenes from the Life of St. Francis* (2001). The
word "trespass" has two principal meanings: the verb, to enter someone's
space, physical or psychological, without their consent, and the noun,
the consequences of such encroachments: a sin, or the crossing of moral
boundaries. In consonance with an overarching theme of Martin's fiction,
the symbiosis of the spiritual and the material, *Trespass* explores the consequences of trespassing: of encroaching upon, defending, expanding, or
dissolving boundaries, tangible and intangible. Boundaries can be gothic
enclosures or welcoming refuges in the contemporary world; modern prisons can be war zones or comfy gilded cages: women remain subject to
imprisonment in a patriarchal script that some have internalized to inflict
upon themselves or others. Unlike the female protagonists of Martin's
earlier work, however, the women of *Trespass* eschew masochistic martyrdoms and passive acquiescence to patriarchal hierarchies; they argue for
their opinions and fight to maintain their boundaries against those they
regard as trespassers. In a more indirect way, Martin also argues against a
major theme of Faulkner and the old white male canon of southern literature, the burden of the past.

Although *Trespass* is set at the turn into the twenty-first century, Martin provides a postmodern dialogue with the historical and literary prec-
edents of current trespasses. Her spectrum of characters is similarly broad:
from those obsessed with trespassing through defensively retaining or en-
larging boundaries by means of hoarding or excluding, to those who want
to repudiate the concept of trespassing through expanding or opening

boundaries, thus sharing and including. A boundary crosser can be a trespasser or a guest, and the boundary-crossed can be a defender or a host, depending on a character's moral imagination. Attitudes toward trespass distinguish the haters from the lovers, the villains from the saints.

Fittingly, *Trespass* begins with U.S. Secretary of State Colin Powell warning the United Nations on February 6, 2003, against Iraq's potential trespasses through putative "weapons of mass destruction." Martin employs this excerpt from Powell's address as her epigraph for *Trespass:* "I cannot tell you everything that we know. But what I can share with you, when combined with what all of us have learned over the years, is deeply troubling. What you will see is an accumulation of facts and disturbing patterns of behavior." As Martin ranges through history, literature, and personality types, she does present us with a "deeply troubling . . . accumulation of facts and disturbing patterns of behavior," but she also provides glimpses of hope through redemptive leaps of the imagination and generously impulsive behavior.

Through the musings of Brendan, an historian, Martin posits that history usually repeats itself, ignorantly and violently. "Now and then [Brendan] gets aggravated enough to point out to friends that the events of the sacrosanct 9/11 were not new and did not actually change anything, that rather than entering a new era, a very old one has only come cycling back into view. The widening gyre, the falcon no longer hears the falconer . . . *the best lack all conviction*" (75–76). Brendan is citing William Butler Yeats's poem "The Second Coming," though he characteristically and optimistically avoids the worst by omitting the lines from the quoted stanza in which boundaries are breached: "Mere anarchy is loosed upon the world, / The blood-dimmed tide is loosed." While sectarian violence, emblematized in 9/11, re-emerges in the early twenty-first century, Brendan is writing a book about the Emperor Frederick II (1194–1250), who tried unsuccessfully to unite the Christian and Muslim worlds in his person. Although the philosopher George Santayana asserted, "Those who cannot remember the past are doomed to repeat it," Martin suggests that despite many reminders, human beings are so territorial, so obsessed with property, that their repetition of the past may be inevitable, in endless cycles of trespasses, real and delusory.

Trespass is steeped in allusions to war and genocide ignited by deep-seated and irrational prejudices, including those determined by race, such as the massacre of hundreds of African Americans by whites in Tulsa, Oklahoma, in 1921 (264–65), as well as Brendan's study of religious hatred in the Middle Ages. The principal historical context, however, is the Serbo-Croatian War (1991–95), which was ignited by religious and nationalist hatreds in which each side justified its violence by perceiving the Other as an alien "race." Martin graphically depicts the consequent physical and emotional carnage through a Croatian family who are refugees from Serbian-occupied Croatia: Branko Drago, who escapes to Louisiana with two surviving children, Andro and Salome; and his estranged wife, Jelena, who finds refuge in Trieste after repeated rape and abuse by Serb soldiers. Another son, Josip, an innocent and defenseless child, was slaughtered by Serbs, with Jelena as witness.

In her acknowledgments, Martin cites Brian Hall's *The Impossible Country: A Journey through the Last Days of Yugoslavia* (1994) as an important source for her understanding of the conflict between Serbs and Croats. One of Hall's central points is that "wars require a dehumanization of the enemy" (K60), a process into which he sees his Serbian, Croatian, and Bosnian friends, acquaintances, and informants descend as war becomes imminent. The Other becomes devoid of individuality, a stereotypically inhuman demon, who can and must be killed with zest and righteousness. Trespasses cannot be forgiven because those perceived as "aliens" have no boundaries, territorial or personal, that must be respected, and so Serb brutality toward Jelena and Josip could be regarded as not only justifiable but also honorable. Both sides participate in the dehumanization: Andro, a Croatian, tries to kill his own mother when he learns that she has a Serbian lover and, years later, strikes his sister Salome and her fiancé Toby when he learns of Salome's pregnancy by this American outsider.

Martin also supplies a literary context for this dehumanization of the Other through her postmodern parodic deployment of Emily Brontë's gothic *Wuthering Heights* (1847). Brendan's wife, Chloe, is an artist, an illustrator currently at work on a new edition of Brontë's novel. *Wuthering Heights* could as easily be titled *Trespass* because the plot is set in motion by a rage for possession of people and property, carried through the generations, that dehumanizes both victors and victims. The characters live in houses with barred gates and doors, supplemented by watchdogs. Heathcliff, perceived and mistreated as a usurping trespasser, repeats the cycle of abuse on young Hareton Earnshaw, whom he disinherits and keeps in poverty and ignorance. As in the sad equation of women and pets that Martin depicts in *The Consolation of Nature and Other Stories,* Heathcliff violently abuses a pet spaniel, as well as two women, Isabella and Cathy Linton, belonging to the enemy family, in place of their men. Similarly, Andro in *Trespass* strikes his mother and Salome to punish the male outsiders who threaten his possession of them. Heathcliff wants vengeance because he was foiled in his obsession with owning Catherine Earnshaw, body and soul, in this world and the next.

In a reprise of the damaged minds of oppressor and oppressed in *Property,* Martin shows that psychic boundaries are as aggressively defended in *Trespass* as they are in *Wuthering Heights.* When Brontë's narrator, Mr. Lockwood, dreams that Catherine Earnshaw is trying to get in the window, in his sleep he tries to repulse her by rubbing her wrist against the broken glass. Those trespassed against, like young Heathcliff or the young Cathy Linton, do not become saintly martyrs but come to resemble their abusers, as Cathy realizes when she asks the internal narrator, the housekeeper Nelly Dean, "How did you contrive to preserve the common sympathies of human nature when you resided here?" (K2310). Similarly, Salome and her brother Andro have difficulty maintaining the "common sympathies of human nature" after their struggle for mere survival in war-torn Croatia.

As Martin's depiction of damaged and damaging victims (who are decidedly not angels purged by suffering) suggests, she does not interpret *Wuthering Heights* as a romantic tale or see Heathcliff as an attractively gothic or Byronic hero. As Chloe reflects on *Wuthering Heights* for her illustrations, she realizes that it is a story about class struggle, involving people as well as property. She describes it as a "tale of two houses" in which Heathcliff has become, "in fact, the owner of both" (194) through his trespasses. Chloe recognizes in Heathcliff "necrophilia, on top of wife-beating and some active assistance in the deaths of his foster brother and his own son. . . . No, he's not the Romantic vision of an over-heated female imagination" (194–95). Instead, she sees him as a trespasser: "He's something new: the vengeful orphan, the ungrateful outsider, the coming retribution of the great underclass (195).

The Serbo-Croatian War, the internecine conflict in *Wuthering Heights,* and the xenophobia in a family of modern American intellectuals: all are Martin's examples of the human inability to learn from stories, fictive or historical. Chloe cannot see her own resemblance to Heathcliff because she is so convinced of her property rights that she believes she can expel a poacher from her and Brendan's property and exclude Salome Drago from her family by preventing her from marrying her and Brendan's son, Toby. As Brendan notes, we remain enslaved to "Homeland Security," which, in the wake of 9/11, "advised people to stock up on plastic sheeting and be ready to seal themselves in their homes" (226).

As in *Property* and *The Unfinished Novel and Other Stories,* Martin conveys her theme through her masterful use of point of view. In keeping with the broad historical and cultural range of *Trespass,* she gives the perspective of multiple characters through third-person limited omniscience, or what Henry James called "central consciousness." The reader is privy to a character's thoughts as conveyed through the writer's description, not through the words of the character, as in a first-person account. Consequently, the characterization is more nuanced and less biased. Martin's techniques of characterization were also changed by her reading of Anton Chekhov during her sojourn in Italy from 1994 to 1997. As Martin told an interviewer, "My characters, instead of being these passive people who just can't really make themselves respond, transformed into these people who bark at one another and are willful and treacherous and mean and gossip about one another and think about politics and reject one another because of their philosophical or political views" (Biguenet Interview 53), an apt description of the characters in *Trespass,* including the women, who argue for their opinions; there are no silent, outwardly acquiescent masochists as in Martin's early fiction.

In *Trespass,* Martin chooses three main characters—Brendan, Chloe, and Toby—as central consciousnesses because their experiences and sensibilities are closest to those of Martin's reading audience: cultured and well-informed Americans who have never experienced the traumas of war at home and consequently can remain, as in the case of Chloe, so dangerously ignorant of their own prejudices that they see such biases as justifiable and righteous indignation. As reviewer Sue Halpern astutely observes, "In creating a character who is probably not unlike many of her readers, Martin is trespassing too, leaving hints that suggest our own self-righteousness, however well intentioned, may not stand up when tested, as Chloe's won't."

Martin's surface characterization of Chloe initially seems sympathetic: a conscientious wife and mother, a committed artist, and an antiwar protestor. Martin, however, strews clues before her readers that Chloe lacks the empathy to open her boundaries to others and share what she has been given and developed. Chloe regards aestheticism and romanticism as entitlements, not liberations, and embraces what Brendan had intended as a criticism: "He was right, she is a bourgeois. She cares about rituals, furniture, flower arrangements, comfort; she dislikes risk. Risk averse, they call it in investing circles. She loves beauty; on this ground she defends herself. If more people did, why would that be such a bad thing?" (108). Chloe has similarly strong convictions as an artist, wishing to emulate "her true gods, the romantic poets. *Those who restrain passion do so because theirs is weak enough to be restrained*" (71), a line from Chloe's favorite Romantic poet and fellow engraver, William Blake ("The Marriage of Heaven and Hell," 1790), though Chloe misquotes and substitutes "passion," her justification for her actions and emotions, for Blake's less grand and less morally defensible "desire." Although her advocacy of beauty and passion initially may appear commendable, her diction points to her need to possess: she "defends herself" against trespassers against beauty, yet believes that she is one of the chosen, the strong, whose passion does not need to observe boundaries, "be restrained," like the "weak." Unlike a truly cultured and sophisticated artist, she cannot tolerate ambiguity and wants a clearly defined "us" and "them": "If only God would send down a new tablet saying which set of outraged "refugees" are the "real" chosen people" (16).

Martin suggests Chloe's complacent hubris through her name since "Chloe" is another name for the goddess Demeter, who was so territorial about her sacred grove that she vengefully punished the hero Erysichthon for cutting down a tree by cursing him with ceaseless and insatiable hunger. Chloe doubly curses Zigor, a Basque poacher on her land, with hunger when she stops his hunting and also causes him to lose his job by informing his employer about his trespassing.

Because Chloe refuses to acknowledge their shared humanity, she cannot see Zigor as her potential savior. Since the threat-du-jour is the Islamic terrorist, Chloe thinks Zigor is Lebanese, although Lebanon is home to many religions, including Christianity. But even Lebanese is just her category for the undifferentiated Other because, according to Toby, "she thinks all Middle Easterners are Lebanese" (45). When she is felled by the stroke that kills her, Zigor, who has come to request her forgiveness for his trespasses and, he hopes, get his job back, remains with Chloe and tries to get her help by calling 911, with the inclusive plea, "Please, help *us*" (201, emphasis mine), which, as Martin ironically notes, "are the last words she hears" (201). The menacing ethnic Other acts like a human being despite Chloe's refusal to hear and recognize their common needs as mortals and to forgive him his trespasses on her property.

Demeter-Chloe is possessive about people as well as property. When Hades abducted her daughter Persephone to the underworld, Demeter was disconsolate and refused to perform her duties to make the earth fruitful. Although she got Persephone back for part of each year, she would not permit anything to grow in the months, winter, when Persephone dwelt with Hades. Similarly, Chloe drives her family away with her jealousy of Toby's love for Salome, and she is left alone in the winter months while Brendan and Toby follow Salome to Trieste, where Salome has found her long-lost mother, Jelena. Chloe's vengeance ironically boomerangs when, left alone with her anger by her family, she dies of a stroke induced by the effect of her rage and frustration on her blood pressure, her failure to eat properly, and her isolation in her cold studio; her imposition of vengeance, hunger, and winter on her familial world fatally redounds on her.

Through Chloe, Martin demonstrates the way that privileging ownership—asserting what is mine as good and what belongs to the Other as bad—can cause people to see the same action in opposite ways. Chloe ostensibly hates Zigor because he kills rabbits on her property, but the same actions are commendable in her cat, "Mike, the murderer she loves" (38). Chloe was recently absorbed in illustrating a critically acclaimed children's version of Henry David Thoreau's *Walden,* but she fails to see in Zigor the same solitary self-reliance in nature that she so esteems in Thoreau, exclaiming "Bastard" when one of Zigor's shots interrupts her reflections on the transcendentalist nature writer and American romantic. Unromantically, in *Walden* Thoreau declares that when he saw a woodchuck, he "was strongly tempted to seize and devour him raw" ("Higher Laws"). Beloved pet, beloved philosopher, or "Bastard" poacher: it depends on whether you are one of us or you are one of them.

Although we tend to associate education and culture with enlightenment, Martin demonstrates that they can also serve as blinders and tools of oppression toward others. Chloe uses her pretensions to culture to justify her xenophobia. In her initial tense encounter with Salome at an elegant and expensive restaurant, Chloe finds Salome rude because she drinks a lot of coffee, which she does not know is characteristic of Croatian culture. When Salome argues with Chloe's dismissive notion that arguing about politics is "boring" (5), Chloe is uncomfortable and affronted. She is ignorant of the life-and-death consequences of politics for a Croatian war refugee. Chloe even distorts her cultural knowledge into a willed ignorance in order to support her prejudices. When Brendan jokingly suggests that they should invite Zigor for dinner, Chloe responds, "It would be like the first Thanksgiving. . . . The settlers invite the savages" (107), conveniently forgetting that the so-called "savages," the Native Americans, were the ones who knew how to hunt and grow food and so provided for the starving Pilgrims. Martin is also reprising Manon Gaudet's incredulity at her slave Sarah's being invited to the tea table by northern abolitionists in *Property.* Chloe, like Manon, cannot imagine the Other as included and nurtured. In another cultural distortion, still thinking that Zigor is Lebanese, she imagines him arriving at his "hovel" to be greeted by "Tiny Khalil," exclaiming, "Allah bless us, every one" (108), perverting Charles Dickens's tale of love, forgiveness, and charity, *A Christmas Carol* (1843), into a religious and ethnic slur, without even bothering to direct it at the right ethnic group.

Most tellingly, Chloe fails to learn from her intimate knowledge of the tragically contested boundaries of *Wuthering Heights*. She cannot see her own attitude toward Salome reflected in Mrs. Earnshaw's rejection of the orphaned child Heathcliff as a "'gypsy brat'" (120), not the "'gift of God'" (120) that Mr. Earnshaw asserts that he is. Nor can Chloe equate Salome, believed to be motherless at the beginning of the novel, with the Brontë sisters, for whom Chloe feels an intense sympathy: "Poor motherless girls, none of them beauties, passionate, intelligent, doomed, preoccupied, by necessity, with death" (50). Ironically, Chloe can identify with the dead Brontë mother, who, "lucky for her, didn't live to see the relentless will to self-destruction that characterized the wasted life of her only son" (50), the fate Chloe fears for Toby through his marriage to Salome. Although Chloe notes that "windows constitute a recurring motif in *Wuthering Heights*" (175) and allow characters to look and to long, but not to touch, she does not see that she has become trapped in that paradigm. In the weeks before her death, she can see her loved ones, Brendan and Toby, only through the "window" of the computer screen when they send pictures from Trieste. For Heathcliff and Chloe, dead at the end of their respective novels, the excluder has become the excluded while the young couples, Hareton Earnshaw and Cathy Linton and Toby and Salome take over the parental homesteads in the hope of starting harmonious new families based on sharing and inclusion.

Through Chloe, Martin uncompromisingly and thoroughly exposes the possessive underside of parental love that she earlier sketched through a vignette in *Salvation* (2001). Chloe's initially mild and unthinking prejudices spiral into a xenophobia that destroys her and causes her to lose the family and land that she is so adamant about defending against trespassers. Saint Francis of Assisi's father "will lock up his wayward son, just as he locks up his grain, and his bolts of fine linen, wool, and silk, and his house and all his furniture and everything that is his" (*Salvation* 213). Like Chloe, he only succeeds in driving his son away and making his family miserable as he obsesses over potential thieves and trespassers. Similarly, in Zagreb, Croatia, Jelena's possessive father drove away his son to the Netherlands and his daughter Jelena to the country and marriage with a farmer, Branko Drago. Lessons are repeated, but humanity does not learn from its mistakes.

In Martin's postmodern fiction, however, nothing is simplistically right or wrong, but can be both simultaneously. Such is the case with Chloe's defensive obsessions. As the saying goes, "Just because you are paranoid doesn't mean they aren't out to get you." One of Salome's first questions to Chloe is "How many acres do you have here?" (48). Recognizing a potential usurper, Chloe made a drawing of Salome with hair comprised of hornets, Chloe's version of Medusa and her snake-locks, with the caption: *"Run for your life; it's that hornet-headed girl"* (94). Chloe may be right about Salome because she does lose her land and her life to the hornet-headed girl. Pregnant Salome will live in Chloe and Brendan's house and perhaps decorate it, as Chloe had feared, in what Chloe deprecates as "Bohunk chic" (196); as with Zigor, she can't be bothered to differentiate among ethnic others; Salome is Croatian from the former Yugoslavia, not a Bohemian from Czechoslovakia. Fittingly, Chloe's nightmare of the undifferentiated Other is realized: "the coming retribution of the great underclass" (195) has arrived, though the "retribution" here is the destruction of the compassionate aspects of Chloe's character and of her family, not the loss of land.

Salome is clearly defined neither as heroine nor as villainess because she is presented through the third-person limited omniscient narration of Chloe, Brendan, and Toby, each of whose observations and judgments complicate any simplistic judgment. Like that of the focal figure of William Faulkner's *The Sound and the Fury,* Caddy Compson, Salome's point of view is not provided, but she is a catalyst for the actions of three main narrators, who seek to understand the "foreign" experience of both: Caddy's as a woman among men in Mississippi, and, in the patriarchal South of Louisiana, Salome's as a refugee from the carnage in Croatia. Chloe regards Salome as a stingingly venomous troublemaker and consummate trespasser, much as the internal narrator of *Wuthering Heights,* Nelly Dean, sees Catherine Earnshaw, but since Martin provides us with Brendan's and Tony's more favorable perspectives on Salome, her character remains ambiguous.

Martin troubles our reliance upon the narratives of history through Brendan. Historians may misread the past to serve their desires in the present, as does Paul in *The Great Divorce,* who could readily be included in Brendan's characterization of such present-focused historians. "The past: as threatening as the future and about as comprehensible, and its eager chroniclers, who make a living sorting through it, trash collectors, recyclers, at best; the enterprise strikes him [Brendan] as a ludicrous folly. Everything cooked up piecemeal and after the fact to serve the needs of the present, trotted out to the public, painstakingly garnished and always, always with an agenda. Like leftovers" (86). Although Brendan, unlike Paul, attempts to be accurate about the past, at the beginning of *Trespass*, he shares Paul's tendency to use the past as an escape from the present, not as a catalyst for action: "Brendan views the present, as he does the past, through a long lens. He seldom has the sensation that he is actually in it" (74). By the end of the novel, through what he learns, he wants not only himself but also his readers to feel the past, "what it looked like, smelled like, what the food tasted like, and most of all what ordinary people were up to" (232). He aspires to depict the Middle Ages with a novelist's attention to the senses and emotions (much like Martin's technique in the medieval setting of *Salvation*) after his own emotions and sensuality have been revivified.

Like Martin, Brendan rejects rigidly defined perspectives and accepts the more problematical ambiguity of life. Because Brendan initially refuses to engage with the present, he is less defensive than Chloe and his view of Salome is more balanced. When he is introduced to her, he, like Chloe, sees a predator: a "sly, vulpine face, very wily and determined, elusive too" (39). Yet, unlike Chloe, he "resolves to draw her out with interest, with kindness" (41) since he can place her in a broader context, in a way that Chloe cannot: "She's a scholarship girl, he reminds himself; her father is a fisherman and an immigrant" (42). He realizes that Salome, like a fox, may have learned predation as a survival mechanism, a necessity in the war-torn world she knew as child. "A cunning little vixen, Brendan thinks, and then it strikes him almost painfully—he would be embarrassed to own the thought—that Chloe, hovering there in her apron, clucking welcoming endearments, encouraging her son and his guest into the warm domesticity of her kitchen, looks very like a foolish, fluttery, and entirely defenseless mother hen" (42). Brendan can see and acknowledge both sides: he understands why Salome feels she needs wiles and determination, but he also recognizes her threat to the sheltered Chloe, who has had no need to hone her defenses against trespassers.

Through Brendan, Martin also delineates the intellectual's tendency to use learning and the past as barriers against the encroachments of a present that might require engagement and action. Initially, Brendan retreats into his learned inaction and lets what he regards as inevitable, the territorial conflicts between Chloe and Salome, Chloe and Zigor, play themselves out:

> The outsiders are insiders now, staking their claims.
>
> And nothing, not patience, kindness, an open mind, good-will, none of the resources Brendan usually brings to bear, nothing he can say or do, will disperse the atmosphere of distrust and hostility in which they must all greet one another at the breakfast table in the morning. (139)

Despite Brendan's fatalism, Salome acts as a catalyst for him, breaking the tense détente, by causing him to act upon his love for his son, Toby. When Salome finds her mother, Jelena, whom she believed killed in the Serbo-Croatian War, alive in Trieste, Toby follows her there, and Brendan joins them to assess the situation and to help Toby.

Brendan grows into his name and comes to resemble St. Brendan, an explorer and discoverer, because he begins to learn from the present as well as from the past, and from his heart as well as from his head, through Salome's mother. He leaves the safely remote zones of the Middle Ages and his rural retreat in America for the strange, multicultural milieu of Trieste, where he transcribes a contemporary account of sectarian conflict: Jelena's story of her life before, during, and after the Serbo-Croatian War. She tells him: "War is a country; that's what I learned, and it always looks the same. The citizens share a culture, which is the culture of trying to save their necks. The soldiers have another culture, the culture of creating havoc. Suspicion is the currency; the economics are despair. I hadn't grown up in this country. I wasn't used to it" (244). Although Jelena's account resonates with Brendan's sense that the past just keeps repeating itself through humanity's compulsions and ignorance, "it always looks the same," Jelena's story holds out the hope that not every victim will turn into a predator. Jelena is the Croatian translation of "Helen," yet Jelena's story does not repeat that of another beauty, Helen of Troy, because her husband, Branko, does not attempt to fight to reclaim her, but lets her go, unlike Helen's husband, Menelaus. Jelena also rejects cruelly unthinking repetition. Despite her experiences of brutal sexual abuse and the murder of her young son by Serbs, she refuses to become "used to it." Brendan recognizes in Jelena "the same effrontery that characterizes her daughter's [Salome's] address. Yet it's warmer, he finds, not unkind, and devoid of cunning" (193).

Martin questions the most famous dictum of traditional southern literature, that of Faulkner in *Requiem for a Nun* (1951): "The past is never dead. It's not even past." In contrast, Martin's Jelena believes "the past is over" (219), and Brendan chooses to start a new life with her in Trieste after Chloe's death. In contrast to the view of Faulkner and the white male traditional canon of southern literature, Martin does not believe that the future must necessarily be overwhelmed by the past, although people are inevitably changed by it, and sometimes are even altered for the better. It is a matter of outcome and temperament in that if Chloe were alive, she would have perceived Salome's catalytic qualities functioning like those of her biblical namesake: Salome handing Brendan's head, like that of St. John the Baptist, to her mother, Jelena, on a platter, as the biblical Salome did for her mother, Herodias. For Brendan, however, his "beheading" leads to a rebirth, not in heaven, but in his "head," where he can now appreciate a wider, more troubling world. Salome has initiated the changes that allow him, like St. Brendan, to expand the boundaries of his known world, in his life and in his writing. He rejects Chloe's fear of trespassers, "her retreat into her habitual long-suffering cynicism, the reliable what-did-you-expect of her strategically low expectations" (132), her wintry attitude, for a "warmer" (193) world of hope and inclusion with Jelena.

Also in contrast to Faulkner and the traditional canon of southern literature, young people are not necessarily burdened by familial traits and heritage. Toby's view of Salome results from his combination of Chloe's need to take impassioned action with Brendan's tolerant perspective. Toby wants an "allowance for passion" (185) that echoes his mother's adulation of Romantics like Blake. "Toby has no wish to be like his father; he has known this for some time now, but this doesn't mean he wants his father to change. He appreciates the ironic distance that characterizes the paternal aura, disinterested, yet benign, fresh as opposed to chilly" (184). He rejects both his father's lack of engagement and his mother's deeply engaged prejudices: "He began to see himself as someone who might change the world. At least, he declared, he did not want to hide from it" (23). Although he cannot save his mother, he acts like his biblical namesake, Tobias: through the consequences of his marriage and journey, he cures his father's blindness.

Toby does not want to reconstruct the past or to cling to the present; he is willing to venture losses for future gains, while cognizant of the risks. Chloe asks Toby if he is sure Salome's baby is his and if he realizes Salome might just be trapping him to "stay in the country" (109) by marrying a U.S. citizen. He has suspicions about an attraction between Salome and their fellow Columbia student Macalister. Amid his new Croatian-speaking connections, he wonders, "Will I be an outsider in my own family?" (223). As Toby crossed the river to Salome's Louisiana home, "he had the sensation that they were crossing some mythical river together, the Lethe or the Styx, on their way to another world altogether, from which they might never return" (98). He is willing to hazard all these risks in exploring the foreign through Salome: "I want to know Salome, I want to know everything about her. That's my mission" (137).

Toby acts as if he is following the advice found in James's *The Ambassadors* (1903) to that novel's innocents abroad: "Live all you can—it's a mistake not to." Tobias is roughly translated from the Hebrew as "God is Good," which denotes Toby's optimism. He is Martin's version of Henry James's innocent abroad who risks all to enlarge his cultural, moral, and emotional boundaries. Like Chad Newsome in *The Ambassadors,* Toby remains abroad because of an older woman, Madame De Vionnet-Jelena. An older man, Lambert Strether-Brendan, is sent as an ambassador by his mother, Mrs. Newsome-Chloe, to get him back. The embassy is an ostensible failure because the older and the younger man both find love abroad. Since they are irrevocably altered by their experience, neither one will ever return as the man he was. They took the risk of opening their borders to experience and expanding their boundaries to include those different from them.

Toby's empathy and his moral imagination are the qualities that permit him to enlarge his boundaries. He can recognize Salome's grasping qualities and see her as "a jaguar among nervous chickens" (11), his version of Brendan's fox and hen, but he understands that there is a traumatized refugee behind the predator. What Chloe regards as Salome's rudeness at their first meeting in the expensive restaurant, Toby attributes to the fact "that she was inadequately socialized" (32). He knows that she came to Louisiana as a small girl and took on the responsibility of helping her father build a fishing business for which she still keeps the books and handles the money. Toby has seen the "shelf crammed with statues of her favorite saints and votive candles, which she lights to solicit favors" (11). He feels compassion for her futile attempts to rewrite the past: "Poor Salome. She really wanted to fix it all, you know, her family. She wanted it to be like it was before the war" (287).

Through Toby's inclusive outlook and actions, Martin provides some hope that the past does not have to be repeated *ad infinitum* as seems to be the case with jealously possessive, psychically wounded "trespassers" like Heathcliff and Salome. In a refugee camp, Jelena informally adopted a small girl named Wilka, a Bosnian Muslim, who has had a crescent moon carved on her cheek by Serbian ethnic cleansers. Even in Trieste, where she now lives with Jelena, Wilka does not speak, fears leaving the apartment, and has fits of screaming and terror. Like the deaf mulatto Walter in *Property,* Wilka has the potential to be saved, but Salome, behaving much like Chloe and like Manon Gaudet of *Property,* cannot recognize a version of herself in this "screaming, gyrating wraith of a girl whose face is hidden by a mass of black hair" (187), and she is jealous of Toby's attention to Wilka. Toby breaks the pattern of the past through his optimism and empathy. He discovers Wilka's passion for ice cream, coaxes her to take walks with him, and even to speak a few words. When he modestly declares, "It wasn't a miracle. I just paid attention to her" (281), he is pointing out that inclusion and sharing are as much a part of human nature as exclusion and trespassing. As Brendan notes, Toby gains by giving, not by grasping: "There's a quality of confidence about him. He has won the trust of a wounded creature and he has a plan to bring her out of suffering and darkness" (263).

Toby demonstrates that empathy can start a new cycle of nurturing and compassion in contrast to the vicious cycles of grasping and despair that much of *Trespass* illustrates. The last lines of the novel suggest the possibility of turning away from the dark depths of human nature with its defensiveness and exclusions and, in the words of the Lord's Prayer, forgiving our trespasses as we forgive those who trespass against us. A patriarchal and hierarchical prayer, "the Lord's," can be repurposed in a new context. With an empathetic moral imagination, men and women could acknowledge and accept each other as wounded by the traumas of the past and welcome the unknown in an enlarged and embracing new family: "The American father and son cease their contemplation of the deep, and turn back across the quay to the old city, where they will join the foreign woman and her daughter" (288).

11

The Unfinished Novel and Other Stories
and The Confessions of Edward Day

THE DÖPPELGANGERS OF ART AND LIFE

*I*talian Fever (1999) was Valerie Martin's first sustained fictional exploration of the relationship between art and life, mainly through a consideration of the meanings, uses, and effects of art for non-artists like her protagonist, Lucy Stark. In that novel, Martin also began a consideration of the artist's relationship with life through two secondary characters, Catherine Bultman and DV. Catherine's painting remains facile because she is too selfish to deeply involve herself in life and so she lacks empathy; she even claims triumphantly that she has never been in love. DV, in contrast, has immersed himself in the banalities of life, including many loves, to the detriment of his fiction, which is formulaic, self-congratulatory, fantasized autobiography. When DV is forced to work hard in solitude and suffering because of Catherine's rejection of his love and the isolation stemming from his inability to speak the language or drive in rural Italy, his fiction improves markedly. In *The Unfinished Novel and Other Stories* (2006) and the novel *The Confessions of Edward Day* (2009), Martin continues to explore the relationship between art and life in much greater depth and complexity, often through the gothic device of the döppelganger. Most significantly, she explodes the cultural script of the gloriously suffering romantic artist as another mask to conceal the selfishness and lack of empathy that ultimately result in a diminished art.

What is the optimal balance between art and life? If artists will not renounce life sufficiently so that they can devote themselves to their art, their art will fail. If artists sacrifice too much life, they will lack experience and empathy, and their art will fail as will their lives. In this balancing act between art and life, artists and their work are subject to myriad threats from accidents, temperament, illness, poverty, fashion, social and gender roles, and more: in short, from both life's predictable and its random vicissitudes. In *The Confessions of Edward Day*, Martin suggests art's vulnerability in this passage about the risks of producing a play: "The backers can go broke before a play goes into rehearsal; the play can close after a tryout; the director may be incompetent, lack nerve, or just lose control . . . ; the play can be difficult, unwieldy, or just banal; the actors may be miscast; illness, divorce, or lawsuits may hamstring the production; critics may hate the play and say so; audiences may fail to show up" (62). Great fiction, including Martin's, shows the difficulties of developing and sustaining a satisfying life, as well as the difficulties and vulnerabilities of art; as depicted in her work, it seems almost miraculous that any great art is created and survives.

In contrast to romantic artists, two great nineteenth-century masters of realism, Henry James and Anton Chekhov, are Martin's partners in the postmodern dialogue of her tales of art and life. In an interview, Martin defines their influence on *The Unfinished Novel and Other Stories*:

> I think if you look at the difference between the stories in *The Consolation of Nature* [1988] and the stories in *The Unfinished Novel* [2006], it's Chekhov that came between. I came to see characters as much more volatile and active; I think that was what I got from Chekhov. . . . [James is] the other influence, and especially his collection *The Figure in the Carpet* which is all stories about artists. I definitely had him in mind as I put together those stories about artists, but the fact that the characters are sometimes so wacky and loud, that's Chekhov. ("Transformations" 29–30)

For Martin's version of chaos theory, James provides the various determined proportions for art and life, while Chekhov provides the chance and randomness within the determined bounds. James's template is found in his short stories about the artist's duty to renounce life for art, particularly those stories collected by Frank Kermode in *The Figure in the Carpet and Other Stories* (1986), as well as those in James's novels about artists such as *Roderick Hudson* (1875), *The Tragic Muse* (1890), and *The*

Sacred Fount (1901). Chekhov's watermark on Martin's work is appropriately more diffuse: his milieu of chance, spontaneity, and the unexpected complicate James's paradigm about binary willed choices, and the plot of Chekhov's novella "The Duel" (1891) is the basis for Martin's postmodern parody in *The Confessions of Edward Day.*

James and Martin often use the gothic technique of the döppelganger to present the conflict between art and life, and as a device to suggest a way out of an enclosure in a claustrophobically selfish point of view. James's paradigmatic tale in this respect is "The Private Life" (1893), in which a writer functions successfully in society and in his art because he can double himself: while one self charmingly engages in social persiflage, the other writes in the silence of his chamber. In her artist tales, Martin also uses contrasting doubles or foils—particularly successful and unsuccessful painters, writers, and actors—but she questions the view that human sympathies and duties should be sacrificed for art as if it were a religious cult. For example, in *The Confessions of Edward Day,* she intensifies the double into a contemporary version of the ominous gothic döppelganger so prominent in the haunted tales of Edgar Allan Poe and in Fyodor Dostoevsky's works such as *The Double* (1846). Edward Day's need to "confess" his guilt about sacrificing a vulnerable young woman's mental health at the altar of art is spurred by his double, who in some ways serves as the voice of conscience as in Poe's döppelganger tale, "William Wilson."

In Martin's narratives of doubled artists, as in those of her literary predecessors, point of view is essential to the works' irony and ambiguity since the reader can perceive events only through the biased and restricted perspective of a single character, either as a first-person narrator or through the third-person limited omniscience of what Henry James would call a "central consciousness." In Martin's "Beethoven," the first-person narrator is a twenty-year-old woman who dropped out of college to experience *la vie bohème* in New Orleans's French Quarter. She waits on tables, occupies a dismal apartment, and begins an affair with Philip, a dedicated but poor painter who is a decade her senior. Philip decides to stop painting the portraits of Beethoven on wallpaper that he can profitably sell to tourists in order to concentrate on the self-portraits and roof-scapes that will not sell, telling the narrator, "Inauthenticity is a fatal disease. It kills you, one day at a time" (76).

Through Philip, Martin points out that creating one's life has its own aesthetic, with the potential to create a masterpiece. While Philip knows that he is "not Monet" (79), or the painterly equivalent of Beethoven, he remains true to his art, but ironically his true genius does not lie in his painting but in his love for Ingrid, who makes money selling her tourist art on Jackson Square. When the narrator sees him looking at Ingrid, he is a Beethoven. "Indeed his [Philip's] expression aroused in me feelings similar to those evoked by the commencement of certain melancholy music, a shiver along the spine, the silencing of the inner colloquy, all the senses arrested by an unwelcome yet irresistible revelation of suffering" (85). Philip makes his love for Ingrid the aesthetic triumph that he cannot achieve with his brush.

Like Lucy Stark of *Italian Fever*, who rejects her vision of the tormented artist DV to return to her life in New York, the narrator plans to leave Philip and return to a life of "sweet reason" (65), but feels a "a perverse but unmistakable throb of dark desire" (89) for Philip and his world of passion and art. The narrator, also like Lucy Stark, chooses bourgeois life over *la vie bohème* after learning from art. Both Philip and the narrator achieve the "authenticity" commensurate with their characters, inclinations, and abilities. In that way they also resemble Lucy Stark in their desire to shape their lives as works of art.

In "His Blue Period," Martin deconstructs the cultural script of the artist as a *monstre sacré*, a great artist who is ruthless in his ambition and in his treatment of others. "Anspach fell in love with a color the way most men fall in love with a beautiful, mysterious, fascinating, unattainable woman. He gave himself over to his passion without self-pity, without vanity or envy, without hope really. It wasn't the cold spirit of rage and competitiveness which he showed for everything and everyone else in his world. It was unselfish admiration, a helpless opening of the heart" (9). During his early period, that color is blue, suggesting the blue period of Pablo Picasso, supposedly inspired by the death of his fellow artist Carlos Castegna. Anspach's deep loss during his blue period is the suicide of his mistress Maria, but he, like Picasso, continues to have a brilliant career.

Martin subverts this cliché of *monstre sacré*. Anspach initially seems to represent the callous artist who sacrifices relationships on the altar of art because we see him through the eyes of a narrator, John, who is mediocre in both art and life. Unlike Anspach, John plays it safe. He loves Maria, but confesses, "I didn't have the heart, or was it the courage, ever to say the words" (5). Instead he marries the hard-working and income-producing Yvonne and his "canvases got smaller and smaller" (20). With Yvonne's steady salary and the occasional sale of a painting, he is comfortable: "It makes me lazy, though, and complacent. Some days I don't paint at all" (23). During a chance encounter, Anspach tells John that Maria had committed suicide in despair over John's choice of Yvonne over her (25), not over Anspach's dismissive treatment. John returns home to tell Yvonne this "news," but Yvonne had known all along. "'How could you not have known that?' she said," the last line of the story (27). Like another John, John Marcher in James's "The Beast in the Jungle," he needs to be told by a woman what he should know himself: avoiding the self-knowledge that passionate commitment demands allowed John to have moderate success and a loving wife and daughter, but at the cost of his development both as an artist and as a human being. Monsters can develop from lack of commitment to art and life, not just from too much commitment, Martin suggests.

In the novella "The Unfinished Novel," Martin presents a female artist as the *monstre sacré* as seen through the narrator, Maxwell, who, like John of "His Blue Period," is evasive, envious, and egotistical, and does everything he can to remain blind to the truth about his life and his art. As a novice writer, Maxwell had an affair with Rita, a leonine and predatory beauty, much like Diana in *Alexandra* (1979) or Donna in *The Great Divorce* (1994). Rita is a fellow writer, but she is Maxwell's superior in both artistic and critical ability (101, 120). She betrays him with a woman and then runs off with his rent money. Years later, on a visit to New Orleans from Vermont, where he has a comfortable relationship with a neighbor, Pamela, and a moderate success as a writer, he encounters Rita, now fat, poor, sick, and unpublished after a life of adventure and passion.

Martin suggests that the inability to take risks and engage deeply in art and life produces inauthenticity in both art and life. Maxwell is not an artist; he plays the role of an artist and he lives a lie. Maxwell is healthy, complacent, and comfortable. "I'm not famous, by any means, but I have a small reputation, or so I flatter myself, and I am able to live in modest comfort on the proceeds from my books" (94). He prides himself on his lack of growth: "Whenever I return [to New Orleans], my friends are always quick to observe that I haven't changed" (92). Although he resembles Valerie Martin in that he says, "I hated the whole gestalt of the Southern storyteller" (97), unlike Martin, he won't respond to contemporary life as it really is, North or South; instead, he attempts to imitate Emerson and Thoreau, by writing, in Thoreau's phrase, "naked speech" (97), but he settles for a fake New England gestalt:

> Of course, when I got to Vermont, I settled down and wrote stories like everyone else. Even if "naked speech" had been within my capabilities, it wasn't likely to sell, and I was, above all, a realist about the requirements of the market. But my characters had names like Winston and Edna, they worked at bookstores, they concerned themselves with ethical questions. By my second year, their inquiries were impeded by blizzards or locals who spoke in monosyllables. I let my beard grow out, discovered the virtues of flannel shirts, wool socks, lined rubber boots. My accent, never strong, faded; my hands were chapped. I had left the South behind, purposefully and finally, and I rejoiced in my new identity. (97–98)

His inauthenticity has cost him his empathy as a human being. When he sees the hungry feral cats in Rita's run-down neighborhood, "hostility toward the human residents of this street animated me. Of course they were all poor, but couldn't they see this suffering in their midst and organize to do something about it?" (104). After Rita's death, he recalls the death of his cat Joey: "If offered the chance to call back to life Rita or Joey, I knew I would choose, without hesitation, the cat" (153), an undemanding and safe companion.

In Martin's tales of artists, envy is the deadly sin that harms the envious much more than the envied, and that damage is magnified when the woman artist is the envied object of a male artist. When Maxwell is agonizing over what to do with Rita's unfinished novel, he has a night-mare about Rita beating him in a race even though she begins the contest wearing high heels (142) that represent her handicap as a woman. When he reads her unfinished novel, he whines, "I felt, as I had not in her living presence, perilously vulnerable to Rita" (132). In a vicious circle, he fears women because he refuses to understand them and does not understand them because he fears them. In their youth, Rita "observed, as others have over the years, that my female characters were shallow, lacking complexity and dimension" (101).

Through Maxwell and Rita, Martin suggests that a pseudo-artist can be more of a monster than a true and committed artist. Rita's reappearance in New Orleans challenges Maxwell's complacent self-image, and so he tries to destroy her and her art. In their final confrontation at his apartment, he attempts to retaliate for her unmasking gaze by refusing to help her, and she responds with a last crushing blow to his ego: "I've read all your books, Maxwell. . . . I'm a much better writer than you'll ever be" (128). As Rita is leaving, she falls down the stairs, the narrator claims, "because I bumped into her and knocked her off balance" (128), but she asserts, "You pushed me" (129). He next kills her art, at least temporarily, by choosing to bury her unfinished novel when it arrives at his Vermont home instead of editing and publishing it.

Since the subject of Rita's novel is "a love triangle, a tale of aban-donment and revenge" (120), Maxwell actually fears Rita's exposure of his betrayed, defensive, and fake self: "Would I find myself dissected, a squirming, quivering creature, flayed and pinned open on a page, my panicked heart throbbing for all to see?" (138). In this image, he sees him-self as the speaker and title character of T. S. Eliot's "The Love Song of J. Alfred Prufrock" (1920), who fears "The eyes that fix you in a formulated phrase" (line 56) and sees himself "formulated, sprawling on a pin" (l.57). As for Prufrock, the eyes Maxwell fears belong to a woman who can judge him for what he is, ineffectual and cowardly. The image also recalls Cath-erine Bultman in *Italian Fever,* who excoriates DV for his poor writing and makes a sketch of DV flayed open "from neck to abdomen" with an understandably "agonized expression" (48) on his face. Martin's pseudo-artists fear the humiliation of exposure even more than physical torment.

Martin shows the power of great art, even over one who fears and envies it. With his usual inability to take decisive action, Maxwell cannot actually destroy Rita's manuscript even though he refuses to get it published. "I was calm. I wasn't vengeful. I'd give Rita a chance. I would put the boxes in a hard plastic case—I had a number of them I used to store my own manuscripts—space-age stuff that would withstand a century or two of the old diurnal roll. I swallowed the last of my cold coffee. Then, with a sense of purpose and well-being, I went out to the shed to get my shovel" (153). In this, the final paragraph of the novella, by relegating her manuscripts to the "old diurnal roll," he attempts to make her as dead as Wordsworth's Lucy in "A slumber did my spirit seal":

> No motion has she now, no force;
> She neither hears nor sees;
> Roll'd round in earth's diurnal course,
> With rocks, and stones, and trees!

Maxwell believes he is "giv[ing] Rita a chance" (153), but he is temporizing. He acknowledges her superiority by not destroying the manuscript, but he can only bury it in the earth as he attempts to bury Rita in his subconscious. Both the manuscripts and Rita's memory could re-emerge. Ironically, he has immortalized her, not obliterated her, within himself because, like Wordworth's Lucy, Rita now "seem'd a thing that could not feel / The touch of earthly years." Like her novel, for him, she will never be finished. And, as in one of Poe's gothic tales of premature burial, that manuscript, either actually or metaphorically, may yet rise to haunt him; the novel and Martin's novella end ambiguously and are, in that sense, unfinished.

In "The Open Door," Martin explores what kind of passion an artist needs to sustain her life and her art, in contrast to Rita and her unfinished novel; part of that sustenance is embracing change in order to avoid stagnation. A successful poet, Edith Sharpe has channeled her passion, her hatred of patriarchy (174) and of the aesthetic and emotional aridity of her childhood (159), into her books, the aptly titled *Sullen Vixens* and *Unnatural Disaster*. Edith believes that "poetry made manners possible. It was her vengeance; she needed no other" (160–61). Now, however, "She had more and more difficulty writing. . . . Perhaps the truth was that she had exhausted the vein of her poetry, and there was nothing left to draw from it, neither blood nor gold" (181). The choice that confronts her is voiced by her lover, Isabel, another of Martin's "overpowering, leonine" (159) female characters, in this case a dancer who proclaims about the American college in Connecticut where Edith teaches, "I can't live in that place. . . . It's like being slowly asphyxiated. I feel alive here. Rome is full of disorder and messiness, all the things Americans are terrified of because they prefer death to life" (179). We do not know if Edith will choose to mine a new vein of experience, based on love and spontaneity, rather than hatred and exclusion, with Isabel in Rome because the story ends with Isabel standing in an open door, asking, "Are you ready?" (185). Isabel confronts Edith with the challenge that a writer faces with each new project, the encounter with the unknown and unfinished.

In "The Change," Martin once again uses the perspective of a male non-artist to compel the reader to think deeply about the attributes of great art and its makers, and the particular challenges faced by women artists. Gina is clearly ready to go through the open door, or, in her case, an open window, to the bewilderment of her somewhat aggrieved spouse, Evan, the central consciousness. Gina no longer follows the convention that women must please, so Evan finds her behavior "churlish" (187) and "uncivil" (187). She ignores the housework and shopping (188), won't dress up with makeup, scent, and jewelry for a party (190), and, at the party, bluntly confronts Vicky, who has had plastic surgery, with "Have you lost your mind? . . . Why would you do something like that? You look awful" (191). He attributes her altered behavior to menopause, "The Change," which he dismisses as just another excuse for women to embrace victimhood, "all the trials of their biology and psychology . . . and the failure of men to comprehend any of it" (193). He does not want either change or "the Change," and wonders, "Why couldn't everything just go on as it always had?" (210).

Gina, as a true artist, embraces change. She transforms herself from a woman caught in a patriarchal domestic script to a goddess-like committed artist. Her sweeping perspective in new prints is even acknowledged by Evan as "terrific" (198). The prints depict nocturnal scenes but have "an almost subterranean glow" (197); "the viewpoint was high" (198), and yet the prints display a remarkable lucidity of detail, including "the small hindfoot of a rabbit, no bigger than his fingernail" (197). In another apparent contradiction, Gina works at night, yet Evan finds her studio empty and the window open. In the tale's final scene, an owl, perhaps Gina, appears to Evan and "a thrill as of discovery, passed through him" (212). Gina now has the vision of an owl: owls are attributes of Minerva, the goddess of wisdom, and wisdom is an attribute associated with age. Thus, Gina does not feel Vicky's need to mimic youth. As he gazes at the owl, the last line of the story indicates that Evan may now realize what Gina already knows, that "it was best to be still in such a presence, which would surely not stay long or ever come again" (212). Change is inevitable, for good or ill, but trying to evade it produces a stagnation that is worse than death, in art and in life.

Artistic inspiration and talent at its greatest pitch "would surely not stay long" because, for Martin, art, vulnerable to all sorts of vicissitudes, is unique and ephemeral, and artists, as well as non-artists who are artists in life, are successful when they can cherish and appreciate its sublime, though momentary, manifestations. As Henry James delineated in his novel *The Tragic Muse* (1890), the art of acting is particularly ephemeral, and Martin displays it as tragically brief in her story "The Bower." The doubles or foils in this story are the limited artist Sandra, a former actress and current drama professor, and one of her students, Carter, who has the potential to be a great artist. He performed so brilliantly as the title character in Sandra's college production of *Hamlet* that the married Sandra becomes enamored with him, has an affair with him, and even wants to vicariously continue her now-defunct acting career by participating in what she is convinced will be his future triumphs on the stage. When she realizes that Carter has tired of her, she recognizes her obligations to her husband and children and lets him go. Carter's great career never materializes because he cannot emotionally recover from an automobile accident that he, as the driver, survived but in which his passenger, a young woman, died in an agony that he witnessed but could not alleviate. Unlike Hamlet, who causes Ophelia's death, Carter does not literally die, but his art is dead; like Sandra, he seems to enact the old saw, "Those who can't do, teach."

Like Maxwell in "The Unfinished Novel," without recognizing their envy, inferior artists see the burial of the superior artist's talent. Sandra cannot convince herself that she is not consumed with envy of Carter's talent, lying to herself that she "admitted that from the start, she had overwhelmed Carter, literally as well as figuratively, because she was bigger than he was" (53). Unlike Maxwell, though, once Sandra realizes that she cannot regain her talent through attaching herself to his career and lets him go, she can hold the beauty of his art in her memory as a pleasure, not the torment it is for the jealous Maxwell. Significantly, Sandra becomes infatuated with Carter at the moment he delivers Hamlet's famous soliloquy choosing life or death in a "bower" erected on the stage. The bower evokes the opening of John Keats's great Romantic poem *Endymion* (1818):

> A thing of beauty is a joy for ever:
> Its loveliness increases; it will never
> Pass into nothingness; but still will keep
> A bower quiet for us, and a sleep
> Full of sweet dreams, and health, and quiet breathing.

In Sandra's memory, Carter's performance will remain that joy though she cannot hold him as the moon goddess did Endymion by having Zeus keep him permanently asleep in a bower, except in the bower of her memory.

In "The Bower," Martin explores some of the situations and themes that she will explore masterfully in *The Confessions of Edward Day.* Both works concern acting, particularly through *Hamlet,* whose title character himself acts many roles and directs a play for his own ends, not those of art. They both depict a young performer whose career is tragically and abruptly abbreviated. In both story and novel, an actor becomes a teacher after he is responsible for a young woman's torment, just as Hamlet, whom Carter and Edward Day played, precipitated Ophelia's madness and death. Yet in both works, despite the ephemeral quality of acting and the messy lives of the actors, it becomes "a joy for ever" in the memories of those who witnessed the performance.

The Confessions of Edward Day also shares themes and techniques with other tales in *The Unfinished Novel and Other Stories:* the self-deceptive narrator, the double, the invidious consequences of envy between artists, the conflict between art and life, and the extreme vulnerability of art to life's vicissitudes. James and Chekhov remain as the poles of disciplined renunciation versus quirky vitality. With James, Martin continues to problematize a religion of art and the worship of the romantic artist as rationalizations to avoid the compassionate commitment of one human being to another. Caring for dependent or needy others, especially through parenthood, seemingly conflicts with the demands of self-realization and art, but the denial of love and its obligations leads to a diminished artistic scope and the artist's unrealized potential—unless, of course, true artistry was never there, as suggested in Chekhov's novella "The Duel," which Martin calls "one of my favorite stories" (Biguenet Interview 53). Chekhov's Laevsky compares his own indecisiveness to that of Hamlet, rationalizing that his artistic soul (that produces no art or work) is too good for mundane cares like a job and family. When he is challenged to a duel by the voice of his conscience, his döppelganger, his confrontation with death causes him to realize and value the woman whose life and reputation he has destroyed; he marries her, and with her leads a life of poverty and simplicity with no further delusions about his sensibility, a fate that Edward Day's life will echo. The spirit of Iris Murdoch's novel *The Sea, The Sea* (1978) also hovers over *The Confessions of Edward Day,* with an actor as a self-deceptive narrator who damages women's lives as he fantasizes a romantic destiny for his artistic self.

As in *The Unfinished Novel and Other Stories,* Martin uses point of view in *The Confessions of Edward Day* to compel the reader to question both her illusion as an artist and that of the narrator or central consciousness, who tries to argue that his actions were justified, like those of Chekhov's Laevsky, by the consequences of romantic victimhood and the demands of an artistic vocation. Although Edward Day titles his memoir *Confessions,* his account is really a rationalization, not a *mea culpa.* Like the two defining works of the confessional genre, the autobiographies of St. Augustine and Jean-Jacques Rousseau, Edward Day's *Confessions* attempt to demonstrate how failings may be diminished, or even appear as virtues, when seen in the context of an entire life, that of a saint and a philosopher. Unlike Augustine or Rousseau, however, Edward Day does not successfully fulfill his vocation and remains tormented and puzzled at the end of his narrative, much like Claude, the unreliable narrator of Martin's second novel, *Alexandra.* Happily, in contrast to Claude's somewhat whining tone, Edward refreshingly uses an actor's charm, the ability to create illusions, to justify his ways to men.

Through Edward, Martin explores the misuse of art by those who deploy it for their own selfish ends or to fill their own emotional vacuums. Edward is not an actor due to his talent or his devotion to the art, but as an attempt to fulfill his own needs and evade obligations that might confine him. He attributes his choice of career to his confusion about his identity as a child and the tragic end of his youth, both of which he ascribes to his mother. She was something of an actress herself since she maintained the illusion that she was a heterosexual wife and mother until she left to live with another woman, Helen. The façade had its chinks, though, and her unmet needs could be glimpsed. She wanted her last child to be a girl, after a series of sons, so when Edward was born she called him by his middle name, Leslie, and read to him from girls' books, while unconsciously providing a role model for a future actor: "Mother was a good reader; she changed her voices for the different characters" (3).

Because Edward cannot develop an identity for himself, he uses art as an evasion of life, not as a confrontation with its profoundly challenging truths. When Edward went to boarding school, he was able to choose a name, but not an identity: "When I went off to school and became Edward, I had no clear idea of myself; perhaps that was why I was drawn to acting. Inside a character I knew exactly who I was, the environment was controlled, and no one was going to do anything unexpected. It seemed a way of playing it safe. Of course, real acting is the farthest thing from safe a person can get, but I didn't know that then" (4). Ironically, he will lose the stage as a refuge years later when he hears onstage the shot that kills his suicidal double and makes his traumatized leading lady into a gothic captive of a male plot. As a college student, though, acting still presents an alluring sanctuary. While Edward spends the night at a party with an attractive older girl, he misses his mother's messages to call him and later learns that she died that night in a suicide pact with her lover, reinforcing his sense that life is uncontrollable so that "for me acting was an egress from unbearable sorrow and guilt" (10).

Edward's first significant role is Hamlet,[1] and for Martin's young men, like Carter in "The Bower" (or like Chekhov's Laevsky in "The Duel"), that is a sign of a dangerous obsession with self that leads to the destruction of others. Edward recognizes that his personal affinities with Hamlet, not his professional skills, make him a success in the role: "My insecurity was part of what made my prince Hamlet so appealing. I was, as he was, a youth, a student, and I had lost a parent in suspicious circumstances" (12). Hamlet, after all, directed a play, not for the sake of the art, but for his own ends in trying to establish his uncle's culpability in his father's death. Like Hamlet blaming Claudius (his mother's lover and now husband) for his father's death, Edward blames his mother's lover Helen for his mother's suicide: "One night I woke from panicked dreams with the idea that I must find Helen and make her pay for what she had done to me" (12). Characteristically, his mind is not on Shakespeare's artistry, but on the play as a safe emotional outlet: "I wept, not for Hamlet, who lived just long enough to avenge his father's murder, but for myself" (12).

Hamlet reinforces what life has already taught Edward: avoid emotional commitment because love is dangerous: too demanding, precarious, and easily lost. Ironically, he fails to see art's warnings about narcissistic self-absorption. Since Edward believes he failed to save his mother, love is, above all, a source of guilt because one can never live up to love's demands. He proves he has learned this lesson in his relationship with Madeleine Delavergne, who could have been the love of his life if he were willing to make such a commitment. Instead, she becomes his Ophelia, psychologically destroyed by his self-involvement. Madeleine's surname, Delavergne, is the actual name of Madame de Lafayette, the author of *The Princess of Cleves* (1678). Madeleine will share the fate of that princess, who is also torn between her husband and the man she loves, and who retreats from the world after her husband's death.

As is typical of Martin's failed fictional artists and failed human be-

---

1. *Hamlet* is first on Martin's top-ten list of literary works ("Top Ten").

ings, Edward is incapable of empathy. Like Claude, the title character of Martin's *Alexandra,* Edward only wants Madeleine when she can live up to his Pygmalion fantasies; he does not value her as she really is, but only for the ways that she can meet his needs. When Edward is initially attracted to Madeleine, he perceives her the way he wants her to be: "Madeleine struck me as unusually stable and confident" (15). In a more intimate relationship, he resents meeting the needs for mutual support of a couple living together: "I was spending far too much energy trying to keep Madeleine's ego properly inflated when my own was sagging well below the recommended pressure level" (80). In Edward's world, where ego is all, compassion is not a virtue, but a debit.

To avoid the draining effects of empathy, Edward decamps to summer stock, forcing Madeleine to return to her own apartment so that he can rent his for the season. Madeleine protests, "'It's not about reason, Edward. . . . It's about feelings.' 'Feelings don't pay rent,' I replied" (93). Madeleine takes this coldly calculating response to heart and does not tell Edward when she discovers that she is pregnant with his child while he is away in summer repertory. When he finds out from his döppelganger, Guy Margate, he sends money, but no emotional support: "I wanted to help her without making any kind of commitment" (130), rationalizing, "Madeleine wasn't some misguided teenager; she was an adult, perfectly capable of making her own decisions" (134). He believes he is saving himself while he is only diminishing his life force as an artist and a person.

In Martin's works, parenthood is the "consolation of nature" for one's own death and disappointments, but in order to attain this consolation, one must be willing to nurture the future through the child. Parenthood is a more binding commitment than a romantic or spousal relationship, and hence more threatening to Edward, who asserts, "I've always known I wasn't cut out for fatherhood. What man is? It's a service role after all, unless one decides to take prisoners and call it family life. I wanted none of it" (162). He wants to be the star, not the "service" or supporting player. When Madeleine, now married to Edward's double, the more attentive Guy Margate, loses the baby and the ability to conceive again, Edward again assesses the situation in terms of his needs: "I confess that I had felt only relief at the news that she would not be able to have a child, which was enormously selfish of me, but there it is. I felt that" (178–79). Edward repeatedly attempts to soften the reader's judgments of him through confessions like this one that are really self-justifications. Interestingly, he only feels guilty discomfort when he sees his failing the mother of his child in terms of acting, not through authentic feeling: "a generalized sadness and a humbling conviction that somehow I had been exposed and that everyone concerned now knew I was entirely unequal to my part" (179).

Martin depicts Edward, like Hamlet with Ophelia, refusing to stop tormenting Madeleine with his attentions and his presence when he decides his ambitions are more important than she is. He masks his egotism in an ostensible devotion to his art as he plans to audition for a part in Chekhov's *Uncle Vanya* (1897). Madeleine is also a contender for a role in the production, but Edward decides to audition despite a plea from his döppelganger Guy Margate, now Madeleine's devoted husband, that he stay away from Madeleine because "she's fragile, she's a fragile woman" (193). Edward prefers to see a different, more convenient Madeleine to whom he has no responsibilities: "Madeleine is an actress. She's a professional" (193), so he can readily rationalize putting his ambitions before his personal relations: "That was how I reached my decision—lightly. Playfully, as an actor, not as a friend of one or a lover of the other, not in defiance or in anger, but as one who is offered a prize and reaches out to take it" (207). His career, his art, remains most important to him. When Madeleine cannot continue on stage after the shot announcing Guy's suicide, Edward finishes that evening's performance with Madeleine's understudy and then completes the run of the play. When Edward tells his friend Teddy that "I don't know what I'm going to do" (255), Teddy is taken aback (252–53) when he finds out that Edward's bewilderment arises from the way that Madeleine's understudy interprets the part differently, not from Guy's death and Madeleine's madness.

Edward's determination to use his art as an excuse for defaulting on his human obligations is reinforced by his mother in art, the acclaimed mature actress Marlene Webern. During the summer of Madeleine's pregnancy, he acts with Marlene in several productions, including the part of the young gigolo of an aging actress in Tennessee Williams's *Sweet Bird of Youth* (1959). Hamlet-like, Edward has a sexual attraction to this mother figure, and he plays a bedroom scene with her in the Williams play that is reminiscent in many ways of Hamlet's exchange with his mother Gertrude in her bedroom. Marlene rejects Edward's advances because she does not want any emotional encroachments on her career. She has a son, only a few years younger than Edward, who has "drug problems" (137) and is "unhappy" (137), "probably because," says Marlene, "his mother is an actress" (137).

Marlene in some ways resembles her character in *Sweet Bird of Youth*, who tells her young lover, "*When monster meets monster, one monster has got to give way. AND IT WILL NEVER BE ME!*" (112–13). She sees the dedicated artist as a *monstre sacré* and tells Edward with regard to the agent to whom she is recommending him, "There's a coldness in you that he'll take offense to, he'll try to root it out of you, but I think ultimately it will be your strength" (138). Marlene fervently advises Edward against the split between man and artist that James posits in his short story "The Private Life": "You're a good actor and you could be a great actor, but only if you understand that your life must be given up to your art. You can have no other life. There can't be Ed having an emotion on the stage and Ed having a strong, pure, deep emotion here in this room and a curtain drawn between. You mustn't sit here and try to push away a powerful emotion because it's painful. As an actor, you have no right to do that" (119–20). She recognizes his tendency to use art as an escape from painful emotions instead of confronting and refining the agony in the alembic of his art. Despite Marlene's counsel, Edward continues to use art as an evasion.

In a novel as filled with doubles or foils for Edward as *Hamlet* is for Hamlet (Horatio, Laertes, Fortinbras, Rosencrantz, Guildenstern), Edward's stage roles are in many ways his chosen doubles, his true döppelgangers. His roles before and after his summer with Marlene are all self-involved men who use and are cruel to the women attracted to them; they will not deeply engage with or help them: the title character in *Hamlet*, Stanley in Harold Pinter's *The Birthday Party* (1958), Jean in August Strindberg's *Miss Julie* (1888), and Astrov in Chekhov's *Uncle Vanya*. Characteristically, Edward fails to recognize himself in his own description of Astrov: "His attraction to Elena, a lazy, selfish, desperate, beautiful siren who enchants him from the first moment he sees her, is serious. He knows this passion could be the wreck of him, yet he can't resist it" (206–207). Like Astrov, Edward only cares about himself, not about his effect on others.

Edward's acknowledged döppelganger, Guy Margate, presents an alternative path; like the döppelganger in James's "The Jolly Corner," Guy indicates what Edward could have become, in this case if he chose love over art. Guy is an actor of obscure origins who physically resembles Edward, though as a literally and metaphorically darker version. He rescues Edward from drowning, but seems increasingly to inhabit the life that he saved. Edward regards him as a hated nemesis because he sees him as a competitor, in art and in love, failing to heed Marlene's advice that "envy can be killing to an actor. . . . It's ruinous in all the arts" (119), as Martin also indicates in her tales of artists in *The Unfinished Novel and Other Stories.* Edward really wants to avoid Guy because, like the döppelganger in Edgar Allan Poe's "William Wilson" (1839), Guy suggests Edward's conscience in that his appearances are timely reminders to Edward of his deficiencies as a human being, culminating in this list of failures in their fraught exchange before Guy's suicide: "Guy had attacked on three emotional fronts: my feelings for Madeleine, my personal sense of obligation to him for saving my life, and my insecurity as an actor" (201).

In Guy, Martin creates a döppelganger who is more than an embodied conscience for, or satirical caricature of, the protagonist. She complicates her use of doubles by employing Henry James's theory of human relationships as closed systems or zero-sum games that he develops in his whimsical novella or *jeu d'esprit The Sacred Fount* (1901). According to the metaphor of the sacred fount, within an intimate relationship there is a fixed amount of vitality or life force, so that when one member of the couple gets more, the other has less. In *The Sacred Fount,* as one member of a married couple seems to get older, his wife appears younger, and one member of an adulterous pair seems more intellectual while his lover becomes more vacuous. While the trope of the sacred fount could be compared to vampirism, it is not a one-way drainage of physical blood, but attempts to represent the complex psychology of an intense relationship in which the balance shifts with life's vagaries. Edward Day moves on, flourishes, and becomes increasingly successful, while Guy Margate, his double in a psychic coupling, becomes old, exhausted, and a failed actor.

In her depiction of Edward and Guy as döppelgangers, Martin combines the metaphor of the sacred fount with another Jamesian doubling, that of his short story "The Private Life," in which a writer succeeds because he can double himself with one self handling an active social life while the other self remains alone, writing masterpieces in a dark room. Martin's use of the sacred fount extends to relationships beyond, but as intense as, the sexual. The sacred fount can represent the energy within the artist, so that Guy Margate is more than a social avatar for Edward Day; he takes over Day's "private life," loving and nurturing Madeleine, thus freeing Edward to pursue success on the stage. After Edward's complaint that "I was spending far too much energy trying to keep Madeleine's ego properly inflated when my own was sagging well below the recommended pressure level" (80), Guy marries the pregnant Madeleine and supports her career for years by working in a bookshop: "I have to do everything, the shopping, the cooking, pay all the bills, keep Maddie calmed down. I never sleep" (190). When Guy kills himself, Edward must resume responsibility for his "private life"; Edward's sacred fount, like Guy's, must now flow in the service of human love. Edward leaves the stage to teach acting and to raise money for a regional theater while caring for the permanently damaged Madeleine, who also no longer acts: "She's Madeleine but not Madeleine, though she doesn't know it . . . she's not passionate about anything including me" (269).

Martin gives her adaptation of the döppelganger a final turn of the screw in the concluding sections of *The Confessions of Edward Day* when she presents us with a new potential double for Edward in the person of his longtime friend, Teddy, who had, many years before, invited Guy to the momentous beach party at which Guy met Edward and saved him from drowning. Teddy is also an actor, but he could not grow professionally until he grew personally. He offended his family and revolutionized his life by coming out of the closet and taking a Chinese American painter, Wayne, as his lover. To the detriment of his career, he devoted himself to Wayne, including nursing him until his death from AIDS. At the end of the novel, he has returned successfully to the theater, but "he has never lived with anyone again. He's working too hard" (270). Teddy's risk-taking and devotion in his "private" life ultimately deepened and enriched his acting.

Unlike Teddy, Edward has been unable to accept and relinquish the past because he never lived it fully or learned from it. Despite Madeleine's Eurydice-like warning, "Don't look back. . . . You might lose me" (272), Edward's jealousy of the long-dead Guy rekindles when he finds an ambiguous note in one of Madeleine's old suitcases. When Edward shows Teddy the note as they are having dinner in a restaurant, Teddy tries to put Madeleine's relationship with Guy in perspective for Edward: "I think he [Guy] was madly in love with Madeleine. And she was fond of him. Sex or no sex, they had a close relationship. Whatever it was that held them together, it lasted several years" (278). Edward rejects this empathetic appraisal: "As Teddy advanced his reasonable interpretation, I tried to eat another bean, but it stuck in my throat" (278). He cannot swallow Guy and Madeleine's mutual affection, however distant in the past it is. Envy once again appears to choke his potential as artist and as a compassionate human being.

As Guy had saved Edward from drowning years ago, Teddy now saves him from choking by thwacking him on the back and dislodging the bean, but he really saves his life by giving him two excellent pieces of advice. First, he tells Edward to ignore the note and send Madeleine some flowers. At this point, Edward finally allows his emotions to surface, weeping copiously in the restaurant, as if he is now mourning all the losses, including that of his mother, that he has repressed for years. After Teddy, seemingly recognizing Edward's obdurate narcissism, observes that "you were moved by your own touching saga" (281), he gives Edward a second sound piece of advice: "It's a good story. You ought to write it down" (281). Although Edward responds that "no one would believe it" (281), he presumably did "write it down" in *The Confessions of Edward Day,* but his narration indicates that he remains oblivious to the significance of his tale and so he cannot relate his art to his life in any mutually enriching way.

Martin's skill is demonstrated by the fact that readers do "believe it," though "it" is not Edward's version of the story. Ironically, the tale that the three men—Edward, Guy, and Teddy—dispute really belongs to Madeleine. Sadly, like Caddy in Faulkner's *The Sound and the Fury* (1929) or Alexandra in Martin's *Alexandra,* Madeleine's sacred fount is so drained by male needs that she is incapable of providing her version of the tale though she is its center. Subject and teller are also doubles that are governed by the sacred fount with the teller usurping the subject's vitality.

As Madeleine's untold story suggests, life and art can be mutually destructive, but Martin ends the novel stressing the ceaselessly powerful ways that life and art can synergistically create and continue. As Edward and Teddy sit at the restaurant table, a well-dressed young man approaches them and tells Edward that he saw his performance as Jean in Strindberg's *Miss Julie* years ago. "When I left the theater, I knew I wanted to be an actor. . . . You changed my life" (283), the last line of the novel. As Martin's repeated use of doubles suggests, change is life, and the sacred fount of art flows on, emerging in a variety of artists and works over time and changing the lives of artists and art lovers. The sacred fount of art is not life's adversary, but a vital part of life, and Martin's oeuvre is simultaneously a postmodern parodic tribute to and dialogue with her predecessors, as well as her own contribution to the sacred founts of life and art.

12

The Ghost of the Mary Celeste

IMAGINATIVE VOYAGING ON UNCHARTED SEAS

*I*n *The Ghost of the Mary Celeste* (2014), Valerie Martin's recurrent themes and techniques are deployed synergistically, culminating in a mature masterwork. Her early preoccupations with female masochism are modulated from extreme sex to more conventional, but equally frightening, Victorian female roles, since, for Martin, in all eras women are subject to boredom and entrapment. As in the works of her middle period, she depicts the romantic and often fatally self-deceptive notion that nature mirrors and responds to human longings, while humans paradoxically and prosaically exploit nature, including their fellow human beings, for gain or property. In *The Ghost of the Mary Celeste,* nature, in the form of the sea, exerts a magnetic attraction upon human hopes and fears because the ever-changing, profoundly mysterious sea represents two vast and uncharted realms: the human psyche and death. Martin addresses human desires and dreads in the face of the unknown as an aspect of her greatest theme: the powers of the human imagination for good or ill, whether deployed by spiritualist mediums or by another sort of medium, authors of fiction.

The structure of *The Ghost of the Mary Celeste*—an amalgamation of documents, diaries, logs, and reminiscences—reinforces the theme of the use and abuse of the imagination. Since Martin provides no solution to the maritime mystery of the ship *Mary Celeste,* readers must employ their imaginations upon these fragments of fact and speculation in order to construct a narrative that satisfies their own predilections. Is the reader, like some of the characters, a romantic who uses fragments of reality to construct a view of life and of an afterlife that offers hope and comfort? Or is that reader, like some of the other characters, a realist who rejects the illusory consolations of an afterlife in favor of valuing the here and now, making the best of life before death's inevitable conclusion? Over the span of her career, including this novel, Martin places characters upon a spectrum from delusory romanticism to a more constructive realism, but it *is* a spectrum, not a division into two distinct categories. No one is invulnerable to the siren call of the imagination as the desires of each individual shape her or his narrative about the mysteries of the human mind and the enigma of death.

Martin gives these mysteries a further Jamesian turn of the screw, with a postmodern twist, by constantly suggesting metafictional layers of narration, like a series of Russian dolls nested within each other. From the flotsam of reality, stories may be constructed by the characters, by Victorian authors, by Martin, and ultimately by the novel's readers if they are imaginatively active. As reviewer Jane Shilling notes, "The only true reality, the message seems to be, resides in the stories that we choose to tell ourselves."

Martin deploys the mystery of the *Mary Celeste* as a screen upon which the characters and the novel's readers project their views of life and death on the fate of the ship, as readers have done for a century and a half. According to Jess Blumberg, "The ship began its fateful voyage on November 7, 1872, sailing with seven crewmen and Capt. Benjamin Spooner Briggs, his wife, Sarah Cobb Briggs, and the couple's 2-year-old daughter, Sophia. The 282-ton brigantine battled heavy weather for two weeks to reach the Azores, where the ship log's last entry was recorded at 5 a.m. on November 25." Another ship, the *Dei Gratia,* found it adrift and in good condition, yet with no one aboard. The *Dei Gratia* towed the *Mary Celeste* to Gibraltar, and the inquiries began and remain unresolved to this day. Why did an experienced and reliable captain abandon ship? Was the ship boarded by pirates? Did all aboard leave suddenly because of the growing and potentially explosive fumes from the alcohol in casks in the hold? Was there a mutiny, perhaps led by the German sailors aboard?[1]

---

1. Blumberg's article, "Abandoned Ship: The *Mary Celeste,*" is a good summary of the mystery; interested readers can find many accounts in digital and print form. As Martin herself said in an interview posted on YouTube, "the research was huge." In that interview, Martin also relates that her interest was piqued in the fifth grade by an article in the *Weekly Reader* about the *Mary Celeste,* and then reinforced by her sea captain father's knowledge of the mystery ("Valerie Martin Discusses . . .").

The conjecture about the ill-fated ship continued and continues, in fiction and in speculative nonfiction. The "ghost" of the *Mary Celeste* cannot be laid because those aboard the *Mary Celeste* vanished as do the dead: we don't know what happened to them, but we want to know and sometimes imagine that we do know. Martin highlights the theme of death through her nineteenth-century Anglo-American maritime setting, as reviewer Christobel Kent elaborates:[2]

> This is a perilous, oppressive world in which women spend months confined in cabins and parlours, waiting for terrible news, or battened in their husbands' quarters; where ships go down with all hands in far-flung seas in the blink of an eye. It is the death-obsessed society of the Victorians, with their bombazine and mourning brooches and séances, a culture that found its apogee in Tennyson's outpouring of grief and despair, *In Memoriam,* here quoted by Martin. Her great creation, the restless, unfathomable sea that swallows the Mary Celeste's crew whole, allows us to draw a line direct from Tennyson's "Nature red in tooth and claw" to the oceanic darkness foreseen by Conrad, emblematic of the chaos of the new century to come, where belief will be sacrificed to stern rationalism.

Through the maritime experiences of her characters (most based on historical personages) and through her allusions to nineteenth-century Anglo-American literature about the sea (particularly that of Joseph Conrad, Edgar Allan Poe, and Herman Melville), Martin provides an array of beliefs, opinions, and speculations about life after death, and the significant ways such imaginative constructions affect life. As reviewer Hope Whittemore observes, "The ship and her ghosts become less important as Martin's convincing characters become stronger, their human voices giving something solid to cling to in a novel of uncertainties."

2. Jane Shilling similarly notes that "gradually we come to understand that it is not just the events aboard the *Mary Celeste* that are unknowable: that mystery is merely a spectacular version of the enigmas that haunt all human transactions" as well as "the way in which her fate exemplifies the 19th-century obsession with mortality and what—if anything—lies on the other side of the fragile membrane that separates life from death."

Initiated by epigraphs from Christina Rossetti and Arthur Conan Doyle, these speculative voices focus on the sea as the symbol of the *mare incognitum* within the human psyche and the *mare incognitum* beyond death.[3] The unknown seas merge in Martin's depiction of Victorian spiritualism as she suggests the ways that narratives about an afterlife spring from the largely unexplored sea of the human imagination. Martin's work is in the tradition of William Dean Howells and Henry James, who, according to Howard Kerr, saw "the entranced medium" as "a psychological rather than a supernatural problem" (21).

Martin invokes another James, William, as she does in her earlier works, to explore the *mare incognitum*. In "The Confidences of a Psychical Researcher," psychologist and philosopher William James speculates that "we with our lives are like islands in the sea" (1263), a "psychic sea" (1264) that encompasses both the "material" and the "mental." If this were true, William James posits, what we regard as the supernatural would only be another manifestation of the material world that we do not yet fathom. James calls himself neither "spiritist" nor "scientist," but a "psychical researcher waiting for more facts before concluding" (1263).[4]

Through her characterization of the real Sir Arthur Conan Doyle, spiritist and creator of the scientific Sherlock Holmes, Martin explores the limits of an imagination that cannot rest and wait in ambiguity but engages in self-deceptive wishful thinking and selfishly uses others to grasp a comforting, if illusory, certainty. Martin contrasts Doyle with the fictive journalist Phoebe Grant, who also seeks truth through her writing but knows how to put people first. Through Doyle and Grant, Martin foregrounds the ethical responsibility of the artist, as a medium of sorts,

---

3. In her study of late Victorian gothic fiction, Hilary Grimes differentiates between these unknown realms: "The supernatural relates to the external, to disturbances in the exterior world, whereas the uncanny is psychological, relating to disturbances in the internal body, or mind" (15).

4. According to John J. Kucich, "While [Henry] James never caught his brother William's intense enthusiasm for spiritualism and other psychic phenomena, he carefully followed William's efforts to use mediums and trance speakers to chart the unconscious. William always maintained a stronger belief in the possibility of spirit communication than in the validity of the mediums he actually studied, and remained a sympathetic, if unconvinced, investigator" (121).

to eschew artistic egotism and cozy evasion in favor of the exploration of life's *mare incognitum* in the "spirit" of courageous engagement and compassion.[5]

In *The Ghost of the Mary Celeste,* the sea reflects these engagements with, or evasions of, life and its aftermath with perfect indifference as in Joseph Conrad's *The Mirror of the Sea* (1906). Martin also mirrors the themes of her own short story "Sea Lovers" in her collection *The Consolation of Nature:* humans cause their own deaths by their romantic fantasies of the sea's beneficence and by their desire to assert their delusory domination over nature to exploit the sea for material gain. As reviewer John Vernon astutely observes, "The sea is virtually a character itself, inherently dangerous and indifferent." Tragedy at sea brackets the novel's contents as the paradoxically romantic materialists, the seafaring Briggs family of Marion, Massachusetts, are largely exterminated by the sea, or die on land as collateral damage. The first chapter is fittingly entitled "A Disaster at Sea." In 1850, aboard the *Early Dawn* shortly before its wreck, Captain Joseph Gibbs's wife, Maria Briggs Gibbs, hears a "soporific churning" that made her think of a child, her child, rocking in his cradle" (6), her son Natie, who soon will die ashore as an orphan. As in "Sea Lovers," Martin evokes Walt Whitman's poem "Out of the Cradle Endlessly Rocking," in which the sea whispers, "death, death, death, death" while a bird sings piteously for a lost mate. In the novel's last chapter, the very recently widowed Sarah Cobb Briggs in 1872 writes longingly of her lost mate, the drowned Captain Benjamin Briggs (brother of the *Early Dawn*'s lost Maria) in the unfinished log of the doomed *Mary Celeste.*

When the news of Natie's death is being delivered to the Cobb family, Reverend Cobb's students are reciting in Latin the shipwreck of Aeneas from Virgil's *Aeneid* (29), but Martin's characters heed neither Virgil's warnings nor the high death toll within the Briggs family but continue to go to sea. They prefer lighter, more romantic, and popular views of the sea, such as these lines from the favorite song (24) of Benjamin Briggs and his fiancée, Sarah Cobb, "In the Starlight," by Hattie Adams Fronk:

5. In *Sympathetic Medium: Feminine Channeling, the Occult, and Communication Technologies, 1859–1919,* Jill Galvan finds that in the literature of the period, "séance or mesmeric channeling" can "become metaphors for textual channeling" (25).

"Where the silvery waters murmur, by the margin of the sea / In the starlight, in the starlight let us wander gay and free." Benjamin Briggs takes his wife Sarah and toddler, Sophy, with him to "wander gay and free" as he makes one last voyage on the *Mary Celeste* in order to make enough money to fund an onshore business. Before leaving land, Sarah sings to her husband (75) Charles Horn's "All Things Love Thee, So Do I": "Gentle waves upon the deep, / Murmur soft when thou dost sleep, / . . . All things love thee, so do I. . . . / When thou wak'st the sea will pour / Treasures for thee to the shore, . . . / All things love thee, so do I." Hope, love, and material needs trump the experience of many deaths at sea among family, friends, and acquaintances or the warnings of great literature like the *Aeneid*. Sarah and Benjamin weigh anchor on the doomed *Mary Celeste*.

As hope prevails over experience of the sea, so it does in the ways the characters respond to the *mare incognitum* of death, in a spectrum from conventional Christianity to the more outré spiritualism. Benjamin's mother, called Mother Briggs, and Sarah's father, the Reverend Cobb, are the voices of Christian resignation before patriarchal authority. Mother Briggs "is stalwart. In her view God knows what must be and what must not be and it is ours to bear it with faith in His wisdom" (14), despite the fact that she has lost two of her six children (Nathan to a shipboard fever and Maria to the disaster on the *Early Dawn*) to the sea and now faces the death of her young orphaned grandson Natie, the drowned Maria's son. Reverend Cobb's authority as the conduit for a patriarchal god is threatened by spiritualism, so he denounces "this insalubrious craze for talking to spirits" (18) and regards spirit messages as "from the devil" (38).

In contrast, Reverend Cobb's deceased wife, Sarah's mother, did not share his and Mother Briggs's Christianity of passivity before an inscrutable Patriarch. Sarah remembers: "'By their fruits, ye shall know them.' That was a favorite saying of Mother's, especially when her children were idle. She took her religion to be a practice, not a test, and she was an active, not a submissive, Christian. She wanted her children to be alive to the possibilities of life, to show in our actions our moral engagement with our fellows" (58). Sarah's mother wanted her children to think for themselves, while being cognizant of the feelings of others. "She never gave orders or forbade actions, unless we were rude in public, which merited a frank rebuke. She had a way of looking at you with sympathy and understanding and hope and then asking the exact question that placed the matter in a clear moral light. The answer came of its own accord, and one cheerfully mended one's ways" (58). Mrs. Cobb exemplifies a member of a conventional religion whose belief in an afterlife did not absolve her or others from the responsibility of thinking and acting in this life to ameliorate the human condition.

Unfortunately, Mrs. Cobb is dead long before the adolescence of her daughters Sarah and Hannah, so they must struggle alone to develop their beliefs about the relationship of life to death and of death to life amid the high mortality rate of their family and neighbors. Sarah misses her mother, particularly her wise counsel and active example, but looks forward, not backward, and considers the effects of beliefs on the living. When a spiritualist, Richard Peebles,[6] visits her father, the Reverend Cobb, presumably to lure him with the prospect of a message from her mother, Sarah imagines her mother's potential spirit message as "Leander, this is disgraceful. Go home at once!" (39). With similar humor, Sarah rejects Peebles's occult warning: "A premonition of great loss! That sounds a fairly safe prediction in this vale of tears!" (38), as well as in this relentlessly seafaring milieu. She is skeptical about both Mother Briggs's and Hannah's views of the afterlife: "My aunt is a puzzle to me. One can't deny that she is a devoted, even a fierce, Christian, but her entire apprehension of God's will is that it is inscrutable and must be submitted to without comment or question. Perhaps she's right, but is it wrong for Hannah to miss the orphan [Natie] she cared for? In what way does her sadness affect the God who has bereaved her? I can't make any sense of it" (35).

Instead, like that of her mother, Sarah's touchstone is the effect of various beliefs on the living. She challenges Hannah, "If the dead see us and care for us and hang about in the air longing to reach us, how can their eternal homelessness be a consolation to us or to them?" (26). Sarah is asking what Justine S. Murison calls the "'*cui bono?*' question," the

6. Possibly suggested by spiritualist James Martin Peebles (1822–1922).

attempt to determine "the benefits of spiritualism to the 'real,' political world" that "haunted spiritualism throughout the 1850s and 1860s" (153).[7]

A practical realist, Sarah attempts to cope with her depressed, fantasizing, motherless younger sister Hannah while hoping for and then planning her own marriage to the handsome young sea captain Benjamin Briggs. When Hannah tells Sarah that she has seen the ghost of Maria Briggs, who she believes has returned to claim her ailing young son Natie, Sarah responds, "Supposing it *is* true. . . . What can anyone do about it?" (17). Similarly, when Hannah later informs Sarah that she saw the dripping drowned Maria leaning over Natie's crib and that the carpet was wet the next morning, Sarah merely asks if she tested the water to see if it were salty (23). Although Sarah recognizes that Hannah genuinely believes in her visions (18), she posits that they are "wishful thinking" (55) and that Hannah's way of coping with overwhelming losses is typical of humans: "I was thinking about ghosts. Who doesn't whisper a confidence at the grave of the beloved when the wind rustles the trees and lifts the petals of the roses planted there? What draws the bereaved to seek the departed still in this world? Is it hope, I wondered, or is it fear?" (19). Sarah thinks about the way her piano playing is a mystery to Benjamin in the same way that his navigation at sea is a mystery to her (24); what we do not understand is mysterious, even if it has easily explicable causes.

Unlike Sarah, Hannah copes with reality, especially mortality, through evasion and denial as she tries to regain the past. Sarah relates that "as a child [Hannah] talked to trees and made up stories. She wrote sweet poems about the dew being dropped from the cups of drinking fairies or enchanted woods where elves had tea parties using mushrooms for tables. It was charming, my sister the fabulist" (16). As she becomes an adolescent, Hannah continues to write poetry that appears to be Martin's amalgamation of Emily Dickinson and Christina Rossetti, two idiosyncratic Victorian poets whose ostensibly charming eccentricities concealed

---

7. In William Dean Howells's *The Undiscovered Country* (1880), disillusioned spiritualist Dr. Boynton answers the "*cui bono?*" question about spiritualism negatively: "All other systems of belief, all other revelations of the unseen world, have supplied a rule of life, have been given us for our *use* here. . . . It [spiritualism] has not yet shown its truth in the ameliorated life of men" (367).

unconventional views of women's entrapment. As described by Sarah, "the poems are on natural themes, the seasons, the beauty of the woods or the sea. They are odd, which they would be given Hannah's peculiar view of the world. Much circling of death, also great value attached to liberty" (49), as in this stanza:

> *Who holds the light that penetrates*
> *The dark above the stair*
> *Must have the heart to celebrate*
> *The spirit lingering there.* (50)

Sarah aptly observes, "There's a dark romantic in my sister" (49).

Hannah's fantasies take an even darker turn as her losses intensify. As Sarah puts it, "This world is not enough for my sister, because her mother has gone from it" (31). In addition, Hannah lost her older cousin Maria, whom she idolized, to death by drowning aboard the *Early Dawn,* Maria's son Natie whom Hannah cared for after Maria's death, and her hope for marriage to Benjamin Briggs, who loves her sister Sarah, not herself. Like many spiritualists of the day, Hannah expressed what Bret E. Carroll calls "dissatisfaction with the conventional clergy" and "suggest[ed] that spirits behaved like ministers in their interaction with those on earth" (85). Consequently, Hannah copes with her losses, not through the conventional Christian heaven of her father, the Reverend Cobb, but through her spiritualist belief that the dead can return to the living, like Maria Briggs's ghost or that of her own dead mother, who she believes visited her to wish her "golden dreams" (31). Hannah's need to hide from life and cling to her memories of the dead is so extreme that she cannot be persuaded to relinquish her mourning veil for hours after Natie's funeral.

Although Sarah and Hannah appear diametrically opposed in temperament and attitude, they actually share a plight and an outcome: boredom in the prison of Victorian female gender roles with death by drowning as the only escape. Before her marriage to Benjamin Briggs, Sarah's energies are confined to assisting her widowed father and trying to console her increasingly distressed younger sister. Consequently, marriage to, and travel with, Benjamin seem a way "to wander gay and free." Sarah genuinely loves Benjamin, who is in many respects a fine young man, but one who fully participates in the gendered conventions of his day, making Sarah's life subject to his as a piece of exclusive property. Early in their courtship, she comments, "I'm as flustered as a chicken before a fox" (19). He sends her this poem in which the bird is not eaten, but caged:

> *Birds at sea sing tunelessly,*
> *But I know one who sings on key.*
> *I long to steal her from the shore,*
> *That she might sing alone for me,*
> *And be my songbird evermore*
> *Sailing on the sparkling sea.* (43)

While he is away at sea before their marriage, Sarah has a dream in which she and Benjamin are running away from something, and she finds "he had gone ahead without me"; she hears their pursuer's possibly vulpine "snarl of rage" and wonders "why Benjamin hadn't waited for me" (59). This dream may either predict Benjamin's death before Sarah's on the *Mary Celeste* or indicate that Sarah subconsciously knows the danger in which her love for Benjamin, and her subordinate position, places her. These dichotomous interpretations reflect the nineteenth-century spiritualist belief in portents from the dead and the later nineteenth-century theories of the active constructions of the subconscious mind by psychologists like William James.

Martin uses Sarah's confinement and boredom on the *Mary Celeste* to represent the plight of the nineteenth-century middle-class Victorian wife. She has no duties, beyond keeping their cabin tidy and minding their toddler, Sophy, and she sighs, "yet another dull day at sea for the captain's wife" (285). When Benjamin is swept overboard and lost, she must remain, for a while, in the ship's hold, representative of the world in which he had placed her. Sarah begins to question various forms of patriarchy. She no longer believes that she is "kept by a Father's hand," that of the benevolent patriarchal God of Andrew Young's 1838 hymn, "There Is a Happy Land," which she sang before the disasters aboard the *Mary Celeste* (289). She states, "And I did pray. But God wasn't listening. . . . I don't think I have the strength to bear this test. I can't say, as Mother Briggs never stops saying, God's will be done. His will *will* be done. Is this His will?" (292–93). She no longer believes in man's dominance over nature or his mission to exploit it for his own ends: "What madness. What vanity of men, to sail about in fragile wooden boxes tricked out with sails, putting their lives, their fortunes, their families at the mercy of this ravenous, murderous, heartless beast of a sea. . . . The sea is my enemy, and it has defeated me" (296–97).

Although Sarah loses her beliefs in religious and commercial patriarchy and in beneficent nature, she still needs hope. She is either given hope or manufactures hope, depending on the reader's belief in the supernatural or in the power of the human imagination. One night on deck with Sophy, Sarah believes she feels Benjamin holding her and saying her name. "I never believed that such things as I now know are possible, were possible. I thought it a species of madness to believe so, but though my heart is broken, I know I'm not mad. I didn't imagine my husband's voice. And I'm certainly not mad enough to ever speak of this night to a living soul. But how I will hold to it, my love. How it will sustain me, whatever comes" (301). Sarah, the pragmatic realist, can even be practical about a supernatural voice or about a delusion that her grief has manufactured; in either case, she will not lose its comfort to the beliefs or skepticism of others, but will keep its comforts to and for herself. Soon, however, the log of the *Mary Celeste* and the novel end, and Sarah's fate is unknown, a mystery like the fate of all the dead.

Hannah, like Sarah, runs away from one patriarchal prison to another, and although she survives longer, also ends up drowned at sea. Like Sarah, Hannah was bored in the Cobb household; as Sarah notes about Hannah's reluctance to part with her mourning veil after Natie's funeral, "She's returned to ordinary life and she balks at the change, because it is so . . . ordinary" (34). In her desperation, Hannah tells Sarah of her own caged feeling, one amounting to premature burial in Marion, Massachusetts: "I'm suffocating here. I can't breathe" (53). She attempts to find relief in corresponding with Boston spiritualists. She sends spirit messages that she has received through automatic writing, under the name of Mercy Dale, to a spiritualist newspaper, until Sarah compels her to cease the correspondence. Unlike Sarah's singing and practical housewifery, Hannah's talent, hearing or imagining she hears the dead, is not appreciated, as she tells Sarah: "I have a gift. . . . It's like a gift for music or painting. I can't just ignore it. I can't make it go away because other people don't like it" (54). Instead, like Sarah, she escapes the confines of Marion by quite literally going away; she runs away to a spiritualist community in upstate New York while Sarah is on her honeymoon, but is taken home by her father until she escapes more permanently (277).

Like Sarah's escape from domestic confines to maritime imprisonment, Hannah just moves from one trap to another, now under the name of the trance medium Violet Petra. Changing the label does not change the contents, and Hannah as Violet remains troubled and restless because spiritualism's promise of more freedom and authority for women mediums is also illusory. According to Alex Owen, spiritualists "privileged passivity and sought to develop it. Passivity became, in the spiritualist vocabulary, synonymous with power. And here lay the crux of the dilemma. For the very quality which supposedly made women such excellent mediums was equally construed as undermining their ability to function in the outside world. Female passivity, the leit-motif of powerful mediumship, also positioned women as individuals without social power" (10). By definition, a medium is only a means of communication between two parties, the spirit and the living person to whom a message is directed. As scholars have demonstrated (see Armstrong, Gitelman, Grimes), spirit mediums were like other Victorian female workers as media: telegraphers and typists. They were not "authors" with "authority," but tools. Unlike telegraphers and typists, though, female mediums were supposed to appear as if they worked without monetary gain, often under the auspices of male managers or patrons, since accepting funds themselves would taint their spirituality or even prove that they were frauds (see Tromp, 21, 115; Owen 50). Like other working women of the day, female mediums were morally suspect. In *Altered States: Sex, Nation, Drugs, and Self-Transformation in Victorian Spiritualism*, Marlene Tromp states:

> Spiritualism was sexy. From its humble beginnings in 1848, this Victorian faith of "sittings," mediums, and spirit contact thrilled its practi-

tioners and detractors alike and broke countless rules of decency and
decorum despite the fact that it was nurtured and developed in the
drawing rooms of the proprietous middle classes. The darkened parlor
of the séance invited and embodied the disruption of the ordinary. In
this world, the linked hands of the sitters violated customary barriers
of age and gender, and the intimate spaces underneath the tipping
tables set the stage for more than just spiritual stimulation. (21)

A number of female mediums of the day were addicted to alcohol or
drugs because, as Tromp points out, "They sought to escape the social
limitations of the non-Spiritualist world that they often successfully betrayed in the séance, to extend their 'improprieties' to the larger social
context in which they lived" (152).

In Hannah Cobb/Violet Petra, Martin presents an almost textbook
case of a woman vainly seeking freedom through spiritualism.[8] Like many
female mediums', Hannah's health was a source of concern in her adolescence and improved once she embarked upon her career (Owen 208).
Also like "many incipient mediums" (Owen 213), Hannah began her career as an automatic writer. As a female medium, Hannah is dependent
upon pleasing others who have no affection for her and she now values
the love she experienced in her family and community, despite its terrifying maritime losses. She tells journalist Phoebe Grant, "I have a terror
of the sea. . . . It has taken everyone I loved. . . . I was too young to
know what a paradise we were in. I felt no one understood me; that I was
trapped and must escape. . . . And I was left on the shore in this charade
of a life" (200), still forced to try to meet the needs and expectations of
others, and like many female mediums of the day, increasingly dependent
on drink for consolation.

Hannah moves from male patron to male patron, often ensconced
in their households with their wives and families, rather than receiving
unlady-like but self-reliant direct remuneration for her talents. Violet tells
Phoebe Grant (who is paid directly for her work), "Often the gentlemen de-

---

8. Hannah's character may be at least partially inspired by that of the medium Emma
Hardinge Britten, who came from a seafaring family (Bennett 46).

velop little crushes on me ... ... I'm just a pet. I'm the in-house clairvoyant. ... Sometimes I play the tyrant, just to keep from dying of boredom" (155). Like many female mediums, and as with Henry James's Verena Tarrant (an inspirational speaker) in *The Bostonians* (1886) or William Dean Howells's Egeria Boynton in *The Undiscovered Country* (1880), her good looks promote her career and male interest. In contrast to the depictions of Verena and Egeria, though, Martin more realistically presents Violet with "the trademark oddity of her left eye, which bulged in its socket, the iris wandering off to one side" (110), suggesting her skewed vision of reality.[9] Martin also presents her as too sexually tainted by her profession, unlike Verena and Egeria, for a conventional marriage, in Violet's case with the briefly infatuated son of a prominent Philadelphia family who sponsors her mediumistic sessions.

Sarah gave up some of her freedom in return for Benjamin's love, but Hannah surrenders much more to an emotionally barren spiritualism. She abandoned her potential creative and interpretive career as a writer, or possibly an actress, to be the transmitter of others' messages. She uses her novelist-like powers of observation and character-reading to tell people what they want to hear. Phoebe Grant observes, "She was an adept at reading the subtlest changes of mood in her audience" (121). When Violet meets Sir Arthur Conan Doyle, he recognizes her thespian qualities: "She made pronouncements with which he was invited to agree. It was like being fed one's lines by a fellow actor" (182). Phoebe comments, "Violet could have been an actress—she had the ability to make her audience see what she saw" (200). Violet becomes poorer and shabbier and drinks more when her genteel private sessions become passé as newer and younger female mediums present dramatic, even spectacular, spirit materializations (Braude 175). Violet's subtler "art" is no longer enough to attract sensation seekers who would prefer a lurid penny dreadful to the nuances of a Henry James novel.

---

9. The bulging eye also could be a symptom of Grave's Disease. "Physicians have long suspected that severe emotional stress, like the death of loved one, can set off Graves' disease in some patients": http://www.thyroid.org/wpcontent/uploads/patients/brochures /Graves_brochure.pdf). In Violet's case, the "graves" are literal, though sometimes empty due to so much death at sea in her family.

When Phoebe asks Violet if she ever really heard the spirit voices, Violet shakes "her head in the negative, while the tears overflowed" (196). She realizes that her creative talents have been channeled into a delusion, rather than a fiction. It is important to realize that Violet is not a fraud, but an example of what William James, in "The Confidences of a 'Psychical Researcher,'" called the unconscious ability to "personate" (1257): "There is a hazy penumbra in us all where lying and delusion meet" (1261). Violet may be more sinned against than sinning in that she has been manipulated to seemingly validate the wishful thinking of others, or as William James puts it, "The subject assumes the role of a medium simply because opinion expects it of him . . . and carries it out with a feebleness or a vivacity proportionate to his histrionic gifts" (qtd. in Kerr 206). She tells Phoebe, "I'm a nonentity. I do nothing. I create nothing. I'm a parasite feeding on the blood of fools who haven't the sense to swat me" (201), and believes "she had been created by the demands of others, by their insatiable appetite for something beyond ordinary life. They craved a world without death and they had spotted her, in their hunger, like wolves alert to any poor sheep that might stray from the fold and stand gazing ignorantly up at the stars" (211). She is not an author, but has surrendered her identity and *author*ity to the fictions of others. When Violet finally asks Phoebe to point a way out of her passivity into agency, it seems too late for a new career. Phoebe can only suggest "a course in typing" (158), another means of being a tool for the messages of others, not an author or creator in her own right.

Although Violet has denied the reality of her voices, near the moment of her death, like Sarah, she believes she does hear voices. Aboard the ship that will take her to England to be examined by the Psychical Research Society, as planned by Sir Arthur Conan Doyle, she reads her favorite poem, "What Would I Give?" by Christina Rossetti in a volume presented to her by her inconstant Philadelphia swain (226).

> What would I give for a heart of flesh to warm me thro',
> Instead of this heart of stone ice-cold whatever I do;
> Hard and cold and small, of all hearts the worst of all.

What would I give for words, if only words would come;
But now in its misery my spirit has fallen dumb:
O merry friends, go your way, I have never a word to say.

What would I give for tears, not smiles but scalding tears
To wash the black mark clean, and to thaw the frost of years,
To wash the stain ingrain and make me clean again.

Violet has lost the warmth of love, and with it her capacity for feeling as
well as a voice of her own. Since she is incapable of overt self-determination,
in her solitary ship's cabin, she hears the voices that she needs to hear:
"The voices came from the sea. They had been waiting for her there. No
one could hear them but her" (230). She envisions what her loveless,
homeless self most longs to see, her sister Sarah who bids her, "Dearest.
. . . Come home now" (233); Violet slips on a railing pursuing her vision
of Sarah and is claimed by the indifferent and inscrutable sea that she has
so feared and hated.

Hannah/Violet is a thwarted artist who falls too easily into the trap,
here highly gendered, of the need to please her audience. Martin presents
Sir Arthur Conan Doyle as another artist who fails to achieve his potential, in part because he needs to please his audience, his readers, to support
his family as his gender demands, including at various times an alcoholic
father, his mother, various siblings, and eventually his own wives and
children. More importantly, though, Martin attributes Doyle's failure to
achieve true greatness to the limits he places on his own imagination for
fear of what he might find. In contrast to Doyle's Sherlock Holmes, Martin depicts Doyle as remarkably unobservant. For example, although he
is a medical doctor, Doyle cannot see that his fellow passenger on a voyage to Africa, Henry Garnet, the African American U.S. ambassador to
Liberia, is fatally ill. His willed blindness leads to his too easy reliance on
clichés and stereotypes, particularly those of racism: the epigraph to the
chapter "On Tour in America" is Doyle's wishful thinking, "The Anglo-
Saxon race will own the world" (171). Like Captain Amasa Delano of
Herman Melville's *Benito Cereno,* Doyle feels uneasy, but keeps reassuring

himself. Also like Captain Delano, he fails to see the murderous potential of wronged blacks; he does not know or bother to find out that Garnet before the Civil War had advocated that slaves should rise up and murder their masters.

Doyle's vague uneasiness over Garnet later surfaces when he transforms him into the vengeful black, Septimus Goring, of Doyle's story "J. Habakuk Jephson's Statement" (1884). This tale is a literary hoax, a fictional "solution," to the mystery of the *Mary Celeste* that Doyle used to launch his career as a popular and well-paid author. Martin implies that Doyle's lack of empathy, an inability to see beyond his own needs, results in his limited artistry. "He'd meant no harm. He was desperate for money. . . . He wasn't thinking that the captain of the *Mary Celeste* might have a family who wouldn't be pleased to see their lost loved ones treated to summary execution. All he had wanted was to entertain the public and especially to attract the attention of James Payn at the *Cornhill,* and he'd been successful beyond his dreams" (253). Martin invidiously compares "Habakuk" to another literary hoax, Edgar Allan Poe's *The Narrative of Arthur Gordon Pym,* in which blackness is ultimately less threatening than the enormous white figure amid the enveloping whiteness that ends, but does not conclude, that narrative. Poe leaves the fate of the passengers, as does Martin, to the reader's imagination, in contrast to Doyle's tidy and racially stereotyped conclusion. Doyle's version of the *Mary Celeste*'s voyage is too full of factual inaccuracies to suggest a realistic solution to the mystery; instead, it merely reflects his own fears and prejudices, and, like the messages often received in séances, is somewhat banal, reflecting quotidian beliefs such as racism, not new knowledge. In contrast, Martin's retelling of the ship's story, based on the facts, points to the greater mysteries of the human imagination before inscrutable nature, including death's aftermath.

Martin also takes aim at Doyle's self-limiting imagination through his sexism as she shows him bested by women in his attempts to be as great a detective as Sherlock Holmes. Although Doyle finds Violet "was . . . as observant as he was, possibly more so" (187), and thus collects all kinds of information about him that she can use as spirit messages for him, he still believes that she is sending him authentic messages from his deceased father. Doyle also fails to solve the mystery of Violet's disappearance from the ship that was to carry her to England. Later, he follows a round of clues, based on his Holmes stories, purposely dropped by Mrs. Blatchford (the wife of the captain who sailed the deserted *Mary Celeste* to Genoa) and Annie Blatchford (an orphan who may be Sophia Briggs, Sarah and Benjamin's daughter). These clues lead him to Sarah Briggs's unfinished log of the voyage. Unable to rest in ambiguity, Doyle anticipates an end to the mystery, but cannot solve it since, as Mrs. Blatchford informs him about the log's putative solution, "Let's just say it deepens it" (268).

Martin gives the metafictions several additional twists. Annie Blatchford, who works "at the telephone exchange" (265), is not merely a medium for the messages of others since she "writes stories herself" (265). Doyle, his amour propre unsettled by these bright and manipulative women, wonders, "Or was it simply another hoax, the desperate ploy of a poor, ambitious young writer, just as he had been [in writing "J. Habakuk Jephson's Statement"], who schemed, just as he had schemed, to captivate the fickle attention of the public by tying a painter to the taffrail of a famous mystery ship?" (270). Doyle suspects that he has become a character in someone else's story, Annie's, as he actually is in Martin's novel.

Doyle's best self, the one he would like to be, may be his most famous fictional character, Sherlock Holmes. Through spiritualism, Doyle, like many others of the era, tried to reconcile science and religion. Martin's Doyle believes that he can solve the mystery of life after death through the "scientific" psychical research in which he wants to employ Violet Petra. By such attempts he tries to unite the two aspects of his character, the rational and the spiritual, a split seemingly reflected in his writing between creating the rational Sherlock Holmes and his spiritualist screeds (Grimes 49). However, as Hilary Grimes points out, "a close reading of Doyle's Holmes stories shows that Holmes's sensitivity to spiritualist insight and connections to hypnotic trance states actually inspire and perfect his deductive abilities" (20). Srdjan Smajić suggests that in *The Hound of the Baskervilles*, "Holmes's investigative procedures suspiciously resemble the practices of spiritualist mediums" (7). Doyle, however, bound by fear and conventions, cannot unite the warring aspects of his psyche as does Holmes.

Violet Petra and Phoebe Grant are actually more like Sherlock Holmes than Doyle is. Jill Galvan points out that "if the séance turned on a dynamic of ignorance and knowledge, it made women into detective devices" (135). Violet observes that Doyle is "like a big child" (200). She can deduce his fear and defensiveness: "He's putting on a good show, but there's something wounded about him. He's nothing at all like his famous detective" (200). When Phoebe undertakes the mission of delivering for Violet a parcel containing, unbeknown to her, Sarah Briggs's unfinished log of the *Mary Celeste,* Phoebe refuses Violet's offer of a small payment and jokes, "Does Mr. Sherlock Holmes take payment for the opportunity to solve an interesting case? . . . Never. Nor shall I" (199). Phoebe does not take money for her transmission of a tragic document, unlike Doyle's hefty payment for his "log" of the *Mary Celeste,* "J. Habakuk Jephson's Statement." Like Holmes, Phoebe's recompense is the satisfaction of getting closer to the truth, but, unlike the cerebral Holmes, Phoebe has a heart and cares about others.

Martin's artistic values are closer to those of Henry James than they are to those of Sir Arthur Conan Doyle. Martin, as demonstrated by her collection *The Unfinished Novel and Other Stories,* places human beings before money, fame, or even art, since, for Martin, a truly great artist would recognize the value of love and empathy over selfishness whether in the service of material gain or of art. Through Phoebe Grant, Martin revises two of Henry James's narratives about artists and their values, but with an emphasis on the value of female friendships and sympathy. Like Henrietta Stackpole with her constant concern for Isabel Archer in James's *Portrait of a Lady* (1881), Phoebe is also a journalist who exhibits repeated and constant compassion for her tragic heroine, Violet Petra. Martin, however, does not present her female journalist as an amusingly likable caricature as James does, but develops Phoebe as a fully rounded character, who one reviewer, Hope Whittemore, finds the "most compelling voice" in the novel. Unlike Henrietta Stackpole, who ends up in a heterosexual marriage, Phoebe embarks on a permanent living arrangement, presumably a "Boston marriage," with another woman, Lucy Dial, whose name invokes feminine solidarity and accomplishment through its allusions to feminist Lucy Stone (1818–93) and the transcendentalist journal the *Dial,* edited by Margaret Fuller (1810–50), author of *Woman in the Nineteenth Century*. Through Violet, Phoebe, and Lucy, Martin reinforces her depictions of female friendships as profound, meaningful, and necessary.

Most significantly, Martin is revising the plot of Henry James's "The Aspern Papers" (1888) through the relationship of Phoebe and Violet. In James's novella, the unnamed narrator is a scholar of the fictional Romantic poet Jeffrey Aspern. The narrator travels to Venice in order to try to get the papers and reminiscences of Aspern's mistress, the superannuated Miss Bordereau. In order to obtain his ends, he employs subterfuges, he trespasses, and he even trifles with the affections of Miss Bordereau's niece. When Miss Bordereau discovers him in her apartment snooping late one night, she denounces him as a "publishing scoundrel" and has the Aspern papers destroyed. In his monomaniacal pursuit of truth and his overweening ambition, James's narrator proves a scoundrel in his inability to put the feelings of the living above his hubristic desire to revivify the dead Jeffrey Aspern. He is an academic, fraudulent, and unsuccessful medium.[10]

Martin's Phoebe Grant, in contrast, comes to the realization that a human being is more than fodder for her ambitions as an author. Initially, Phoebe seems fully imbued with the masculine priorities of her profession, which are much like those of James's "publishing scoundrel": "When a heartfelt account moves the teller to tears, the natural response of anyone with ordinary human feeling is to offer kind words of sympathy and consolation, but my profession precludes such natural expressions, and the sight of tears tends to stir in me nothing so much as a sense of predatory expectation" (153), so that, Phoebe recalls, "I wanted to expose" Violet (123). Yet when Violet confesses to Phoebe that she does not really hear the voices of spirits, Phoebe's reaction is compassionate concern made possible by their shared plight as women; she eschews a triumphant rush to the newspaper office to print an exposé:

---

10. James even uses spiritualistic language about his narrator's pursuits: "A person observing me might have supposed I was trying to cast a spell upon it [Miss Bordereau's door] or attempting some odd experiment in hypnotism" (K19646); "That was what the old woman represented—esoteric knowledge (K19653); the narrator is "wondering what mystic rites of ennui the Misses Bordereau celebrated in their darkened rooms" (K19678).

For a few minutes Violet wept while I watched. I confess I've seldom experienced such a profound sense of companionship. I didn't try to comfort her, nor did she seek reassurance; she just wanted to cry. I had the unexpected realization that I liked her. We were two middle-aged women with not much in common, but we had arrived, through our several conversations, which didn't total more than a few hours over ten years, at a surprisingly resilient bond. . . . I had no sense of triumph over Violet, though surely she had just made a damning confession. Instead I felt protective and kindly toward her. (196–97)

Reality is not limited to the bluntly and materially obvious, the true or the false of an exposé. More finely grained and subtler nuances are also a part of reality to those with the ability to perceive them, and that is what Phoebe provides in her sympathetic yet discerning portrait of Violet in her memoirs. Phoebe's "mediumship" of the deceased Violet's voice is recompensed with the continuation of Phoebe's own voice after death through Lucy Dial, who edits Phoebe's memoirs. This chain of compassionate sisterhood is in stark contrast to James's isolated "publishing scoundrel" and the defensive Doyle, a "publishing scoundrel" to the Briggs family through "J. Jephson Habakuk's Statement."

Martin has stated that she tries to correct her romantic tendencies with realism so that she won't end up like the suicidal Emma Bovary (Martin's website; Biguenet Interview 47), or like the women who follow romantic dreams to their deaths in this novel, like Sarah and Hannah Briggs. But the eminently practical and realistic, like Phoebe Grant, sometimes have their romantic or mystical moments. Shortly after her mother's death, Phoebe believed she heard her voice (129) when she most needed to hear it. When she parted from Violet, she "felt [Violet] was being swallowed up [by the steam from the train she was standing beside] and though I was perfectly aware that this was not the case, I had a strong premonition of something dark, something like doom gathering around" her (170); Phoebe senses Violet's loneliness, despondency, and self-destructive tendencies and packages them in a "premonition." As T. S. Eliot noted, "Human kind cannot bear very much reality" (*Burnt Norton*), so even the most rational people, like Phoebe, sometimes look for William James's "white crow": as the eminent doctor Weir Mitchell (historically real) explains to Doyle: "[James] says to disprove the statement that all crows are black you needn't look at all crows; you need only produce one white one" (175). Humankind continues its longings and quests for the white crow.

Martin's novel, however, does not end with a white crow, but with a carved owl, evoking the human longing for a goddess of wisdom, Minerva. In the last line of the novel, toddler Sophia Briggs, whose first name also means wisdom, points at the owl and says, "Whoo-whoo" (302). This is an apt ending to a novel suggesting the awe-inspiring capacities of the human imagination before the unknown and its endless struggles to articulate its hopes and fears in words, or in narratives like this novel and the many narratives enclosed within it. Indeed, the marvels, wisdom, and folly of the human imagination comprise the figure in Martin's carpet. Martin's readers, in turn, exert their own imaginations on Martin's figures in an attempt to chart the *mare incognitum* of life and death with words and stories as hopeful, wondering, and suggestive, but ultimately as enigmatic, as Sophy's "Whoo-whoo."

13

Sea Lovers

METAMORPHOSES IN NATURE AND ART

$\mathscr{A}$lthough the title *Sea Lovers* (2015) would suggest another maritime tale like its immediate predecessor, *The Ghost of the Mary Celeste,* this collection of short stories evokes a more metaphoric sea, the human longing for effortless transformations in nature and the imagination as signified by the fluidity of water. As Ovid writes in his *Metamorphoses,* "in all this world, no thing can keep / its form. For all things flow; all things are born / to change their shapes. And time itself is like / a river, flowing on an endless course" (XV, 520). The human desire for, and fear of, metamorphosis is simultaneously assisted and thwarted by humanity's membership in the animal kingdom as well as the human's mind's capacity to imagine realms beyond the laws of nature. Martin writes in her introduction, "The question 'Are we animals, or are we something else?' has engaged my imagination throughout my writing career, and I have addressed it most particularly in short stories. These Acadiana stories [the final two in the collection] offer an answer at once whimsical and disturbing: We are neither, and we are both" (2–3).

Martin explores the ambivalence of human nature through ten previously published tales—five from *The Consolation of Nature and Other Stories* (1988) and five from *The Unfinished Novel and Other Stories* (2006)—and concludes the collection with two new stories. To emphasize the divisions inherent in human nature, she divides the stories into three sections: "Among the Animals" ("Spats," "The Cat in the Attic," "The Consolation of Nature," and "The Freeze," from *The Consolation of Nature*); "Among the Artists" ("His Blue Period," "Beethoven," "The Unfinished Novel," and "The Open Door," from *The Unfinished Novel*); and "Metamorphoses" ("The Change" from *The Unfinished Novel,* "Sea Lovers" from

The Consolation of Nature, and the new stories, "The Incident at Ville-deau" and "Et in Acadiana Ego").

Martin does not include any stories from her first collection and first book, *Love* (1977), commenting, "My early stories have a young writer's excitement about formal innovation, as well as a young woman's preoccupation with personal relationships. They appear unsophisticated to me now, innocent, unguarded, and sometimes uncouth" (1). Although Martin does not discuss gender in her introduction, the stories in *Sea Lovers* continue the exploration of the power dynamics between women and men that she began in *Love.* The principal difference is the wry, whimsical, and highly ironic sense of humor in her later tales, arising from the consideration of lovers within the ceaseless flux of the larger "sea" of nature, humanity, and art. Love, like the imagination manifested in art and in identification with nature, offers the promise of completion and immortality through metamorphosis. The promise is unfulfilled since, as the lovers of "Et in Acadiana Ego" conclude, "You're divided" (289), and death announces in the title that, "I am even in Acadia."

In *Sea Lovers,* Martin performs her own artistic metamorphosis on previously published stories by placing them in a new context and order so that the tales in "Among the Animals" and "Among the Artists" (see chapters 4 and 11, respectively, for detailed discussions of these stories) appear much more closely linked in juxtaposition. In the stories in "Among the Animals," the human imagination, artistry applied to life, uses animals to their detriment in an attempt to cope with or defy the exigencies of love and mortality. In "Among the Artists," animals, particularly cats and rabbits in "His Blue Period" and "The Unfinished Novel," receive more consideration and better treatment than human beings from second-rate artists who prefer to believe that animals are more easily manipulated and understood than human beings. In Martin's stories, like the waves of the sea, nature and humanity arise in thematic prominence and dissolve into ambivalence; they are "neither" and "both" (3); we remain "among" as the titles of the collection's first two sections suggest.

Like many of the women in Ovid's *Metamorphoses,* Martin's women experience metamorphosis in order to evade masculine power, whether in social control or physical force. This is evident in the two previously published stories now gathered in the section "Metamorphoses." When placed in this context, "The Change," which appeared earlier as an artist tale, becomes a story as much about nature as about art. The metamorphosis is the artist Gina's new ability and wisdom to accept the physical or animal part of human nature as in the "change" of menopause with its suggestion of mortality, a change her husband is unwilling to accept. As Ovid wrote in his long narrative poem, "Just so, our bodies undergo / the never-resting changes; what we were / and what we are today is not to be / tomorrow" (XV, 521). Consequently, Gina's greater vision, as manifested in her masterpieces depicting precise and luminous nature, is signified by her putative transformation into an owl, an attribute of Minerva, the goddess of wisdom. "Sea Lovers," the title story, previously published in *The Consolation of Nature,* in the context of this collection becomes as much a story about art as about nature. The human need for imagined control of nature, an artistry attempted in life, is refuted by the mermaid, part fish and part woman, who kills in order to follow the imperative of her nature to lay and fertilize the eggs that will presumably be transformed, a metamorphosis, into more beings that link nature and humanity.

Martin's capacity for metamorphosis as an artist is one of the hallmarks of her career and a principal catalyst for her literary achievement. To attain the engaging composite of fantasy, realism, and humor of the two new stories that conclude both the "Metamorphosis" section and the collection, "The Incident at Villedeau" and "Et in Acadiana Ego," Martin looks to her past with a fresh perspective. She recognizes what she calls her "evolution" in her introduction (1) and in the dedication to University of New Orleans professor Kenneth Holditch, "who got me started" by introducing her to those virtuosos of the short story Nathaniel Hawthorne and Henry James in her student days. Martin also returns to another great influence from her past, Lyle Saxon (1891–1946), whose tales of colorful, often spooky, Louisiana characters and events she devoured as a child in New Orleans. Specifically, she turns to his jewel of a short story, "The Centaur Plays Croquet" (1927), for the apparently objective narrator of "The Incident at Villedeau," for the love story between a centaur and a woman in "Et in Acadiana Ego," and for the droll social commentary in both stories.

The key to the fantastic nature of "The Incident at Villedeau" is provided in the epigraph to the tale: "I am a man upon the land," from "Child
Ballad No. 113" (255). The traditional song concerns a mythic being, a "selkie," who is a seal in the water and a "man upon the land"; he has a child
with a human woman whom he presents with a bag of gold in exchange
for the child while predicting that she will marry a gunner who will kill
both father and child. Accordingly, Martin's Felix Kelly, who has eyes
that "were strangely round, black, and placid beneath a thick overhang of
brow" (257), is taken from the water near Villedeau in mysterious circumstances. He fascinates and impregnates the upper-class Odile Chopin, but
refuses to marry her. She marries her cousin, Octave Favrot, and they live
with the child Michel, who is blind with "a filmy silvery lining behind the
retinas" (262) and who, like Felix, has "thin, translucent webbing" (262)
between his toes. After Felix absconds with Michel, Octave shoots both
Felix and the child in the woods, claiming that he thought he was shoot-
ing a bear. In the aftermath, the locals attempt to find out how the gold
that Felix had accumulated ended up buried under the porch of Odile's
mother's house and why Octave shot Felix: accident, homicide, or fate.

The charm of Martin's story lies in the humor evoked in the clash of
social norms, realism, romantic expectations, and the fantastic. Octave
is acquitted of the slaying, mainly because he is a gentleman and Felix is
an outsider who lives by his wits in nature and his handiwork in a black-
smith's shop. The sheriff, perfectly content with Octave's denial that he
has the gold, does not want the house searched. After Michel's death,
Octave and Odile part. Octave at first prospers, then loses all in the fairy-
tale number of three, but his triple calamities are mundane, not magical:
sheath blight on his rice crop, a financial panic, and a fire. He does not
fall into romantic despair, but lives, like the man/selkie he killed, close
to nature with "admirable fortitude" and a "stoical solitude" (275) until
his drowning years later. In contrast, Odile at first acts the part of the
tragic heroine: she "stubbornly refused to thrive and kept her thoughts
on death" (276), spending much time in solitary contemplation of Felix's
grave. Eventually, though, she moves with her mother to New Orleans,
where she takes "a lively interest in her cousin's two young children" (278)
until she succumbs to a yellow fever epidemic. Life, Martin may be sug-

gesting, does not consist of a single and consistent genre, but is a wild juxtaposition of tragedy, comedy, realism, fairy tales, and fantasy.

Like the professorial narrator of Saxon's "The Centaur Plays Croquet," Martin's lawyer narrator in "The Incident at Villedeau" tries to make sense of a seemingly fantastic story by presenting varying explanations of the "incident." As one might expect in a "town of water," as Villedeau's name could be translated, the narrator is frustrated by the fluidly slippery nature of the facts that keep pointing to a realm beyond objective reality. As if attempting to evade the legal fictions that provide no satisfactory explanation for the incident at Villedeau, he tries to keep his own life firmly in the realm of reality through specializing in "trusts and real estate transfers" (277). He cannot, however, part with his romantic fantasies about Odile, whom he prefers to remember not in domestic content in New Orleans, but "dancing under the stars in the arms of a callow admirer to the lilting strains of an Acadian waltz" (277). Unlike Saxon's narrator, however, who believes that the testimonial of many witnesses will elucidate the tale of the lady and the centaur, Martin's narrator has the wisdom to acknowledge the limits of human knowledge; he understands that without the unknown, life would be unbearably banal: "the fathomless sea conceals no mystery more recondite than that which may flicker beneath the surface of a neighbor's distracted greeting on a summer's day" (278). Martin's readers become "sea lovers" as our imaginations remain mesmerized by the ineluctable mysteries beneath the tale of the woman and the selkie and by the wavelike shifting of the lines between nature, humanity, and the fantastic until their final dissolution in death.

In "Et in Acadiana Ego," Martin continues to explore the "neither" and "both" (3) of animal and human nature through a story about a woman and a centaur in pre-modern Louisiana. As Martin explains, "Acadia is the name given to the eighteenth-century French settlement in Nova Scotia by the residents thereof. It is a variant of the word *Arcadia:* the paradise of Greek myth inhabited by fantastic creatures, the playground of the gods. When the French were driven out of Acadia by the British, they made a long and difficult journey to Louisiana. The bayous and swamps where they settled, surviving by fishing and trapping, became known as Acadiana" (2). It is a watery, mutable world, this region of "bayous and swamps," so in "Hauteville," where the story takes place, the inhabitants attempt to maintain their "high town" above the water, as well as the intricate structure of bridges that link the houses on both sides of the river, signifying the complicated and vulnerable social network that the story's protagonist, Mathilde Benoit, challenges. Neither society nor its challenger can prevail against nature; the story's last paragraph reveals that after a hurricane, water has reclaimed all, as do time, change, and death.

Martin's postmodern tale playfully alludes to two stories of division: once again, Saxon's "The Centaur Plays Croquet"; and Gaetano Donizetti's highly romantic opera *Lucia di Lammermoor* (1835), which the woman and the centaur see in New Orleans. In the opera, Lucia is torn between her love for her family's enemy, Edgardo, and her loyalty to her family, embodied in her brother Enrico. Under the impression that Edgardo no longer loves her and the advice of her clergyman, she agrees to marry Arturo for the good of her clan. When Edgardo unexpectedly appears and reproaches her as "ingrata," Lucia goes mad and kills Arturo, then dies. The opera ends with Edgardo's decision to join Lucia in heaven by stabbing himself. In Saxon's "The Centaur Plays Croquet," the protagonist Ada Calander, unlike Lucia, defies society and the church, and fatally breaks her husband's heart, all for her love of the centaur Horace; she ends her life as a recluse on her decaying Louisiana plantation after Horace's death. The woman of the romantic era crumbles before powerful social and religious forces; to her detriment, the woman of the modern era defies and rejects a society and religion that Saxon portrays as absurdly and comically petty and literal-minded through the fact-finding narrator. Women pay for challenging patriarchal norms.

In Martin's postmodern revision of Donizetti's (see chapter 7 for more of Martin's revised "Lucy" stories) opera and Saxon's tale, the focus is not on the forces of a patriarchal religion and society; Martin quickly neutralizes them near the beginning of the tale. In the aftermath of the death of Mathilde's father, we are told, "There were suitors, there were rumors, there was resistance to the very idea of a young woman of means doing as she pleased, but not even the priest could force Mathilde to marry, so she did not. She set up a charity school for orphans and turned over the management of the bank to her father's partner, thereby satisfying the nuns who had educated her and the investors who relied upon her. She occupied herself with her horses in the country and with music in the city. She was free" (283). Mathilde demonstrates her freedom from religion by not even taking seriously her priest's demand to remove the statue of the centaur Chiron from her home. Instead, she "collapsed in giggles" (303) and tells Nikos, her centaur, "with fake solemnity, 'I have abandoned my God for you'"(304). She prevails against religion, unlike the tragic Lucia or Saxon's Ada, whose minister destroys her centaur statue. As in Saxon's story, the woman and the centaur clandestinely visit the opera in New Orleans, but since religious strictures against selling one's soul to the devil are not at issue, they do not attend *Faust* as in Saxon's tale. Instead, they see *Lucia di Lammermoor,* and Nikos's response to that opera shows Martin once again parodically reversing gender roles. Nikos finds the opera "overwhelming" and begins the drinking that eventually contributes to his death. He risibly experiences Mathilde's ride on his back after the opera as a loss of virginity: "No one has ever been on my back before. . . . It was so unexpected, so wonderful and strange. I felt we were one. . . . I am completely yours" (297–98).

Although Mathilde is relatively free from the forces of religion and patriarchy, she is not free from the forces of nature, as becomes immediately and humorously apparent upon the arrival of Nikos. While he is quite obviously divided between animal and human, Mathilde proves to be equally so. Nikos is as attracted to Mathilde's filly as he is to her: "What a rider she was! And what a rump on that filly!" (284). Mathilde is as driven by sexual attraction to Nikos as is her filly and "felt as restless as her horse" (285). Nikos does not die from a romantic duel or as a broken-hearted suicide or at the hands of religious fanatics. He dies of natural causes, felled by a disease of horse's hooves called founder or laminitis, to which his "human" diet of oat porridge and alcohol (excessive carbohydrates) may have contributed. He could not successfully deny the animal half of his nature. (Saxon's centaur Horace also drinks to excess, as do the brawling centaurs in Ovid's *Metamorphoses.*) After Mathilde's futile attempts at curing the disease, she shoots Horace at his request to relieve his agony. Following his death, "Mathilde withdrew from the world, at first because she was too heartbroken, and then because she was too ill" (314): Martin immediately undercuts the romantic suggestion of a fatal broken heart with the "natural" cause of an illness.

The forces of nature overwhelm Mathilde, Nikos, and the flooded town of Hauteville, with one exception: "when the waters recede, the two gravestones are still in place" (315). On Horace's stone, Mathilde had ordered carved, "His soul goes whinnying down the wind" (315). In one sense, this is an acknowledgment that Nikos is an animal in nature. It is also a tribute to art that can—sometimes, temporarily—outlast the forces of nature and death. The line itself is a work of art in miniature in its alliteration, its imaginative vision of Nikos as immortal, and as an homage to the playful artistry of Lyle Saxon, whose centaur Horace has these same words on his tombstone. At the end of *Metamorphoses*, Ovid asserts that he will gain immortality through his art: "my name and fame are sure: I shall have life" (XV, 549). Martin is much more ambivalent: "Are we animals, or are we something else? . . . We are neither, and we are both" (2–3). Thus, stories, imaginative metamorphoses of nature and art, continue to be created as attempts to resolve the contradictions of human nature; in turn, each story contributes to a new story in a metamorphosis like the waves of the sea. As Ovid wrote, "wave follows wave, and every wave is pressed, / and also presses on the wave ahead; / so, too, must moments always be renewed. / What was is now no more, and what was not / has come to be; renewal is the lot / of time" (XV, 520).

Conclusion

*I*n Henry James's tale "The Figure in the Carpet" (1896), the great novelist Hugh Vereker attempts to explain "the particular thing I've written my books most for" (368), the "figure in the carpet" of his fiction: "Isn't there for every writer a particular thing of that sort, the thing that makes him apply himself, the thing without the effort to achieve which he wouldn't write at all, the very passion of his passion, the part of the business in which, for him, the flame of art burns most intensely?" (365). For Valerie Martin, that figure in the carpet, that "very passion of" her "passion," is her intense scrutiny of the uses of the human imagination across time and space, particularly as it is manifested in theories of life that include romanticism (including romantic love and masochism), science, religion, philosophy, materialism, social systems, and art. Her writing simultaneously participates in and interrogates southern literature, postmodernism, and the gothic. Her persona is that of the impassioned observer so valued by William James and Henry James.

Martin views people as part of nature, with both humans and nature subject inexorably to death. In the face of this existential dilemma, she explores the ways that human beings can use their imaginations for good or ill, with the condition of women often serving as the touchstone—or the canary in the coal mine—to determine the efficacy and morality of various imaginative constructs. Science, religion, philosophy, property, social systems, and art can be employed in a vain attempt to conquer death or to pretend that death is not real. In Martin's works, such evasive uses of the imagination result in domination over the ostensibly inferior "other"—women, ethnicities, races, classes, and nature—in a futile effort to rationalize away powerlessness in the face of death.

But the imagination, for Valerie Martin, can also be used as a force to ameliorate the harsh realities of death and the various systems of domination that try to evade death through delusive shows of power. In contrast, the imagination can provide pleasure and broaden narrow perspectives in ways that lead to the compassionate fellow feeling that makes life and its end bearable. James's novelist in "The Figure in the Carpet" tries to evoke this response in dialogue with the tale's narrator: "Well, you've got a heart in your body. Is that an element of form or an element of feeling?" (368). "Forms" are imaginative constructs that are inextricably linked to "feeling" in the ways that they manifest emotions toward others and in the ways that they make others feel. For Martin, a great imagination, as applied to art or life, manifests itself in empathy, a feeling that leads to compassionate actions, forms, that alleviate human suffering and provide pleasure through imaginative play or the recognition of truths. The capacious intertextuality of Martin's works exemplifies a great imagination as a means of dialogue, a process that encompasses the responses and feelings of others in order to create an endless succession of imaginative endeavors leading to greater empathy. As realized through her versatility and mastery of technique, Valerie Martin's work reveals such imaginative greatness, in artistry both timely and timeless.

Works Cited

BOOKS BY VALERIE MARTIN

Alexandra. 1979. New York: Pocket Books, 1991. Print.

The Confessions of Edward Day. New York: Vintage, 2009. Print.

The Consolation of Nature and Other Stories. Boston: Houghton Mifflin, 1988. Print.

The Ghost of the Mary Celeste. New York: Doubleday, 2014. Print.

The Great Divorce. New York: Vintage, 1994. Print.

Italian Fever. New York: Vintage, 1999. Print.

Love: Short Fiction. 1977. Seattle: Lost Horse P, 1999. Print.

Mary Reilly. New York, Vintage, 1990. Print.

Property. New York: Vintage, 2003. Print.

A Recent Martyr. New York: Vintage, 1987. Print.

Salvation: Scenes from the Life of St. Francis. New York: Vintage, 2001. Print.

Sea Lovers. New York: Doubleday, 2015. Print.

Set in Motion. 1978. Baton Rouge: Louisiana State UP, 2001. Print.

Trespass. New York: Vintage, 2007. Print.

The Unfinished Novel and Other Stories. New York: Vintage, 2006. Print.

OTHER WORKS CITED

Ahl, Diane Cole. "Benozzo Gozzoli's Cycle of the Life of St. Francis in Montelfalco: Hagiography and Homily." *Saints: Studies in Hagiography.* Ed. Sandro Sticca. Binghamton, NY: Medieval & Renaissance Texts & Studies, 1996. 191–213. Print.

Armstrong, Tim. "Distracted Writing." *Modernism, Technology, and the Body: A Cultural Study.* Cambridge: Cambridge UP, 1998. 187–219. Print.

Babinsky, Ellen. Rev. of *Salvation* by Valerie Martin. *Christian Century* 118.22 (1 Aug. 2001): 33. Print.

Barrow, Bennet H. *Plantation Life in the Florida Parishes of Louisiana, 1836–1846.* Ed. Edwin Adams Davis. New York: AMS P, 1967. Print.

Bauman, Zygmunt. *Intimations of Postmodernity.* London and New York: Routledge, 1992. Print.

Becker, Susanne. *Gothic Forms of Feminine Fictions.* Manchester: Manchester UP, 1999. Print.

Bennett, Bridget. *Transatlantic Spiritualism and Nineteenth-Century American Literature.* New York: Palgrave Macmillan, 2007. Print.

Biguenet, John. "An Interview with Valerie Martin." *Brick* 88 (2012): 46–56. Print.

Blake, William. "The Marriage of Heaven and Hell." 1790. The William Blake Archive. Web. 30 Aug. 2011.

Blumberg, Jess. "Abandoned Ship: The *Mary Celeste*." *Smithsonian Magazine.* November 2007. http://www.smithsonianmag.com/history/abandoned-ship-the-mary-celeste-174488104/. Web. 16 June 2014.

Bone, Martyn. *The Postsouthern Sense of Place in Contemporary Fiction.* Baton Rouge: Louisiana State UP, 2005. Print.

Braid, Barbara. "Victorian Panopticon: Confined Spaces and Imprisonment in Chosen Neo-Victorian Novels." *Exploring Space: Spatial Notions in Cultural, Literary and Language Studies.* Ed. Katarzyna Molek-Kozakowska and Andrzej Ciuk. Newcastle upon Tyne: Cambridge Scholars, 2010. 74–82. Print.

Braude, Ann. *Radical Spirits: Spiritualism and Women's Rights in Nineteenth-Century America.* Boston: Beacon P, 1989. Print.

Brontë, Emily. *Wuthering Heights.* 1847. Shelfari Community E-book.

Broyard, Anatole. Rev. of *Set in Motion* by Valerie Martin. *New York Times on the Web.* 23 June 1978. Web. 3 Jan. 2011.

Calinescu, Matei. *Five Faces of Modernity: Modernism, Avant-Garde, Decadence, Kitsch, Postmodernism.* Durham, NC: Duke UP, 1987. Print.

Carr, John C. "An Interview with Walker Percy, 1971." *Conversations with Walker Percy.* Jackson: UP of Mississippi, 1985. 56–71. Print.

Carroll, Bret E. *Spiritualism in Antebellum America.* Bloomington: Indiana UP, 1997. Print.

Chopin, Kate. *The Awakening.* In *The Complete Works of Kate Chopin.* Ed. Per Seyersted. Baton Rouge: Louisiana State UP, 1969. 881–1000. Print.

"Claire Danjou." Myspace. Web. 20 Aug. 2011.

Coleridge, Samuel Taylor. "Chapter 13: On the Imagination." *Biographia Literaria.* 1817. Literature Network. Web. 16 Aug. 2011.

———. *Collected Letters.* Vol. 1. Ed. Earl Lesley Griggs. New York: Oxford UP, 1956. 974. Print.

———. "Work without Hope." 1825. *The Poems of Samuel Taylor Coleridge, 1787–1833*. Global Language Resources, Inc.: DjVu Editions E-Books 2001 Global Language Resources Inc. Page 415. Web. 30 August 2011.

Cowart, David. "Fathers and Rats: *Mary Reilly* and *The Strange Case of Dr. Jekyll and Mr. Hyde*." *Literary Symbiosis: The Reconfigured Text in Twentieth-Century Writing*. Athens: U of Georgia P, 1993. 85–104. Print.

Cremeens, Carlton. "Walker Percy, the Man and the Novelist: An Interview." *Conversations with Walker Percy*. Jackson: UP of Mississippi, 1985. 16–39. Print.

Cullwick, Hannah. *The Diaries of Hannah Cullwick, Victorian Maidservant*. Ed. Liz Stanley. New Brunswick, NJ: Rutgers UP, 1984. Print.

Davis, Thadious M. *Southscapes: Geographies of Race, Region & Literature*. Chapel Hill: U of North Carolina P, 2011. E-book. Kindle.

Dickinson, Emily. "A Narrow Fellow in the Grass." *The Complete Poems*. 1924. Bartleby.Com. Web. 30 Aug. 2011.

———. "The Soul Selects Its Own Society." *The Complete Poems*. 1924. Bartleby. Com. Web. 30 Aug. 2011.

Donaldson, Susan V. "Telling Forgotten Stories of Slavery in the Postmodern South." *Southern Literary Journal* 40.2 (2008): 267–83. Print.

Eliot, T. S. "The Love Song of J. Alfred Prufrock." *Prufrock and Other Observations*. 1920. Bartleby.Com. Web. 30 Aug. 2011.

Ellis, Kate Ferguson. *The Contested Castle: Gothic Novels and the Subversion of Domestic Ideology*. Urbana: U of Illinois P, 1989. Print.

Fischer, John Irwin. "Masochists, Martyrs (and Mermaids) in the Fictions of Valerie Martin." *Southern Review* 24.2 (1988): 445–50. Print.

Fronk, Hattie Adams. "In the Starlight." http://www.designtrain.com/genealogy/Burtnettfamhistory/Inthstarlight.htm. Web. 17 June 2014.

Frugoni, Chiara. "Saint Francis, a Saint in Progress." *Saints: Studies in Hagiography*. Ed. Sandro Sticca. Binghamton, NY: Medieval & Renaissance Texts & Studies, 1996. 161–90. Print.

Galvan, Jill Nicole. *Sympathetic Medium: Feminine Channeling, the Occult, and Communication Technologies, 1859–1919*. Ithaca, NY: Cornell UP, 2010. E-book.

Ganner, Heidi. "Intertextuality and Paradigm Shifts in Valerie Martin's *Mary Reilly*, Emma Tennant's *Two Women of London: The Strange Case of Ms. Jekyll and Mrs. Hyde*, and Robert Swindell's *Mrs. Hyde*." *The Self at Risk; in English Literature and Other Landscapes*. Ed. Gudrun M. Grabher. Innsbruck: Verlag des Instituts für Sprachwissenschaft der Universität, 1993. 193–202. Print.

Gitelman, Lisa. *Scripts, Grooves, and Writing Machines: Representing Technology in the Edison Era*. Stanford, CA: Stanford UP, 2000. Print.

Goddu, Teresa A. *Gothic America: Narrative, History, and Nation*. New York: Columbia UP, 1997. Print.

Gray, Francine Du Plessix. "The Ephemeral Triangle." Rev. of *Alexandra* by Valerie Martin. *New York Times*. 5 Aug. 1979: 10, 15. Print.

Gray, Richard. *A Web of Words: The Great Dialogue of Southern Literature*. Athens: U of Georgia P, 2007. Print.

Green, Jeremy. *Late Postmodernism: American Fiction at the Millennium*. New York: Palgrave Macmillan, 2005. Print.

Grimes, Hilary. *Late Victorian Gothic: Mental Science, the Uncanny, and Scenes of Writing*. Farnham, Surrey, GBR: Ashgate, 2011. E-book.

Guinn, Matthew. *After Southern Modernism: Fiction of the Contemporary South*. Jackson: UP of Mississippi, 2000. Print.

Hall, Brian. *The Impossible Country: A Journey through the Last Days of Yugoslavia*. New York: Random House, 1994. E-book. Kindle.

Halpern, Sue. "Love Croatian Style." Rev. of *Trespass* by Valerie Martin. *New York Times Book Review*. *New York Times on the Web*. 16 Sept. 2007. Web. 1 Apr. 2011.

Hardy, Thomas. "The Subalterns." 1901. Academy of American Poets. Web. 27 Aug. 2011.

Harrison, Kathryn. "Balance of Power." Rev. of Valerie Martin's *Property*. *New York Times Book Review*. 108.8 (2003): 10. Print.

Hobson, Fred. *The Southern Writer in the Postmodern World*. Mercer University Lamar Memorial Lectures No. 33. Athens: U of Georgia P, 1991. Print.

Horn, Charles. "All Things Love Thee, So Do I." http://freepages.genealogy.rootsweb.ancestry.com/~hartsman/Horn/CEHWorks/AllThingsLoveThee/all%20things%20love%20thee%20.html. Web. 17 June 2014.

Horner, Avril, and Sue Zlosnik, eds. *Gothic and the Comic Turn*. New York: Palgrave Macmillan, 2005. Print.

Howells, William Dean. *The Undiscovered Country*. Boston: Houghton Mifflin, 1880. Print.

Humphries, Jefferson. "The Discourse of Southernness: Or How We Can Know There Will Still Be Such a Thing as the South and Southern Literary Culture in the Twenty-First Century." *The Future of Southern Letters*. Ed. Jefferson Humphries and John Lowe. New York: Oxford UP, 1996. 119–33. Print.

Hutcheon, Linda. *A Poetics of Postmodernism: History, Theory, Fiction*. New York: Routledge, 1988. Print.

Jaggi, Maya. "A Woman's Lot." Rev. of *Property* by Valerie Martin. *The Guardian (London)*. 31 May 2003: 25. Print.

James, Henry. "The Aspern Papers." 1888. *The Essential Henry James Collection.* E-book. Kindle.

———. "The Beast in the Jungle." 1903. *The Essential Henry James Collection.* E-book. Kindle.

———. *The Bostonians.* 1886. Cambridge: Cambridge World Classics, 2011. E-book. Kindle.

———. *Italian Hours.* 1909. E-book. Distributed Proofreaders. Kindle.

———. *Letters, Volume IV, 1895–1916.* Ed. Leon Edel. Cambridge, MA: Harvard UP, 1984. Print.

———. *The Sacred Fount.* 1901. New York: Scribner's, 1901. Public Domain E-book.

James, William. "The Confidences of a 'Psychical Researcher.'" *Writings, 1902–1910.* Ed. Bruce Kuklick. New York: Library of America, 1988. Print.

———. *The Varieties of Religious Experience.* 1902. E-book produced by Charles Keller. E-book. Kindle.

Jordan, Patrick. "Saint Francis of Assisi." Rev. of *Salvation: Scenes from the Life of St. Francis* by Valerie Martin. *Commonweal* 128.18 (2001): 25. Print.

Kaus, Alaina. "Speech and Silence: The Irony of Voice in Valerie Martin's *Property.*" Unpublished essay.

Kean, Danuta. "Valerie Martin tells Danuta Kean about her fascination with the theatre and what she has learnt from observing actors." Orion Books. Web. 31 Aug. 2011.

Keats, John. *Endymion.* 1818. Academy of American Poets. Web. 30 Aug. 2011.

Kent, Christobel. Rev. of *The Ghost of the Mary Celeste* by Valerie Martin. *The Guardian,* Wednesday, 19 Feb. 2014 04.00 EST. Web. 17 June 2014.

Kerr, Howard. *Mediums, and Spirit Rappers, and Roaring Radicals: Spiritualism in American Literature, 1850–1900.* Urbana: U of Illinois P, 1972. Print.

King, Amy K. "Valerie Martin's *Property* and the Failure of the Lesbian Counterplot." *Mississippi Quarterly* 63.1–2 (2010): 211–31. Print.

Kreyling, Michael. *Inventing Southern Literature.* Jackson: UP of Mississippi, 1978. Print.

———. *The South That Wasn't There.* Baton Rouge: Louisiana State UP, 2010. E-book. Kindle.

Kucich, John J. *Ghostly Communion: Cross-Cultural Spiritualism in Nineteenth-Century American Literature.* Hanover, NH: Dartmouth College P, 2004. Print.

Leach, Laurie F. "A Fuller Statement of the Case: *Mary Reilly* and *The Strange Case of Dr. Jekyll and Mr. Hyde.*" *Beyond Adaptation: Essays on Radical Transformations of Original Works.* Ed. Phyllis Frus and Christy Williams. Jefferson, NC: McFarland, 2010. 83–94. Print.

Lowe, John. "Introduction." *The Future of Southern Letters.* Ed. Jefferson Humphries and John Lowe. New York: Oxford UP, 1996. 3–19. Print.

Lyotard, Jean-François. *The Postmodern Condition: A Report on Knowledge.* Trans. Geoff Bennington and Brian Massumi. Minneapolis: U of Minnesota P, 1984. Print.

Martin, Sandra. "Sex, Lies, and Slavery." Interview with Valerie Martin. *The Globe and Mail* (Canada) 12 Mar. 2003: R3. Print.

Martin, Valerie. "An Interview with Valerie Martin." Rob Smith. *Contemporary Literature* 34.1 (1993): 1–17. Print.

———. "Top Ten." *Top Ten: Writers Pick Their Favorite Books.* Ed. J. Peder Zane. Web. 30 Aug. 2011.

———. "Transformations: An Interview with Valerie Martin." Nancy Dixon and Veronica Makowsky. *Florida English* 10 (2012): 25–37. Print.

———. "Valerie Martin Discusses *The Ghost of the Mary Celeste.*" *https://www.you tube.com/watch?v=JcEMK_WpR-c.* Web. 16 June 2014.

———. *Valerie Martin Online.* Web. 20 Aug. 2011.

Massé, Michelle. *In the Name of Love: Women, Masochism, and the Gothic.* Ithaca, NY: Cornell UP 1992. Print.

Maurer, Christopher. *Fortune's Favorite Child: The Uneasy Life of Walter Anderson.* Jackson: UP of Mississippi, 2003. Print.

McCay, Mary A., and Christine Wiltz. "An Interview with Valerie Martin." *New Orleans Review* 21.1 (1995): 6–24. Print.

McHenry, Susan. "This Property Is Not Condemned." Interview with Bebe Moore Campbell and Valerie Martin. *Black Issues Book Review.* Sept.–Oct. 2003. *Arts Publications Online.* Web. 21 Apr. 2010.

McPherson, Tara. *Reconstructing Dixie: Race, Gender and Nostalgia in the Imagined South.* Durham, NC: Duke UP, 2003. Print.

Merkin, Daphne. "Escaping Relations." Rev. of *Set in Motion* by Valerie Martin. *New Republic* 61 (1978): 15–17. Print.

Meyers, Helene. *Femicidal Fears: Narratives of the Female Gothic Experience.* Albany: State U of New York P, 2001. Print.

Miquel-Baldellou, Marta. "Mary Reilly as Jekyll or Hyde: Neo-Victorian (Re) Creations of Femininity and Feminism." *Journal of English Studies* 8 (2010): 119-40. Print.

Moorhouse, Geoffrey. "The Patron Saint of Greenies." Rev. of *Salvation: Scenes from the Life of St. Francis* by Valerie Martin. *New York Times Book Review.* 11 Mar. 2001: 13. Print.

Morrison, Toni. *Playing in the Dark: Whiteness and the Literary Imagination.* 1992. New York: Viking 1993. E-book. Kindle.

Murison, Justine S. *The Politics of Anxiety in Nineteenth-Century American Literature.* Cambridge: Cambridge UP, 2011. Print.

Nicol, Bran. *The Cambridge Guide to Postmodern Fiction.* Cambridge: Cambridge UP, 2009. E-book. Kindle.

Oates, Joyce Carol. "Property of: Valerie Martin's *Property.*" *Uncensored: Views and [Re]Views.* New York: HarperCollins, 2005. 131–41. Print.

O'Connor, Flannery. *Mystery and Manners: Occasional Prose.* Ed. Sally Fitzgerald and Robert Fitzgerald. New York: Farrar, 1969. Print.

O'Connor, Rachel. *Mistress of Evergreen Plantation: Rachel O'Connor's Legacy of Letters, 1823–1845.* Ed. Allie Bayne Windham Webb. Albany: State U of New York P, 1983. Print.

Ovid. *The Metamorphoses of Ovid.* Trans. Allen Mandelbaum. San Diego: Harcourt, 1993. Print.

Owen, Alex. *The Darkened Room: Women, Power, and Spiritualism in Late Victorian England.* Philadelphia: U of Pennsylvania P, 1990. Print.

Percy, Walker. *Conversations with Walker Percy.* Ed. Lewis A. Lawson and Victor A. Kramer. Jackson: UP of Mississippi, 1985. Print.

———. "The Message in the Bottle." *The Message in the Bottle.* 1975. New York: Farrar, Straus & Giroux, 1981. 119–49.

Petersson, Robert T. *The Art of Ecstasy: Teresa, Bernini, Crashaw.* New York: Atheneum, 1970. Print.

Raper, Julius Rowan. "Inventing Modern Southern Fiction: A Postmodern View." *Southern Literary Journal* 22 (1990): 3–18. Print.

Roberts, Bette B. "The Strange Case of *Mary Reilly.*" *Extrapolation* 34.1 (1993): 39–47. Print.

Romine, Scott. *The Real South: Southern Narrative in the Age of Cultural Reproduction.* Baton Rouge: Louisiana State UP, 2008. E-book. Kindle.

Rossetti, Christina. "What Would I Give?" *The Complete Poems of Christina Rossetti: A Variorum Edition.* Ed. R. W. Crump. Vol. 1. Baton Rouge: Louisiana State UP, 1979. 142.

"Saint Clare of Assisi." *Encyclopaedia Britannica Online.* Encyclopaedia Britannica, 2011. Web. 20 Aug. 2011.

Saxon, Lyle. "The Centaur Plays Croquet." 1927. *N.O. Lit: 200 Years of Louisiana Literature.* Ed. Nancy Dixon. New Orleans: Lavender Ink, 2013. 339–52. Print.

Shilling, Jane. Rev. "Water Spirits: *The Ghost of the Mary Celeste* by Valerie Martin." *New Statesman.*15:27 (28 Feb. 2014) (http://www.newstatesman.com). Web. 17 June 2014.

Showalter, Elaine. "Solitude, Work, Humility." Rev. *Mary Reilly* by Valerie Martin. *Times Literary Supplement.* 1–7 June 1990: 586. Print.

Smajić, Srdjan. *Ghost-Seers, Detectives, and Spiritualists: Theories of Vision in Victorian Literature and Science.* Cambridge: Cambridge UP, 2010. Print.

Smith, R. McClure. "*A Recent Martyr:* The Masochistic Aesthetic of Valerie Martin." *Contemporary Literature* 37.3 (1996): 391–415. Print.

———. "The Strange Case of Valerie Martin and *Mary Reilly.*" *Narrative* 1.3 (1993): 244–64. Print.

———. "Valerie Martin's Revisionary Gothic: The Example of 'Sea Lovers.'" *Critique* 34.3 (1993): 171–81. Print.

St. Thérèse of Lisieux. *The Story of a Soul: The Autobiography of a Soul.* Ed. T. N. Taylor. London: Oates & Washbourne, 1912. Public Domain E-book.

Taylor, Elizabeth. *At Mrs. Lippincote's.* 1945. London: Virago P, 2008. Print.

Tolson, Jay. *Pilgrim in the Ruins: A Life of Walker Percy.* New York: Simon & Schuster, 1972. Print.

Tromp, Marlene. *Altered States: Sex, Nation, Drugs, and Self-Transformation in Victorian Spiritualism.* Albany: State U of New York P, 2006. Print.

Vella, Christina. *Intimate Enemies: The Two Worlds of the Baroness de Pontalba.* Baton Rouge: Louisiana State UP, 1997. Print.

Vernon, John. Rev. "The Vanishing: *The Ghost of the Mary Celeste* by Valerie Martin." *New York Times Sunday Book Review.* 24 Jan. 2014. Web. 16 June 2013.

Washick, James. "The Elision of Christ in *Mary Reilly.*" *Christianity & Literature* 44.2 (1995): 169–79. Print.

Weese, Katherine J. *Feminist Narrative and the Supernatural: The Function of Fantastic Devices in Seven Recent Novels.* Jefferson, NC: McFarland, 2008. Print.

Whitman, Walt. "Out of the Cradle Endlessly Rocking." *Leaves of Grass (1892–93).* Bartleby.Com. Web. 28 Aug. 2011.

Whittemore, Hope. Rev. of *The Ghost of the Mary Celeste* by Valerie Martin. *The Independent.* Sunday, 23 Feb. 2014. Web. 17 June 2014.

Whitton, Natasha. "A Rat in the Garden: Teaching Valerie Martin's 'The Consolation of Nature.'" *Eureka Studies in Teaching Short Fiction* 9.1 (2008): 47–55. Print.

Woods, Tim. *Beginning Postmodernism.* Manchester: Manchester UP, 2009. Print.

Wordsworth, William. "A Slumber Did My Spirit Seal." *Romantic Poetry: An Annotated Anthology.* Ed. Michael O'Neill and Charles Mahoney. Oxford: Blackwell, 2008. 123. Print.

Young, Andrew. "There Is a Happy Land." http://library.timelesstruths.org/music/There_Is_a_Happy_Land/. Web. 17 June 2014.

Index